THE UNITED STATES
AND THE REPUBLIC OF KOREA

HOOVER INTERNATIONAL STUDIES
Richard F. Staar, director

THE UNITED STATES AND THE REPUBLIC OF KOREA

Background for Policy

CLAUDE A. BUSS

HOOVER INSTITUTION PRESS

Stanford University | Stanford, California

*The Hoover Institution on War, Revolution and Peace,
founded at Stanford University in 1919 by the late President
Herbert Hoover, is an interdisciplinary research center for
advanced study on domestic and international affairs in the
twentieth century. The views expressed in its publications
are entirely those of the authors and do not necessarily
reflect the views of the staff, officers, or Board of Overseers
of the Hoover Institution.*

Hoover Press Publication 254

© 1982 by the Board of Trustees of the
   Leland Stanford Junior University
All rights reserved
International Standard Book Number 0-8179-7542-X
Library of Congress Catalog Card Number 81-82077
Printed in the United States of America

Design by L. Ziedrich

CONTENTS

EDITOR'S FOREWORD

When on August 15, 1945, Japan accepted terms to end the war, American leaders scarcely could have foreseen the crucial role the United States was destined to play in East Asia. Nowhere were problems greater than in Korea.

Japan's colonial rule had failed to prepare Korea for political independence. The postwar division of the Korean peninsula into the communist North and the noncommunist South led to civil war in 1950, with Americans and South Koreans fighting valiantly side by side. Hostilities ended with the signing of the armistice agreement in 1953. Since that time the United States and the Republic of Korea (ROK) have been allies in maintaining peace in Northeast Asia and the western Pacific.

The relationship between the two countries has not always been smooth despite their Mutual Defense Treaty. Much misunderstanding has resulted from the enormous cultural differences and from conflicting perceptions of the American security commitments. The highest order of statesmanship will be required in both Washington and Seoul if doubts and recriminations are to be subordinated to the necessity of continued cooperation.

As this study by Professor Claude Buss shows, the mutual interests of the United States and the ROK must be constantly re-evaluated, with full consideration given to the ever-changing strategic environment. The most powerful determinants of the bilateral relationship include such external factors as the rising challenge of the USSR, the continuation of the Sino-

Soviet dispute, the burgeoning strength of Japan, and the re-emergence of Mainland China as an active member of the world community. The long-range struggle for markets and raw materials, especially oil, also will have its effect.

No international situation is more fraught with danger than that prevailing in the Korean Peninsula. North and South exist in delicate balance. Behind the North stands the might of the communist powers; behind the South is the United States with its friends. Miscalculation could lead to war. This study describes the efforts of two allied nations to preserve the peace, maintain stability, and contribute to progress throughout Northeast Asia.

RICHARD F. STAAR
Director of International Studies
Hoover Institution

PREFACE

Since the end of World War II, the Korean Peninsula has been divided between the Democratic People's Republic of Korea (DPRK) in the north, supported by the Soviet Union and the People's Republic of China; and the Republic of Korea (ROK) in the south, an ally of the United States. Because the Korean War ended in an uneasy truce, not in peace, both sides have lived in fear of renewed hostilities since 1953.

The Korean Peninsula, where the interests of the major powers converge in Asia, is a flashpoint that could ignite a global war. In this respect, Korea is as flammable as Poland in Europe, Iran in the Middle East, and Afghanistan in South Asia. Although the focus of international politics is momentarily located elsewhere, a deliberate provocation by the communist powers, a miscalculation, or an aggravated incident might quickly bring Korea back into the headlines of the world.

Since the American withdrawal from Indochina, an atmosphere of apparent tranquility has settled over East Asia and the western Pacific. This momentary calm, however, gives no indication of the profound changes under way in every nation in the region. And it is the decisions of these nations that will settle the issue of peace or war.

President Reagan confronts a crossroads in American relations with South Korea. From Presidents Truman to Carter, South Koreans regarded the United States as their chief support and the preserver of peace. President Carter's policy of withdrawal diluted their faith in the American commitment. When President Reagan assumed office with the overwhelming mandate of the American people, it became his responsibility—and his opportunity—to chart anew the diplomatic path the United States would follow. In dealing with the ROK, the United States must concern itself not only with that nation, but with the Soviet Union, Japan, and China as well. It matters greatly to the United States that each of these powers is at a critical juncture in determining its policy for the future.

The USSR, as devoted as ever to its ideology and political system, has reached its own crossroads. In aggressively building up its military strength and pursuing its nationalistic objectives, is the USSR gaining prestige and power or overreaching itself? If stymied by internal economic problems or by the antagonism aroused by aggressiveness, the USSR might—in frustration—be driven to greater militance and recklessness in the world community. Much depends on the temperament and the moderation of the successors to Secretary Brezhnev.

In Asia, the USSR shows no intention of abandoning any part of the strong position it has achieved. Having gained strategic footholds in India and Vietnam, the Russians have built an offensive capability in the northern islands off the coast of Japan and have stationed some 51 well-equipped, well-trained divisions along their frontier with China. They have stepped up their naval activities in the Pacific and can threaten the security of Japan and the sea-lanes vital to Japan. The preservation—perhaps the strengthening—of the Soviet alliance with North Korea would seem to be a key element in whatever plans the USSR has for safeguarding or expanding its future interest in Northeast Asia.

It is primarily the threat of Soviet hegemonism that has converted China from its perceived role as a communist coconspirator to a friend and well-wisher, if not an ally, of the United States. China's future role would appear to be to preserve the status quo rather than to champion revolution. A successful U.S. policy toward the two Koreas could encourage China in that direction. Since China says that it wants a peaceful solution to the Taiwan problem, a friendly relationship with South Korea that would not, at the same time, require the PRC to desert its longtime North Korean ally, would seem to be in China's interest. China can afford to be flexible in dealing with Korea so long as the Deng Xiaoping leadership concentrates on the successful accomplishment of the Four Modernizations. But one can never be sure how long China will continue on its present course.

Similarly, Japan has reached a stage where it must make decisions regarding its place in the world. Japanese media and political and economic circles readily admit that Japan can no longer be content with a merchant's view of diplomacy. No matter how painful the results may be, the Japanese are discussing rearmament, including the possibility of nuclear weapons, and the need to bear a larger share of the burdens of defense and peace-keeping. There is no need to remind the Japanese of the importance of Korea to their security.

Both sides of the 38th parallel in Korea are at watersheds in their development. In the North, Kim Il Sung is firmly in command, apparently strong, but inexorably nearing the end of a long career. Will the succession be engineered peacefully? Will the successor government choose to pursue a communist, militant philosophy, or will it accept the possibility of peaceful coexistence with the South? In the South, the moment is also critical. Will the new regime be able to continue to provide security and prosperity and, at the same time, cope with burgeoning economic problems and meet the growing demands for more freedom to exercise individual human rights?

In addition to the complexities of the international situation, President Reagan must operate within the ordinary limitations of the decision-making machinery. His appointees to sensitive positions in the State Department, the Pentagon, and the National Security Council support his ideas; nevertheless, he is not free of precedent or immune to the time-consuming processes of bureaucratic compromise. He also must bend, to a certain extent, to the demands of Congress, the budget, and public opinion. The president faces the same problems that challenged his predecessors: how to deter the DPRK and its communist supporters; how to help defend the ROK should deterrence fail; how to assist in the development of the ROK while contributing to its defense; how best to utilize the ROK in plans for global defense against the USSR; how to preserve American credibility in the eyes of American allies; and how to mesh bilateral U.S.-ROK relations with worldwide diplomatic and military commitments.

Since a successful working democracy depends on close links between the government and the people, this study is intended primarily for the concerned person who wants more information on which to base his own judgments about relations between the United States and the ROK. It is not intended for specialists, bureaucrats, or professional diplomats who have at their disposal a massive mixed bag of source materials for use in decision making. If this effort to inform the citizenry provides ideas or suggestions of benefit to the establishments in Washington or Seoul, it is an extra bonus. The purpose of this study is to show how U.S.-ROK relations have evolved and to set forth the variables that must be considered in formulating a national strategy for the future.

Because of the nature of the international system and the rapid changes in the strategic environment of East Asia and the Western Pacific, the United States has not followed a consistent course or pursued a clear-cut strategy in dealing with the ROK. Decisions have been made ad hoc and in response to temporary conditions or situations. The lack of consistency, however, may have been due not to lack of desire or lack of will but to the sheer inability of the United States, or any other power no matter how strong, to control the march of events. Diplomatic tactics may zig and zag, but the objective of protecting the national interest remains constant.

Crucial policy decisions are seldom choices between white and black—between good and bad. They are usually between the partially good and the slightly bad, between the certain good and the possible better, or between the tolerable and the distasteful. Decisions on Korean affairs never depend on ourselves alone or on ourselves and the South Koreans. The sentiments of our friends and allies, the perceived intentions of our adversaries, and the policies of other powers—great and small—with influence in Northeast Asia also play a role.

When President Reagan took office, the Korean Peninsula was deceptively calm. The passions aroused by such incidents as the capture of the *U.S.S. Pueblo,* the shooting down of an American reconnaissance plane and a military helicopter, and the killing of American officers in the tree-trimming incident in the Demilitarized Zone (DMZ) had cooled. Nevertheless, tensions persisted due to the repeated efforts of the North to infiltrate agents into the territory of the South.

Although Presidents Chun and Reagan began their administrations on a happy note when the former visited Washington, the dangers in the Korean situation could neither be ignored nor underemphasized. If hostilities between North Korea and South Korea again erupt, the chances are that under present circumstances, the Russians on one side and the Americans on the other would be involved immediately in another war on the mainland of Asia. This makes it imperative to search out the roots of potential conflict, to consider what the United States can and cannot do in seeking to protect its interests, and to explore the international ramifications of the U.S.-ROK relationship.

Issues other than security between the United States and the ROK are annoying but scarcely vital. Economic relations have generally been complementary and harmonious, but they could become bothersome should profitable cooperation give way to intense competition, as in the case of Japan. "Koreagate," the activities of the Korean Central Intelligence Agency in the United States, and the rather awkward Korean efforts at influence peddling made some American congressmen sufficiently angry to advocate a halt in military assistance to the ROK. On the other hand, the Carter human rights campaign brought to the surface—in Korea—a considerable amount of resentment, occasionally referred to as incipient anti-Americanism.

The present work does not pretend to be a crystal ball. It suggests alternative directions that U.S.-ROK relations might take and argues for strenuous efforts, both in Seoul and in Washington, to promote mutual security, to continue economic cooperation for mutual benefit, and to preserve goodwill.

Many of the ideas in this study originated in the author's previous experience in writing *The United States and the Philippines: Background for Policy.* It is again his pleasure to acknowledge, with thanks, the inestimable help given to him by friends and colleagues at the Naval Postgraduate School in Monterey and Stanford University, and in Washington, D.C., Tokyo, and Korea. He is especially grateful to the Hoover Institution on War, Revolution and Peace for underwriting this study.

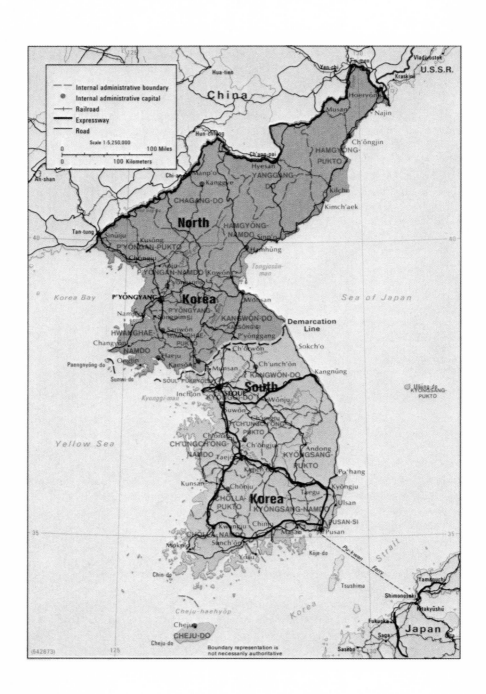

1 | THE GROWTH AND DEVELOPMENT OF THE REPUBLIC OF KOREA

For any American interested in acquiring a solid background for making judgments on relations between the United States and the Republic of Korea (ROK), whether bureaucrat, businessman, missionary, reporter, academician, or citizen, the beginning of wisdom is the clear recognition that the two nations have distinct approaches to the problems of international relations. Operating within a unique environment and conditioned by geography and history, each nation has its own political and social values and national priorities. The ideals of one are not transferable to the other. The United States and the ROK must pursue such goals as liberal democracy with guarantees of individual liberty and a free, competitive market system differently. Within the international system of sovereign equality, neither nation has any right to assert its own superiority or pass judgment on the correctness of acts and intentions of the other.

The United States perceives the primary threat to national security as the power and aggressiveness of the USSR; the ROK sees it as another invasion of the South by the communist North. All foreign policy in the United States, even that dealing with the ROK, must be formulated as a function of relations with the USSR. In contrast, all matters of foreign policy in the ROK must be adjudged in terms of the North Korea–South Korea confrontation. The interests of the United States and the ROK can never be identical; they can, however, be harmonious.

What is vital to one nation may be peripheral to the other. That which in the United States may seem to be distant or of little consequence may be regarded as a matter of life or death in the ROK. Since differences in perception are root causes of disagreement or conflict, the reconciliation of these differences in perspective and points of view is the basis of mutual understanding.

The vigorous nationalism of the American people is matched by an equal sense of national pride on the part of South Koreans. They are proud of their country and cultural heritage. Although they hope for the eventual reunification of all Koreans into a single nation, their immediate concern is to preserve the South Korean state as they are building it.

To the ROK, relations with outside powers—particularly the United States, the Soviet Union, Japan, and China—are important only as they contribute to national survival. The maintenance of peace on the Korean Peninsula, a prerequisite for national growth, is of far greater importance to the ROK than the creation of a new balance of power or a new world order designed primarily to ease or contain U.S.-USSR tensions. As a first step toward understanding Seoul's point of view in world affairs, this chapter emphasizes the domestic factors that shape the foreign policy of the ROK.

The Land and the People

Any statement about the land and the people of the ROK posits that it is only half of a divided peninsula—half of a divided nation. The concept of the territorial integrity of the entire Korean Peninsula is dear to all Koreans whether in the North, the South, or overseas. Any personal characteristics and behavior patterns ascribed to Koreans in the South can generally be extended to Koreans in the North. Individual variations within the Korean Peninsula are no greater, for example, than variations in the land and people of Italy.

A word of caution is in order. Many South Koreans insist that the experience of North Koreans under the communist system has profoundly modified traditional Korean ways of thinking and behavior patterns. On the other hand, many North Koreans say that South Koreans have been wooed away from their ethnic and cultural roots by slavish imitation of the ways of the West. Despite common blood and a shared language, some Koreans on both sides of the demarcation line voice serious doubts about the oneness of Korea.

The Korean Peninsula, bordering on China and the Soviet Union, points like a dagger at neighboring Japan. This strategic location is the meeting place of all the major powers in Northeast Asia. The ROK, about the size of Portugal or Pennsylvania, occupies a little under half the total area of the peninsula. The ROK is neither weak nor small and in no way conforms to the impressions and memories of the average American veteran of the Korean War.

In 1981 the population of Korea was about 55 million, with some 17 million in the North and 38 million in the South. Approximately 40 percent of the population in the North and 34 percent in the South are under fifteen years of age. As a result of the Korean War, nearly 2 million Koreans, or one person in ten in North Korea, "voted with their feet" and migrated to the South. The largest community of Koreans in a foreign country—the three million across the Chinese border in Manchuria—would acquire extreme political significance in the event of a war between China and the Soviet Union. More than 600,000 Koreans, two-thirds of whom have roots in North Korea, reside in Japan. The ties of the Koreans in the United States, numbering nearly 500,000 and increasing by 20,000 every year, are naturally with the ROK.

The Koreans, whose ancestors migrated initially from Manchuria and Central Asia, are a homogeneous people racially and culturally. Their history goes back to the third milennium B.C., with their first record as a unified country dating from the Silla dynasty in the seventh century A.D. Neither the centuries of domination by China nor the modern annexation by Japan obliterated the Koreans' strong racial consciousness and sense of unity.

Koreans throughout the peninsula speak a common language thought to be related to the Altaic or Tungusic language families. Modern Korean stems from the dialect originally spoken around the capital city. Chinese loan words form roughly half the vocabulary, but the modern trend is to substitute Korean words and concepts as much as possible for Chinese characters and expressions. Both North Korea and South Korea are modifying the language by coining new words and ordering official terms to cover science and technology, philosophy and ideology, and trends in their respective life-styles. Koreans write with a distinctive phonetic script. No agreement has been reached in efforts, North or South, to devise a replacement for the foreign McCune-Reischauer romanization system.

Recent exhibits of Korean art objects throughout the United States make it unnecessary to underscore the vitality and individuality of Korean culture. Koreans of distinction rank with the best in the arts of architecture and ceramics, woodwork and metalcraft, sculpture and painting, dance and drama, poetry and literature. In the distant past, some Korean masters of Chinese arts and crafts served as bridges for the transmission of ancient skills and materials from China to Japan.

In modern times, Korea was exposed to ideas from the West, primarily by way of Japan. Nothing is more exciting in contemporary intellectual life than the endeavor of South Korean scholars and intellectual leaders to define and perfect their cultural identity. They seek to achieve the optimum blend of philosophy, religion, art, and science of the East and West to make the quality of life within Korea commensurate with the international dignity and honor that they expect to achieve.

In many respects, the people are the richest resource of the ROK. Koreans are tough and hardworking and possess a healthy, robust sense of humor. Many Koreans say, only half in jest, they would get along just fine if only their leaders would let them alone and stay out of their personal affairs.

The Changing Social Fabric of the ROK

From earliest times, the people of Korea enjoyed a tightly knit social fabric woven to a large extent on the warp of Confucianism. Eighty percent of the people lived in small villages, where they grew rice and conducted their own local affairs with a minimum of interference from officials of the national government. Sharp distinctions were drawn between the *yangban,* or upper classes, who enjoyed prestige and privilege, and the *sangnom,* or commoners, who were the sons of soil and toil. As late as 1950, three out of five Korean farmers were tenants.

In their social code, Koreans were more Confucian than the Chinese. The rules of human behavior were to be found in the five basic relationships: parent and child (from which the others stemmed), king and minister, husband and wife, elder brother and younger brother, and friend and friend. Because the Koreans attached such importance to the family and the clan, they regarded loyalty to kin as paramount over loyalties to the state or to friends and neighbors.

Korean adaptations of Confucian tenets regulated village life. The prime duty of the individual was to be a good family member, venerating his ancestors and producing children to carry on the family tradition. This system provided satisfactory social security, but severely hampered opportunities for change or progress. The standard of living for most villagers was slightly above the level of subsistence, allowing for few comforts and no luxuries. Holidays, festivals, ceremonies, and such special events as births and deaths interrupted the daily routine of life. When Koreans were driven to break the bonds of social restraint, however, they often went to extremes of cruelty and violence.

Religious practices among Koreans were associated with a primitive spirit worship, overlaid with Confucian ancestor worship, Mahayana Buddhism, and a variety of forms of Christianity. Education in premodern times reflected the Chinese prototype of education for the scholar-gentry. The goal of Korean education was the mastery of the Chinese classics, with an emphasis on philosophy, art, and calligraphy. Following the ancient Chinese pattern, the aspiring young scholar pursued learning to pass the official examinations that would embark him upon a government career.

Confucianism tended to make the average Korean villager a complaisant citizen. Peace and sufficient food were signs that a ruler was blessed with the mandate of heaven. If a ruler failed in his mandate, he was likely to be overthrown or assassinated. That was the Confucian equivalent of the will of God. The villager, seeking only stability and food, found no difficulty in transferring his loyalty from one ruler or one dynasty to the next. The ordinary villager was no more immediately concerned with the fate of the ruler than with the mandate of heaven.

Beyond the villages, the ties of kinship and a sense of history combined to stress loyalty to a particular locality rather than to promote a sense of national identity. In the north, the southeast, and the southwest, people were more acutely conscious of the ancient local kingdoms of Koguryo, Paekche, and Silla than of the concept of an overall, united Korean nation. Even modern-day politicians owe a great deal of their strength to local provincial bases. Kim Dae Jung was identified with the poor area of South Cholla; Kim Young Sam with Pusan; and Kim Jong Pil with the more prosperous South Choong Chong. Presidents Park Chung Hee and Chun Doo Hwan originally came from the neighborhood of Taegu in North Kyongsang. In Korean politics, the right birthplace and the right local connections were always accepted as excellent credentials for favors, appointments, and concessions.

However important a common provincial origin may have been in fashioning political life and influence, it was the capital city, Seoul, that was the showplace of Korean culture and the symbol of national life. It was in the capital city that the king and his ministers, most of the satellite bureaucracy, and the *yangban* lived the life of glamor and tinsel that ordinary villagers could only dream about. It was there that wealth, aristocracy, and political power merged. Persons in authority seldom came to the villages except as tax collectors or imperial policemen. Yet, with all the distance between Seoul and the villages, the national capital was closer to the Korean countryside than to any foreign culture or civilization.

Other than the Chinese, the first foreigners to make a deep impression on the traditional patterns of Korean life were the Japanese. After Korea was opened by Japan in the 1870s, an alliance between Korean aristocrats and Japanese colonial administrators quickly sprang up. The Japanese took charge of such industrialization as there was—railroads, shipping, public buildings, and small factories—and gave the best jobs to Korean collaborators. Even in the countryside, a distinction developed between the ordinary Korean subsistence farmer and the Japanese agricultural entrepreneur who acquired substantial landholdings for his crops of rice, beans, and fruit. Such cash crops were grown more for the Japanese than for the Korean market. As a new class stratification based on economic prosperity rather than social rank came into being in Korea, the gap between the elite and the masses widened.

The changes wrought in Meiji Japan by contacts with the West were soon transplanted to Korea. Radical changes in behavior patterns and political concepts occurred. With growing Japanese influence came new styles in clothing, housing, and everyday behavior. Korean children went to school in Japanese-style uniforms, studied Japanese textbooks, and played Japanese games. Everyone was exhorted to learn the Japanese language.

The imperial court, the law courts, commercial offices, and government bureaus adopted Japanese procedures. Japanese signs were placed in public buildings, and a Japanese press was established. The imprint of Japan was stamped heavily and deliberately on the entire Korean Peninsula. In Korea, much of the hatred of Russia is a part of the heritage from Imperial Japan.

The effects of these imports from Japan were only skin-deep. Although changing the surface patterns of social behavior, they did not profoundly modify the fundamental Korean value system. Both Korea and Japan were variations on a theme by Confucius. Koreans had no difficulty in accepting the rules and regulations imposed by Japan; however, they resented the imposition of change by decree—a symbol of alien sovereignty. The basic Korean—human—love of liberty was such that changes, no matter how beneficial or useful, were scorned or rejected because they were identified with a foreign conqueror.

The impact of Western nations—England, France, and the United States—was too limited to make a deep impression on Korean society. This is not to underestimate the deep and lasting influence of Christian missionaries on the educational system of Korea and the life-styles of many individual Koreans. Western influence burgeoned, however, after World War II and the subsequent partition of Korea. In the North, the Communists turned their backs on the Confucian heritage, with help from their Russian and Chinese mentors. In the South, the American model practically took over. Americans were identified with affluence and national salvation. Copying the United States in industry, education, politics, and— above all else—the armed forces became the order of the day. But in all these matters, the American models were superstructures erected on the traditional base of the enduring Korean way of life.

During the first years of Korea's rebirth as an independent nation, President Rhee needed all his energies to guarantee national survival. Neither the new leaders nor the ordinary people had time to think about the continuity of their social heritage or the blending of tested traditions with the benefits of modernization. Basically they went on living as they had for centuries.

President Park Chung Hee brought a new spirit to the Blue House. (The Blue House, so named because of the color of its tile roof, is the South Korean equivalent of the White House.) On entering office in 1961, he set about to modernize—by exhortation if possible, by revolution if necessary—the social fabric of his people. His intent was not to destroy the traditional way of life. Born in rural Korea, he had a profound respect for his own society, which had demonstrated its ability to survive and satisfy the needs of its people through centuries of hardship, civil war, and foreign invasion. He perceived, however, flaws that needed eliminating. The standard of living in South Korea's 36,000 small villages would have to be improved and the moral fiber of the urban areas would have to be strengthened.

His attention centered on youth and their education. Toward the end of his administration in 1977, some 9.7 million students, or one-fourth of the population of the ROK, were in school. Of these, 357,000 students were attending one of the ROK's 302 colleges and universities. The literacy rate for the entire nation was said to exceed 90 percent.

The subject matter of the education system from the primary through the graduate and professional levels was thoroughly modernized. A "reverse brain drain" between the ROK and the United States became apparent as many Koreans who had left in the 1950s and 1960s for advanced training in the United States began to return to the ROK for lucrative jobs in academia, industry, and the government. Discussions among educated Koreans came to resemble those among thoughtful Americans. Topics that mattered included the good life, public health and welfare, the role of women in society, the energy crunch, inflation, environmental pollution, the management of scarce resources, demands for political reform, and social justice.

As the years passed, the conflict between democracy and communism as forms of government and social systems became deeply imbedded in the social consciousness of Koreans, North and South. In contemporary South Korea, democracy is universally accepted as a common ideal, but it is defined in essentially Korean terms. It implies a parliamentary system, based on free, popular elections by secret ballot, such human rights as protection against police brutality, arbitrary arrest, and summary trial, and guarantees of such individual freedoms as that of speech and the right to peaceful assembly. South Koreans insist, however, that no matter how precious such rights may be theoretically, they can never be granted at the cost of endangering the state. At the proper time, Koreans may enjoy the benefits of democracy, but not so long as the ever-present danger of an attack from the North hangs over their heads like a sword of Damocles.

The people of the ROK are passionately anticommunist. It is the basic ingredient of their faith and the root of their political and social action. They *hate* communism and the Communists for the destruction and death they caused by the Korean War. "We are not soft on Communists," say the South Koreans." Unlike the South Vietnamese, we will never permit a fifth column in our midst."

South Koreans make no pretense of precisely defining "Communists" and "communism." They apply the terms loosely and indiscriminately to anyone considered an opponent whether a rambunctious student, a political philosopher, an indefinable Marxist, a suspected Russian spy, an unorthodox economist, a labor organizer, a traitor, an infiltrator, anyone from the North—and until recently—a Chinese. The anticommunist atmosphere in the ROK is reminiscent of McCarthyism at an earlier period in the United States.

During the presidency of Park Chung Hee, evidence of wholesome social mobility began to proliferate. The middle class became larger and more influential, as it was given better opportunities for advancement. Whether because of education, economic progress, or mass communications, old shibboleths began to lose much of their force. Newspapers, magazines, radio, movies, and television invigorated the whole social structure, infecting the entire nation with a very evident "can do" spirit.

The effects of social change are noticeable in both the countryside and the cities. In rural South Korea, a drastic change in the proportion of village population to total population has occurred. Although the number of rural households remained practically constant, the proportion of rural inhabitants dropped from 80 percent in the 1950s to 60 percent in the 1960s to 30 percent in the 1980s. Either the rural birthrate was dropping or youngsters were leaving the farms for the cities. Thanks to land reform programs originally launched during the American occupation, South Koreans do not suffer the blights of excess tenancy and landlessness. Being 95 percent literate themselves, farmers send all their children to primary and middle schools, with four out of five going on to high school.

In 1980, the village family's annual income reached $3,000, comparing favorably with the income of urban families. Most rural families eat well and have adequate living quarters. They have money for doctors when sickness strikes, and they can afford televisions and radios. Field wages are often better than those of skilled workers in the cities, ranging from $8–10 per day, plus meals, rice liquor, and cigarette allowances. Farm work is made easier by such power machinery as tractors, rice transplanters, hullers, and irrigation pumps. Farm life has become more profitable due to improved technology, subsidized grain prices, rapid transport, and an insatiable urban market. South Korea ranks among the highest countries in grain production per acre. All other indicators of agricultural progress—income, the growth rate, the number of machines, exports, and farm size—have increased steadily.[1]

In 1971, President Park initiated the *Saemaul Undong,* or New Community Movement. Somewhat similar to the New Life Movement in Nationalist China or the New Democracy in the Philippines, the New Community Movement generated a certain amount of ballyhoo for discipline, self-help, and cooperation. After a decade of operation, it can be credited with substantial achievements.

In the name of the New Community Movement, the government has provided subsidies for small bridges, feeder roads, and small-scale irrigation and reclamation projects. It also has made modest grants and loans to enable farmers to improve roofs, kitchens, and toilets. Construction and repairs are practically oriented since the government supplies the money or the materials and the farmers themselves do the work. Through frequent visits to the countryside, President Park himself gave impetus to the village beautification and construction of community meeting halls, publicizing the movement by participating in ribbon-cutting ceremonies and by personally awarding prizes to farmers for work well done. He constantly harangued his cabinet officers and provincial officials to encourage rural development. It is not too much to say that President Park was as popular with farmer fathers as he was unpopular with their university-student sons.

The progressive changes in village life have moved South Korea toward a more open society, and it now compares favorably with any agricultural country in Asia. In South Korea, boys and girls in the rural areas may meet together socially, have improved chances for education, and can equally aspire to jobs in the city should they want to leave the farm. In the countryside, however, the Confucian ethic lingers on. In the city, students may riot and demonstrate against the government, but in the villages, the people are more interested in law and order. The villager is still inclined to see in Confucianism a philosophic justification of government by a benevolent bureaucracy under a virtuous ruler. The old mandate of heaven philosophy still provides the yardstick by which the government is measured.

President Chun Doo Hwan is following Park's lead in emphasizing the idea that state and family are mirror images: government and citizen must be to each other as father and son. He seems to be equally aware of the importance of rural South Korea to maintaining the social stability of his nation and equally devoted to *Saemaul Undong* or any other program designed to better the countryside.

The changes in rural South Korea have been more than matched by social development in the urban areas, particularly in Seoul. Even the smaller cities, including the provincial capitals, are caught up in the problems of industrialization and modernization.

Seoul is the one city in the ROK that every foreigner knows. It is the center of diplomatic life and international finance. A gigantic metropolis replete with deluxe hotels, acres of high-rise apartments, and miles of freeways and subways, it throbs with a vitality that approaches the tempo and scale of Tokyo. The eighth largest city in the world, with eight million people, it contains 85 percent of the wealth of the entire nation. Lying within 30 miles of the Demilitarized Zone (DMZ), it is ominously exposed to tank attacks from the North and lies within easy bombing or artillery range. The vulnerability of Seoul is the chief concern of those responsible for the defense of the ROK.

The major social problems of Seoul are similar to those of Paris or Manila, where responsibility for the government and the economic development of the nation is lodged in the same cadre of officials. The need for talent is monumental, and the shortfall of any bureaucracy, Korean or otherwise, is legendary. Extravagance, corruption, influence peddling, bribery, and nepotism are unavoidable, and their bad effects are magnified by the life-style associated with any big city.

President Park endeavored to adapt the principles of the rural New Community Movement to urban areas, advocating a kind of Moral Rearmament for city dwellers. He issued guidelines on diligence and frugality, forbidding government officals, for example, to eat out for lunch, to go to luxurious entertainment spots, including *kisaeng* (geisha) houses, to use public vehicles for private convenience, or to give welcome or farewell parties for provincial dignitaries visiting the capital. He urged all citizens to assume responsibility for maintaining order, to follow high moral standards in their own lives, to help their less fortunate neighbors, to save energy, and to clean up their city.

The programs of social improvement fostered by President Park may have achieved less than he hoped, but they did not die with him. President Chun Doo Hwan is, if anything, more fanatically devoted than his predecessor to the goal of a just, pure, and equitable society as an integral part of the national identity of the ROK. A seemingly religious person and an exemplary family man, austere and uncompromising in his own behavior, he is dogged in his faith in the virtue of the traditional Confucian-Korean morality. But he and thousands of South Koreans like him are caught in the whirring gears of social change. They see the shattering of the old value system by the impact of the West as the root cause of the corruption that has permeated the entire social structure.

President Chun is not convinced of the superiority of Western liberalism. He is not impressed with concepts of freedom, which he sees as a cloak for laxness and permissiveness on the part of Americans. He is determined to eradicate moral flabbiness among the politicians, bureaucrats, and businessmen with whom he associates. His crusade for purification enjoys a substantial amount of popular support.

The president finds himself in a Catch 22 situation. He must utilize the talents of progressive elements if the ROK is to continue its spectacular record; yet progressive elements must be curbed lest they create social chaos and make it possible for North Korea to march in. In the name of security, he finds it necessary to continue, even to tighten, the regime of martial law. He has cracked down not only on gangsters, hooligans, and hoodlums, but also on preachers, priests, poets, journalists, writers, professors, students, and labor union leaders who have been charged with disturbing the peace or inciting rebellion.

There is little doubt that President Chun and his regime can achieve social stability in the short range. It is also clear that social stability must be achieved if the country is to be secure, if democratic government is to be brought about, and if the economy is to be made sufficiently prosperous to provide the better jobs, opportunities for education, housing, and medical care that the populace increasingly demands. The danger is that excessive repression for short-range goals may produce negative long-term results. Individual frustrations may drive impatient or dissident elements to desperate actions, thus aggravating or multiplying the dangers that repression was designed to prevent.

Political Evolution Under Park Chung Hee

Because of the political uncertainties of the divided Korean nation at the time of liberation from Japan, the Korean people were given no opportunity to demonstrate their readiness to construct and operate an independent government. When the Russians in the north and the Americans in the south turned over their mandates to their respective indigenous regimes, neither Kim Il Sung nor Syngman Rhee could pretend to leadership of a popularly based, representative democracy. In the ROK, Dr. Rhee acted like a dictator until ousted by student riots in 1960.

After a brief democratic interlude, General Park Chung Hee seized the reins of government following a military coup ably supported by a nephew of his wife, a young lieutenant colonel named, Kim Jong Pil. Park had been an officer in the army of Manchukuo, trained by the Japanese and assigned to North China. Returning to Korea at the end of World War II, he engaged in controversial politico-military activities during the dramatic, confused early years of the American occupation. Although arrested for communist activities, he was released in circumstances that are not clear. He performed unspectacular duties during the Korean War and steadily gained in competence and command experience until thrust into prominence by the events of 1961.

In 1963 he gave up his army affiliation and, as a civilian, was elected to his first four-year term of office as president. For the first eleven years, he devoted himself to strengthening the armed forces and developing the country. With the passage of time, he restored public order and organized an efficient administrative machine, complete with a harsh police apparatus and the newly established Korean Central Intelligence Agency (KCIA). He launched his economic programs with uncompromising intensity, tolerating no opposition and showing no patience with mediocre performance. He created his own political machine, the Democratic Republican Party (DRP), with himself at its head.

Having no love for the trappings of democracy, he set out to redirect the processes of government according to his own ideas. Looking on the legislature, the National Assembly, as an irresponsible debating society, amenable to bribery and corruption, he strengthened the executive branch of the government. Since the old corrupt practices continued, President Park increasingly resorted to police power and the KCIA to keep the citizens in line. The more severe his repression, the more determined became the opposition.

He was re-elected for a second four-year term in 1967. The press criticized him unmercifully, and the students periodically took to the streets to protest against his autocratic methods. Thanks to a constitutional amendment pushed through in 1969, President Park ran for a third term in 1971, winning re-election by an uncomfortably slim margin over Kim Dae Jung. The primary focus of the issue-oriented campaign was corruption, redistribution of wealth, and neutralization of the Korean Peninsula. Kim's organization, the New Democratic Party (NDP), managed to win one-third of the seats in the National Assembly.

The coincidence of internal developments in the ROK with the U.S. withdrawal from Vietnam and the Nixon visit to China caused a drastic hardening of President Park's policies. In the fall of 1971 he called out the troops to quell riots on seven university campuses in Seoul and one in Kwangju. In December of that year he declared a state of emergency. After cautiously opening negotiations with North Korea, he needed a strong position at home as a basis for bargaining.

On October 17, 1972, President Park declared martial law and suspended major portions of his own constitution. Dissolving the National Assembly and banning all political activity, he closed the country's colleges and universities for six weeks and assumed control of the media. He forced through the *Yushin* (Revitalizing) Constitution, which did not abandon democratic ideals, but sidelined them for the sake of security, stability, and economic progress.

The president's term of office was to be for six rather than four years, and he was to be elected by a carefully chosen electoral college called the National Conference for Unification. He was given authoritarian powers and could be re-elected without limit. The National Assembly was reduced to rubber-stamp status; one-third of its 231 members, collectively known as the *Yujong Hoe,* or Revitalizing Reforms Political Associations, were to be named by the National Conference for Unification on recommendation of the president. The South Korean people were given no firm guarantee of their civil or human rights.

Shortly after the adoption of the *Yushin* Constitution, President Park presented himself to his dutiful new electoral college for election for another six years, 1972–1978. He replaced martial law with rule by decree, prohibiting criticism of the constitution and the president and severely curbing such rights as freedom of assembly and freedom of the press. Enforcement was entrusted to the police and the ubiquitous KCIA.

The decrees were especially hard on academic and student leaders, missionaries and churchmen, lawyers, writers, editors, reporters, poets, social workers, and outspoken political opponents. These intellectuals were subdued, but not silenced; they engaged in a continuous cat-and-mouse game with the authorities. Protesting against the harshness and the uncurbed, pervading corruption in government, they occasionally risked demonstrations on college campuses or city streets.

These dissidents were neither organized nor unified, and they failed to arouse any mass discontent. The bulk of the citizens went about their business in the usual way. The poor urban laborers, farm workers, clerks, and civil servants were, as always, dissatisfied and restive. But the ordinary man on the street seemed to feel that his lot was improving and was not disposed to join any movement against a government holding out real hope for a better future. Life grew increasingly comfortable.

Within two weeks of the fall of Saigon in April 1975 and simultaneously with the disclosure of infiltration tunnels under the DMZ, President Park issued a series of emergency decrees out of a genuine concern for security. Even the opposition NDP recognized the seriousness of the situation and temporarily supported the president. The harshest decree, no. 9, forbade criticism of the government, the president, or his family and ordered prison terms of not less than one year for anyone engaged in any activity deemed dangerous by the government. The head of any organization, school, or company was made responsible for the behavior of subordinates.

This decree manacled newspaper editors and publishers, and forbade student riots. Dissident professors and administrators were dismissed or placed under close supervision. Antigovernment student leaders were jailed or expelled. No uncontrolled or independent organizations were allowed on campuses, and all students were forced to join the paramilitary National Student Defense Corps. Activists outside the educational world were either jailed, placed under house arrest, or cowed into silence by close police surveillance.

The most courageous of Park's opponents, including former ROK President Yun Po Sun and minority party leaders Kim Young Sam and Kim Dae Jung, signed a Declaration for the Democratic Salvation of the Nation, which was read on March 1, 1976, in the Myongdong Cathedral in the heart of Seoul. The declaration defiantly called for restoration of full democracy, a more active effort for peaceful unification, and an economic policy that would make the ROK less dependent on foreign capital. Supporters of the declaration were arrested and held for as long as two years.

At the conclusion of President Park's six-year term of office in 1978, he was re-elected without fuss or incident; but the National Assembly elections on December 12, 1978, produced a shocker. The opposition NDP outpolled the government's DRP by a margin of 32.8 to 31.7 percent. Although the NDP did not gain a majority in the National Assembly because of the operation of the *Yujong Hoe,* it became more outspoken in its attacks on President Park and the entire *Yushin* apparatus.

In May 1979, the dynamic Kim Young Sam was chosen as the new head of the opposition NDP, displacing the milder Lee Chul Sun. Kim immediately challenged the government's authority to act as the only channel for dialogue with the North. Kim restrained his attacks on President Park during President Carter's visit to the ROK, but once the American president left, Kim resumedthe initiative. From the floor of the National Assembly, Kim called for an investigation of the *Yushin* Constitution, the resignation of Park, and a return to full democracy. Some of Park's advisers apparently called for drastic punitive action against Kim, but the president himself was more tolerant.

On September 10, Kim brazenly demanded the overthrow of Park and called on the ROK army to stay out of the political arena. For nearly a month the country was gripped with uncertainty. On October 4, the National Assembly voted to expel Kim, and in protest, the entire NDP membership of the Assembly resigned. Throughout the nation public uneasiness reached the explosion point. Students and workers demonstrated in Pusan and Masan in the southern part of the country, forcing the government to bring in the army to restore order. The head of the KCIA, Kim Jae Kyu, censored Park for letting things get out of hand, and the chief of Park's bodyguard counseled Park to get tough with the dissidents. This policy dispute led to the assassination of the president and the chief of his bodyguard on the night of October 26, 1979.

Interregnum—From Park Chung Hee to Chun Doo Hwan

In a brief interlude between Presidents Park Chung Hee and Chun Doo Hwan, the prime minister under the assassinated president, Choi Kyu Hah, assumed the presidency. By providing an outlet for pent-up political pressures, he managed to maintain domestic stability when the country might easily have slipped into chaos. If the long struggle between the Park regime and the dissidents—compounded by the increasingly difficult problems of security, social change, and economic development—had led to anarchy, the North might have been tempted to invade. In that case, the United States could scarcely have escaped involvement.

Park's assassination immediately brought the KCIA into disrepute. The Korean army, still under U.S. operational command "for action against aggression from the outside," became the dominant factor in the political scene. Regardless of generation, South Korean officers were united in their opinion that if students or other activists got out of hand, the officer corps would have to rise above factionalism and restore order. The army would not remain neutral and indifferent to the political future of the ROK.

President Choi's cabinet selections further proved his adroitness. Military men were given the posts of home minister (controlling the police), minister of government administration, and, naturally, minister of defense. The powerful and influential General Chun Doo Hwan, although not given cabinet rank, was retained in the prestigious position of commanding general of the Defense Security Forces. It was only after December 12 that he became the architect, engineer, and driving force of the new regime. Business interests were placated by the appointment of Shin Hyon Hwak, former president of the Federation of Korean Industries, as prime minister. Educational circles were mollified by the selection of Dr. Kim Ok Gill, president emeritus of the prestigious women's university EWHA, as minister of education. Other posts were distributed among technocrats, bureaucrats, and political persons of good reputation and proven merit.

As a temporary expedient, the new government quickly adopted some popular liberalizing measures. It abolished the hated Emergency Decree no. 9 and released hundreds of political prisoners. Civil rights were restored to more than 600 detained dissidents, including opposition leader and former presidential candidate Kim Dae Jung. Censorship of the press was eased somewhat, although readers of the *Asian Wall Street Journal* or the *Far Eastern Economic Review* might find that the censors had neatly scissored out any article considered damaging to the best interests of the

ROK. Since riot squads, plainclothesmen, and KCIA agents were no longer allowed on university campuses, students breathed easier. They were permitted to elect their own officers in the National Student Defense Corps and granted freedom to assemble on campus. Throughout the entire country, the atmosphere of repression brightened considerably.

President Choi, a man of circumspection rather than force and clearly under the domination of the military, was in no position to accede to the more extreme demands of the opposition. He let it be known that he would not renounce all the precepts and procedures of the previous administration, with which he had been so closely identified. As deeply devoted to the prevailing policies for national security and principles underlying economic development as his former chief, President Park, Choi was not to be pushed into making rapid changes in these areas. He was quite willing to bear the brunt of criticism engendered by inflation and mounting business difficulties. His philosophy was that Koreans were ready for change, but not desperate for it.

His greatest challenge was to respond to the popular consensus demanding political evolution and "modernization." He promised a new constitution and a revamped process for electing presidents. He would not, however, totally negate the *Yushin* Constitution. He would not give the press total freedom or allow students the unrestrained right to assemble, protest, and demonstrate. He would listen to the voice of the National Assembly in framing a new constitution, but he would not surrender to the legislature the executive's right to draft the constitution. He would not entrust the political future of the ROK to the whims of "office seekers" clamoring for more freedom and democracy. Because of his ideological dilemma, he was slow to make decisions. For a long time, the complaint was frequently heard in Seoul: "It is all very mysterious and confusing; we do not know what is happening, or where we are going, or why we are moving so slowly."

Perhaps greater safety lay in glacial speed. At the moment of President Choi's succession to office, the basic necessity for the nation was to remain on an even keel while the new administration tackled the long-range problem of political development. How could the ROK evolve toward a state structure that would provide for rapid upward social mobility and economic development and, at the same time, establish a government that, reflecting the needs and aspirations of the South Korean people, would ensure domestic tranquility, promote the common welfare, and carry out an effective foreign policy?

For a time it looked as if a liberal, Western-style democracy would be given a new lease on life in Seoul. True, democracy had not entirely disappeared during the Park regime. Careers remained open to talent; a capable bureaucracy was created; and political compromises were frequently made between President Park and his opposition. President Park was never able to make himself the complete autocrat. Recognizing the value of consensus in the Korean environment, the president sought advice even from those with whom he had little empathy—intellectuals, business tycoons, and politicians.

There were such attributes of representative government as political parties and legislative assemblies, but they were held in low esteem because of their shortcomings and abuses during previous administrations. The practice of universally recognized human rights was delayed because of the twin crises of security and economics. The ideals of an open society, a welfare state, a free competitive economic system, and a responsive popularly based representative government were accepted as goals for the future—not achievable in the present.

The people of the ROK were obliged to face up to the dilemmas inherent in any democratically based, responsible society. Can a government combine individual self-fulfillment with acceptance of social responsibility, permit wide participation in decision making while maintaining a capacity for effective action, reconcile requirements for law and order with the right to dissent, preserve the best of traditions while promoting social change, derive the maximum benefit from scarce resources while assuring the most equitable distribution of profits and earnings from the nation's total economic activity, and protect the vital interests of the state while discharging its international obligations?

In the troubled times immediately following the assassination of President Park, the caretaker government was pressed to make a new constitution and to prepare for the election of a new chief executive. A hectic fight for that office was in the offing. President Choi, reputedly disliking the responsibility thrust upon him and lacking any power base of his own, was generally considered an unlikely candidate for a regular term of office as president. The most obvious candidates were three Kims: Kim Jong Pil, Kim Young Sam, and Kim Dae Jung.

Kim Jong Pil, relative and longtime associate of President Park, founder of the KCIA and former prime minister, and president of the DRP, was the probable favorite. However, he had made many enemies in his long and distinguished career. Sometimes accused of being too pro-United States, or too pro-Japan, he claimed to be most devoted to the enshrinement of Korean culture and to the creation of a government system adapted to Korean needs and Korean character. Describing former attempts to build a democracy and open society on Western models as "messy," he advocated a new approach that would in his view stem from the Korean psyche itself. His election would have brought few changes in economic and foreign policy and the least tampering with the *Yushin* Constitution.

Kim Young Sam and Kim Dae Jung were rival leaders of the opposition party, the DNP. Kim Young Sam was the titular head of the party and enjoyed a substantial provincial power base in Pusan. He boasted of his integrity and his courage, insisted that he would put national needs ahead of personal ambitions, and promised that he would not compromise national security while working for democratic reform. He conceded nothing to his rivals in his hatred of communism, but let it be known that he would work more aggressively than past leaders for reunification.

Kim Dae Jung, born in Mokpo near Kwangju, was perhaps the most charismatic of the three. Going abroad after his narrow defeat in the presidential election of 1971, he was kidnapped from a Tokyo hotel in 1973 by KCIA agents and mysteriously brought back to Seoul. He declared that he would have been dumped into the sea had it not been for international publicity. For his continued defiance of martial law, he suffered imprisonment, house arrest, and loss of civil rights. His activities in 1976 have already been noted.

Because the Korean Army regarded Kim Dae Jung as pro-communist, it was not certain in 1979 that the army would allow him to be a candidate or permit him to take office if elected. Kim Dae Jung promised that he would fight for more democracy and advocated a strong ROK, and a conscious, genuine effort toward peaceful reunification. Like everyone else in the ROK, he opposed the withdrawal of American forces.

Each of the three Kims had his merits and demerits; each had his detractors and fervent supporters. Which might have been victorious in a democratic election will never be known. The scheduled election was never held. General Chun Doo Hwan's rise to power summarily halted the trend toward political liberalization.

The Rise of Chun Doo Hwan

On the night of December 12, 1979, a scant six weeks after the assassination of President Park Chung Hee, a power struggle within the military signaled a warning to overzealous proponents of a rapid move to liberal democracy. Chun Doo Hwan, charged with investigating the assassination, arrested his superior, General Chung Seung Hwa, who by virtue of his position as chief of staff of the Korean armed forces was also martial law administrator. Chung was one of the old guard, not noted for soldiery, who had risen to power through political influence and the right connections after the Korean War. Chun, on the other hand, prided himself on his military competence (he graduated in 1955 with the eleventh class of the Korean Military Academy—the first class to take a full four-year curriculum).

The two generals represented distinct factions within the military. General Chun had been too young for a command in the Korean War but was a Korean division commander in Vietnam. He and his classmates (all from Taegu in North Kyongsang province) felt that old-timers like General Chung should be retired from the top jobs to make room for the younger generation of genuine military professionals. General Chun, the younger, arrested General Chung, the elder, for questionable performance of his duties at the time of President Park's assassination. Chung was tried and sentenced to ten years in prison, but later released on grounds of ill health.

Some thirty senior generals were relieved of their positions to make room for younger officers. Lee Hi Song was named the new martial law commander, Ro Tae Woo the Seoul garrison commander, Chung Ho Yung Special Forces commander, and Kim Bok Dong, chief of staff of the Third Army, which is stationed in and around Seoul. General Chun, emerging as first among equals, made sure that no threat to his authority would arise in the vicinity of the national capital.

Acting on the authority of President Choi, General Chun took over the KCIA and proceeded to clean house. Although he pledged to refrain from interfering in legitimate political processes, Chun quickly concluded that government was too serious a responsibility to leave to politicians. The military's function would be to set goals and standards, and technicians and bureaucrats *with integrity* would conduct daily affairs. The rigidity of Chun's character and the firmness of his decisions became apparent immediately. He was less inclined than President Park to bend to the will of Washington and more xenophobic. He was convinced that in its own interest, the United States would keep its troops in the ROK indefinitely.

Working behind the scenes, he supported President Choi's promise of a new constitution by the end of 1980 and new elections by 1981. But as the rigors of the *Yushin* spirit relaxed, General Chun became more and more disturbed by the unrest spreading throughout the country. Tumultuous demonstrations against the police in Seoul on May 15, 1980, were followed by riots in Kwangju, the capital of South Cholla province. Beginning on May 17, this city of 800,000 people, led by armed and angry elements, was in open revolt. Even in Park Chung Hee's most repressive days, citizens had never taken up arms against the government. After ten days, regular troops were brought in to restore order. Without doubt the seething situation in Seoul and Kwangju convinced the military that Kim Dae Jung, the symbol of protest, would have to be removed from the political scene. To make sure that the North would not be tempted to invade the South because of domestic disorder, General Chun also took positive steps toward outright control of the government.

Still acting as an agent of the regularly constituted civilian administration, General Chun had political leaders Kim Jong Pil and Kim Dae Jung jailed and placed Kim Young Sam under house arrest. With one stroke, he removed the three leading presidential candidates from the scene. Martial law was proclaimed throughout the country; party headquarters and universities were closed; and the National Assembly was dissolved. Paratroopers were put on guard at universities, newspaper offices, and public buildings. All political activities were banned, and government was put in the hands of the military. Thousands of politicians (including cabinet ministers and vice-ministers), businessmen (including heads of prestigious quasi-public conglomerates), and other leaders and dissidents were dismissed from office. Some were held for trial.

On May 31, President Choi appointed a Special Committee for National Security Measures—a junta of 24 individuals including fourteen active and three retired generals—to take effective charge of the government. This further move away from democracy produced the deepest rift in U.S.-ROK relations in a decade, but the military was not to be deterred. Although ostensibly an advisory body, the Special Committee completely took over political and economic administration, superseding the cabinet and martial law authorities. It operated through some fourteen subcommittees, each with eight or nine members and headed in all but two cases by military personnel. These groups were responsible for such matters as constitutional development, agriculture, justice, economy, foreign affairs, domestic affairs, finance, social purification, culture, and information. Throughout the government and the quasi-public corporations, these committees fired bureaucrats and technocrats, intimidating those who remained.

On June 20, it was announced that Kim Jong Pil and nine other senior officials accused of corruption had agreed to turn over their fortunes (estimated to total $147.6 million) and to retire from politics in exchange for the government's promise not to prosecute them. Kim Jong Pil alone was said to have accumulated a fortune of $36 million from bribes, payoffs, rebates, and gifts during his eighteen years in office. The guilty included Park Chong Kyu, former chief of the president's bodyguards; Lee Sae Ho, former army chief of staff and commander of the Korean forces in Vietnam; Oh Won Chol, President Park's senior economic secretary, in charge of heavy and chemical industries; and Lee Hu Rak, former head of the KCIA. During his defense, Lee Hu Rak commented: "When you carry so many sacks of flour on your shoulder, you must expect that white will get on your coat."

On August 16, President Choi resigned in favor of Prime Minister Park Choong Hoon, who remained in office only eleven days. Meanwhile, the social and political purification continued. Programs were conducted in every office, factory, school, and village. Men, women, and children had to listen to lectures on the evils of luxurious living and the values of social responsibility. Thousands of officials, employees, and teachers were fired or held for trial on grounds of corruption, inefficiency, or irregularities. Crackdowns on riffraff, racketeers, gangsters, and gamblers netted a reported 30,000, of whom 1,000 were tried by court-martial. Eight thousand were released after questioning, and the rest were sentenced to a four-week re-education program. These measures infuriated some people and scared others, but this sincere effort to eradicate evil and punish wrongdoers also generated a substantial amount of public approval. Certainly it helped General Chun broaden his power base before his emergence as the dominant political figure.

On August 22, ending a 29-year military career and retiring as a four-star general, Chun Doo Hwan announced his readiness to uproot corruption and injustice from the country. Representing a policy of New History, New Wave, and New Determination, he would restore democracy and create a new welfare state. His priorities would be national defense, reduction of inflation, creation of new political parties, and honest elections that would make bureaucrats servants of the people.

Five days later, he was elected temporary president of the ROK by the National Conference for Unification acting as an electoral college. He chose Nam Duck Woo, a distinguished economist, as his prime minister and named the capable diplomat Lho Shin Yong as minister of foreign affairs. He retained the four-star general Choo Young Bok as minister of defense, perhaps because as an air force officer, Choo would not become too deeply involved in army intrigues. Chun pledged that the new constitution, providing for a strong president, eligible for a single seven-year term, would be adopted on schedule and that regular elections for president and the National Assembly would be held in the spring of 1981.

Until that time, he chose to chair a military-dominated Legislative Council for National Security, with emergency powers, which would serve as an interim legislature. He permitted universities to reopen and authorized the reappearance of political parties. Nearly a thousand ex-leaders were barred from political activity; nevertheless, old groupings re-emerged with new names. The Korean National Citizens' Party, the Democratic Socialist Party, and the Democratic Korea Party were among the newcomers. The government's own Democratic Republican Party, rechristened the Democratic Justice Party, named Chun Doo Hwan as its candidate for the presidency in 1981. He was elected for a seven-year term without significant opposition.

The long-standing anticommunist law was repealed, and the KCIA was renamed the Agency for National Security Planning. Martial law was lifted, and the military courts were dissolved. Some prisoners, including the poet Kim Chi Ha, were released, and hundreds were granted clemency. The sentence of death imposed on Kim Dae Jung was commuted to imprisonment for life. President Chun promised a policy of harmony and reconciliation.

To better control public opinion, the government reorganized the media, eliminating superfluous newspapers, radio, and TV. The two existing news agencies were consolidated into a single state-controlled organization, the Hankook, or Korean National News Agency. The free press was transformed into a government mouthpiece.

Chun realizes the importance of his role in the political development of the ROK. He appreciates the individual Korean's greater love of liberty than of public order. He is aware of the twin dangers of too much freedom on the one hand and too much repression on the other. He wants democratic government and the welfare state in his own way, at his own pace. Whether he can accomplish his goals depends on his success in achieving the requisite economic progress while providing for national defense.

Economic Future of the ROK

For nearly a decade after the Korean War, the ROK could do little more than keep its people alive. Even that would not have been possible had it not been for American aid. After President Park took over, he launched a development program that, in less than two decades, brought the ROK from agricultural poverty to the threshold of a modern industrialization.

Park was a relentless driver; to him hard work and national survival were inextricably linked. He pushed through the First Five-Year Plan (1962–1966), which ignored consumer demand and mobilized national energies for the creation of a massive export industry. He called on the nation's financial institutions to provide the funds to accomplish these ambitious goals.

Without substantial natural resources, the ROK sought to become self-sufficient in grains and other foodstuffs. For industrial development, President Park looked abroad for loans and technical advice. He was given extraordinary assistance by Japan after the normalization of relations in 1965 and by the United States in the form of lucrative contracts in connection with South Korean efforts in the Vietnam war. During the first Five-Year Plan (1962–1966), and the second as well (1967–1971), he relied primarily on Korea's skilled, industrious labor force. He was tough on labor. Workers received low wages and no such fringe benefits as medical care or unemployment insurance. There was no opportunity to protest against harsh working conditions.

Toward the end of the Second Five-Year Plan, President Park received a rude economic jolt when the United States announced in 1971 that it would withdraw half of its troops from South Korea. Coupled with the U.S. rapprochement with China, the collapse of the Bretton Woods international financial system, and the 1973 oil crisis, this announcement spurred further self-reliance—particularly in the field of heavy industry for the indigenous production of war materials. Despite the necessity of adapting to these exigencies, the ROK achieved through its first three five-year plans what is often called the economic miracle on the Han River. The ROK began modestly to think about the possibility of catching up with Japan.

The growth rate of the ROK, averaging 10 percent annually for the decade 1967–1977, reached 13 percent in 1978, but slowed to 6.4 percent in 1979 during the Fourth Five-Year Plan. Under President Park, the gross national product (GNP) approached $60 billion and per capita income surpassed $1,500 (compared with a mere $100 in 1962 when the economic drive began).

In international trade, "export madness" drove the ROK above the $15 billion level in 1979, somewhat under the $19 billion worth of imports. Much of the deficit was made up by the earnings of invisibles, including shipping services, tourism, and remittances from South Korean workers in the oil-rich countries of the Middle East. At the time of Park's death, his nation enjoyed an excellent credit rating, with more than $5 billion in reserve to cover a $10 billion debt.

While zealously developing its agricultural resources, the ROK scored its most spectacular gains in such industries as textiles and clothing, footwear, electronics, electric and other machinery, steel, autos, shipbuilding, petrochemicals, plywood, fertilizers, and food processing. By the end of the 1970s, the ROK lagged behind Japan in economic development by only a decade.

Of the 253 companies listed on the Seoul stock exchange in 1979, more than a dozen posted aftertax earnings of more than $10 million. Fourteen firms exceeded $100 million in exports, and four exceeded $300 million. Four giant Korean-based multinationals, handling such diversified lines as automobiles, televisions, radios, cosmetics, footwear, and textiles, each reported $2 billion or more in sales. One spectacular South Korean success story, the Daewoo organization, grew from a single company with five employees and $1,000 in capital in 1965, to a conglomerate of 22 companies and sales of $2 billion in 1978.

As the ROK reached the takeoff point as a fully developed nation, it encountered new difficulties. The old problems of the ROK as a less developed country (LDC)—low wages, high unemployment, poor standard of living, unmanageable trade deficits, and extreme maldistribution of income—were aggravated by the problems that plague all rapidly industrializing countries—shortages of skilled labor, inflation, high costs of oil and other scarce resources, rising consumer demand, and calls for protective tariffs in other countries. The ROK began to feel the sting of opposition to its exports of textiles, footwear, automobiles, televisions, radios, and their parts to Japan, Western Europe, and the United States.

Economic danger signals began to emerge even before the death of President Park. Like other nations, the ROK seemed to be in the grip of "stagflation" (stagnation of productivity and galloping inflation). Economic growth turned negative toward the end of 1979. Unemployment passed 750,000, or 5 percent of the work force. Wages failed to keep pace with rising prices. Layoffs, low pay, and tough working conditions caused laborers to make common cause with student dissidents. Jobs became harder to find for the 3 percent of the working population who entered the job market each year. Wholesale and consumer prices moved ahead at an annual rate of approximately 25 percent. Costs of food, clothing, housing, fuel, and electricity rose steadily. At one fell swoop in January 1980, the price of domestic heating oil jumped 60 percent and electric rates 36 percent. The cost of gasoline passed $4.50 per gallon.

Short supplies of overpriced consumer goods, too little money in the pockets of those who needed it, and job shortages—particularly in export industries—forced the government to take action. In a way, President Park was handicapped in his freedom to maneuver. He was surrounded by a combination of bureaucrats, industrialists, traders, bankers, and military types flanked by an array of engineers, management specialists, and economists. At the center of this galaxy, he laid down the rules for loans, subsidies, grants, and concessions. Political and economic elements were so intertwined that Park could not crack down on his associates and underlings without hurting himself. He had created economic giants, and he was limited by their resultant political power.

In the face of mounting political and economic unrest, Park undertook remedial measures that were little more than cosmetic. Expressing exasperation with "corrupt politicians, conscienceless capitalists, and selfish technocrats" in his own entourage, he shuffled his advisers from job to job or dismissed them entirely.

Much to the chagrin of favor-seeking entrenched interests with influence at the Blue House, President Park launched a stabilization program on the advice of the most respected of his economists. He tightened credit policies and raised interest rates toward the 25 percent mark. He stopped all new heavy-industry projects and ordered a shift in emphasis from export-promotion industries to import-substitution industries catering to the home market. He liberalized import rules, decontrolled prices on many consumer items, and generally shifted the government's priorities toward consumer welfare. He permitted some increase in wages but kept them behind the inflation curve.

After Park's death, the vital role of economists and economic institutions in the destiny of the nation became more apparent. During the interregnum between Park and Chun, the lack of leadership was embarrassingly acute because of the social malaise following the assassination and the horrendous increase in the price of oil. Only modest steps were taken to cope with mounting economic woes. The *won* was devalued, budget cuts were announced, credit rates were manipulated as demanded by the money supply or other economic indicators, and compromises with labor leaders were worked out to meet some of the workers' most pressing needs.

When General Chun came to power, he breathed new life into the economic stabilization program. His wholesale dismissals at the outset showed that he intended to enforce new ethical standards in economic performance. He decreed an end to bribery, corruption, and feathering of personal nests at the expense of the public interest. Some skeptics remarked that they had seen this before, but soon they, too, were impressed by Chun's sincerity of purpose. With unmistakable directness, he accomplished by fiat what credit control, monetary squeeze, or bureaucratic pressure could not.

Within the bounds of the Fourth Five-Year Economic Development Plan (1977–1981), Chun took immediate steps toward restructuring and redirecting the nation's economy. He wanted a strong economy as much for a strong national defense as for the improved welfare of his people. He announced subsidies to reduce the cost of transportation and other basic necessities for low-income groups. To provide selective stimulus to the economy and to foster employment, he supported agriculture and small- and medium-sized industries and ordered construction of housing, highways, and other public works. He further liberalized rules for foreign investment, opening the consumer and service industries to foreign participation, lowering the minimum that foreigners could invest in a particular enterprise from $500,000 to $100,000, and increasing the percentage of a given enterprise that foreigners might own.

Turning his attention to large corporations, he announced a new policy of landholding disclosure and divestiture. The amount of unused land held by corporations and offered to banks as loan collateral was scandalous. Companies were forced to disclose their holdings, sell idle lands, and repay their loans. Chun also ordered conglomerates to dispose of affiliated companies in excess of management capabilities—in effect, to get out of operations that were far outside their main area of business.

His major attack was on giant conglomerates that had become top-heavy and uneconomical thanks to cheap credit, defense contracts, and tax concessions. They owned and operated shipyards, steelworks, petrochemical projects, and huge engineering establishments. Due to rising energy costs, overcapitalization, and shrinking markets, many units had become economic disaster areas. In the interest of eliminating wasteful competition, the government tightened credit, even though this forced some companies into bankruptcy or reorganization. Mergers were ordered in the manufacture of autos, diesel engines, and electric power equipment and in copper refining, among other fields. The purpose was to reduce government support and government control, thereby making industry freer but more responsible for making its own way in a market situation.

During Chun's first full year in office, economic performance dipped badly before beginning to rise again. In 1980, wholesale prices rose 44 percent and retail prices 35 percent. Unemployment rose from 3.8 to 5 percent. Wage increases lagged behind rising prices. Consumer spending and savings fell off, while industrial production declined. Oil prices skyrocketed. To top it all off, bad weather led to a miserable grain harvest. Due to economic recession and the accompanying political unrest, for the first time since 1962 the GNP registered a negative growth rate—down 5.7 percent. Per capita GNP increased slightly in *won* values, but in U.S. dollars it decreased from $1,597 in 1979 to $1,508 in 1980 because of the government's devaluation of the Korean currency.

The 1980 budget rose to $10 billion (up 31 percent over 1979), with the per capita tax burden rising to $276. National defense expenditures in 1980 represented 37 percent of the total budget, or 6 percent of the GNP. These figures explain why South Koreans deeply resent what they view as Japan's unfair economic advantage due to its free ride in national defense.

Foreign trade was the one bright spot in the ROK's dismal economic picture. Largely due to further devaluation of the *won,* exports increased from $17.4 in 1979 to $17.2 billion in 1980 and imports from $19.1 billion to $21.9 billion. Despite a substantial deficit in its service account, South Korea had no trouble borrowing sufficient capital to cover its obligations. At the end of 1980, its foreign reserves amounted to a respectable $6.5 billion, with the debt service ratio standing at 14 percent—well within the standards of the World Bank.

Although by no means out of the woods, the Korean economy had made remarkable progress on the road to recovery. President Chun immediately strove to reduce the government's subsidy program as quickly as possible. After the bad harvest, his grain support program was so costly that he could have bought rice more cheaply in California at world market prices than from Korean farmers. He needed to stimulate productivity but curb inflation. He sought to promote the general welfare without incurring unmanageable budget deficits.

Chun adopted a program directly aimed at realizing the nation's growth potential. His methods were to implement public works, stimulate residential housing construction, improve industrial structures, promote small- and medium-sized industries, and raise productivity in agriculture in order to provide jobs and improve living conditions. He put thousands to work on subways, highways, railways, power plants, factories, and projects to modernize the communications systems.

At the same time, he made concerted efforts to promote exports and to strengthen the balance of payments position. Under his direction, the Economic Planning Board mapped out ways of increasing exports to $20.5 billion in 1981 and $25 billion in 1982 while keeping imports within $26 billion in 1981 and $30 billion in 1982. Export promotion measures included holding the line on wages, improving quality control, and pursuing more aggressive marketing methods. The ROK hopes to expand its income from exports by diversifying products and markets and by shifting from such labor-intensive products as textiles to capital-intensive products such as computers and other electronic equipment.

On the import side, the government pinned its hopes on greater consumer purchasing power and encouraged local manufacture of a broader range of consumer goods. It tried to reduce reliance on foreign oil by stricter conservation policies and by rushing ahead with its power development program. Oil costs surpassed $6 billion in 1980. The ROK expects to cover 80 percent of its own energy requirements within the next decade through newly constructed nuclear and coal-fueled power plants. To strengthen the balance of payments position, the government counts on annual remittances of approximately $2 billion from Korean workers overseas, particularly those in the Middle East.

For the immediate future, South Korean economists expect that the shortfall in the income account will be met by profits from service operations and short-term loans. Operating capital requirements of $7.7 billion for 1981 should be raised from public and private sources without difficulty. The credit rating of the ROK with the World Bank, the International Monetary Fund, the U.S. Export-Import Bank, the Asia Development Bank and with Japanese, U.S., Saudi, Kuwaiti, and German commercial banks remains excellent. For private loans from international banking syndicates, Korean borrowers are required to pay a premium of less than 1 percent over the London international rate.

The government hopes that by controlling the money supply and interest rates it can decelerate inflation to 15 percent in 1981 and keep food prices and public utility rates stable. By the end of 1981, it hopes to restore the GNP to the level of 1979. It expects a slight improvement in unemployment and a renewed upward trend in per capita income, which it hopes will exceed $1,900 in 1982. The increase in the national budget for 1981 was fixed at 18 percent over 1980, with the per capita tax burden rising from $276 to $340. The South Koreans tax themselves heavily, collecting 61 percent of their revenue from internal sources.

President Chun, like President Park, wants to redress inequities in income distribution and to expand the scope of social services. His program provides for aid to farmers and coal miners, expansion of medical insurance for urban workers, better educational opportunities for the disadvantaged, and improved housing for low-income persons. He aspires to a genuinely democratic welfare state, with an equal chance to a better life for every individual. In Chun's view, his aim of high growth with stability and equity can best be accomplished through private initiative and a competitive market system functioning in an open and foreign-oriented society.

After purifying the economic establishment he inherited, President Chun demands unalloyed loyalty to his programs and philosophy. Like President Park when he first took office, President Chun is a strong character, and is surrounded by able technocrats. There is every reason to believe that he will continue the excellent record of the 1960s and 1970s.

Enjoying a good balance between agricultural and industrial resources, the South Korean people are hardworking, pragmatic, and confident of a better future. Skilled workers, capable managers, and imaginative entrepreneurs, they are welded together into a national unit dedicated to general prosperity. They have created an educational system geared to their national needs and an institutional framework able to harness and guide their productive energies, whatever turns might occur in their political development.

The immediate fate of the Chun administration rests on its economic performance. Its ultimate fate depends on such factors as "sunshine in August" (for a good harvest), a high rate of utilization of factory capacity, a reasonable relationship between wages and productivity, continued prosperity in the world market system, and the price of imported oil. Contributing their own hard work and managerial skills to their continued growth, the South Koreans look forward to the fullest cooperation from their American and other allies and trading partners.[2]

2 | THE FOREIGN POLICY
OF THE REPUBLIC OF KOREA

The first step toward a better understanding of U.S.-ROK relations is to consider the growth and development of South Korea. The second, inseparably linked with the first, is to study South Korean foreign policy. An analysis of Seoul's perspective and its priorities in safeguarding national interests should indicate where the ROK can afford to compromise and where it cannot.

According to the ROK constitution, the national goals are to consolidate national unity, to destroy all social vices and injustice, to afford equal opportunity for individual development, to help each person discharge those duties and responsibilities concomitant with freedom and rights, to promote the welfare of the people, to strive for lasting world peace, to promote international prosperity, and thereby "to create a new era in our history, ensuring security, liberty, and happiness for ourselves and for our descendants forever." This happy mingling of the philosophy of the American Declaration of Independence and the Preamble to the American Constitution shows the absolute compatibility of the South Korean and the American concept of government as the servant of the people and of the two states' basic approach to the existing world order.

As a minor power allied with a superpower, the ROK realizes that its freedom of choice in foreign policy is limited by decisions of the United States. Because of differences in strength and influence, the priorities of the ROK have to be arranged to accord with the will and intentions of its major ally. Whenever the United States changes its assessment of—and consequently its operating policies on—such matters as communism, dé-tente, totalitarianism, or human rights, the ROK must accommodate itself as best it can. Often feeling deserted or outraged by unfathomable (to them) American inconsistencies, the South Koreans have intensified their efforts toward greater self-reliance in the international, as well as in the domestic, field. Under President Chun, they are following up on new diplomatic initiatives undertaken by President Park.

The dominant objective of the foreign policy of the ROK is national security (that is, guaranteeing survival should hostilities be renewed by the North). The steps taken and the problems encountered by the ROK in endeavoring to achieve this objective are the subject of this chapter.

Divided Korea, the War, and the Armistice

Meeting in Cairo in November 1943 to plan the new order in Asia, Roosevelt, Churchill, and Chiang Kai-shek declared that after the defeat of Japan "the three great powers are determined that in due course, Korea shall be free and independent." At Teheran Stalin endorsed this declaration. At Yalta, the anticipated entry of the USSR into the war in East Asia obliged Roosevelt and Churchill to make provision for Soviet interests in Northeast Asia. Subsequently and hastily, due to the sudden collapse of Japan, the Allied High Command agreed on the 38th parallel as the dividing line for the acceptance of the Japanese surrender in Korea.

The Russians arrived in northern Korea on August 12, 1945, after a lightning campaign in Manchuria. The Americans, preoccupied with Southeast Asia, China, and Japan, did not land in southern Korea until nearly a month later. From this beginning, the Korean Peninsula was divided, with the Russians in control in the north and the Americans in the south. At Moscow, in December 1945, the Big Three (the United States, Great Britain, and the Soviet Union) agreed to move toward unification by establishing a provisional government under a four-power trusteeship—the Big Three plus China, then under Chiang Kai-shek. This denial of immediate independence infuriated South Koreans.

Representing their respective zones of occupation, the United States and the Soviet Union formed a joint commission to consult with Korean political parties and social organizations to establish a free and independent government. Due to the intensifying cold war, sessions of the joint commission were fruitless. The temporary division of Korea, originally a military stopgap, gradually became permanent.

Despite stiff Soviet opposition, the United States dumped the problem of unification in the lap of the United Nations. In 1947, the General Assembly advocated the holding of nationwide elections under international supervision. The North refused to adhere to this plan, but the South unilaterally decided to carry out the recommendations of the General Assembly. On May 10, 1948, balloting *in the South only* resulted in the election of a "national" assembly—although it represented only the South—to meet in Seoul. This assembly adopted a constitution and elected Syngman Rhee president of the Republic of Korea.

The new state, recognized by many countries including the United States and China, received the mandate of government from the American military government. A resolution passed by the U.N. General Assembly on December 12, 1948, referred to the government of the ROK as the "only lawful government in Korea."

Considering these procedures in the South as illegitimate and itself the only true representative of the Korean people and the Korean nation, the North set up its own state and government under the auspices of the Russians. On August 25, 1948, the North elected a Supreme People's Council. Within two weeks, a constitution was ratified and the Democratic People's Republic of Korea proclaimed. The Russians lost no time in exchanging ambassadors with the DPRK and concluding an agreement on economic and cultural cooperation.

In this manner, Korea—which had been one in culture and civilization for over a thousand years—was divided into two hostile parts, each representing an opposing ideology and great power. Each half pretended to legitimacy as the sovereign of the entire country. Both used the word "Korea" in their official designation. The North, supported by the USSR, and the South, backed by the United States, immediately initiated schemes for unification. The South lost the support of China when Mao Zedong ousted Chiang. With this change, the problem of Korean unification was absorbed into the global struggle of the anticommunist powers against the communist.

Far more concerned about the containment of communism in Europe than in Asia, the United States underestimated the seriousness of the situation in Korea. Except for a small military advisory group, the United States withdrew its forces from Korea. The Russians simultaneously withdrew from the North. The United States did not consider Korea vital to its interests, and Secretary of State Dean Acheson declared the peninsula outside the defense perimeter of the United States. It was scarcely noticed that the arms and equipment left behind by the Russians were far superior to the materiel left by the Americans. The North was sufficiently confident of its ability to unify Korea by force that on June 25, 1950, it launched an invasion across the 38th parallel.

The Korean War was the focus of a global contest between collective security—the dominant theme of the United Nations—and the use of force, as symbolized by the communist powers. The war was fought primarily between North and South Korea, but more significantly between the North, backed by the USSR and the PRC, and the South, backed by sixteen members of the United Nations, led by the United States. The U.N. Security Council's July 7, 1950, resolution called for the establishment of a unified command under the United States for U.N. forces in Korea. This resolution still forms the legal basis of United Nations' Command (UNC) in the ROK.

Even after the actual fighting began, the United States set limits on its military objectives, operational areas, and the weapons used. General Omar Bradley referred to the Korean War as the war to prevent World War III. As far as both the ROK and the DPRK were concerned, however, it was not a limited war. They suffered far too much destruction of life and property.

Military stalemate led to the signing of an armistice on July 27, 1953, by the DPRK and the PRC (not the USSR), and by the United States for the UNC. President Rhee, respresenting the ROK, would not sign the agreement since he felt that it did not guarantee the national security of the ROK and Kim Il Sung, commander of the North's forces, would attack anytime he judged the time to be ripe.

The armistice defined the military conditions ensuring complete cessation of hostilities. It established a military demarcation line and a demilitarized zone between the hostile forces and set up the Neutral Nations Supervisory Commission (NNSC), the Military Armistice Commission (MAC), and inspection teams intended to enforce the agreement. The agreement still controls the military status quo on the Korean Peninsula and will remain in effect until superseded by a peace treaty.

The day the armistice was signed, the sixteen nations that had sent troops to support South Korea stated that in accordance with the U.N. Charter, they would support the establishment of a united, independent, and democratic Korea; that they would again commit troops to Korea in case of a future armed attack; and that any future war would not necessarily be confined to Korea. Fifteen of the nations withdrew their troops, leaving the United States to carry out the armistice.

It proved impossible to move from armistice to peace treaty. The final diplomatic effort to unite Korea peacefully was the Geneva Conference in the spring of 1954. The ROK proposed genuinely free, nationwide elections under international supervision, but the other side adamantly refused to recognize the United Nations' authority or competence to deal with the Korean problem. Neither side would compromise its right to achieve unification under its own influence and in accordance with its own ideas. The United Nations could only repeat its commitment to a "unified, independent, and democratic Korea under a representative form of government."

Since the failure of this last international gesture for peace and unification, the Korean Peninsula has been surrounded by an atmosphere of hostility and mutual distrust. Peaceful coexistence has been possible only because it was preferable to another war.

Existing Tensions and National Security

The tensions between the ROK and the DPRK result from their dia-
metrically opposed ideological systems, from their deep-seated economic
rivalry, and from the arms race accompanying the military imbalance. In
the view of the South, any of these tensions could provide the North with
an excuse, should it need one, to invade.

Competing Ideological Systems

The ideological foundation of the DPRK is a combination of Marxism-
Leninism, *juche* (sometimes romanized *chuche,*) or self-reliance, and the
cult of Kim Il Sung and his family. (The South regards Kim as irresponsible, bizarre, and possibly quite mad.)

Usually referred to as Beloved and Respected Leader, Kim was a guerrilla fighter against the Japanese in northern Korea and Manchuria during
the 1930s. Forced to withdraw into Siberia in 1941, he resurfaced in September 1945 in Wonsan, North Korea, in the uniform of a Soviet army
major. As soon as the Russians organized their people's democracy at
Pyongyang, they made him—rather than better-known nationalists—first
secretary of the North Korean Central Bureau of the Korean Communist
Party. With Russian support, he was chosen prime minister of the DPRK
in 1948. The next year he was appointed chairman of the Korean Workers'
Party, the successor of the Korean Communist Party. He became a fighting leader and a national hero during the Korean War, but it was not until
1958 that he got rid of the last of his North Korean rivals for power. By
playing off his new-found Chinese allies against his traditional Russian
backers, he was able to establish an independent power base on which to
construct his *juche* program.

Kim's power is unlimited. He is general secretary of the party and head
of state; he is chairman of the MilitaryAffairs Committee (party), chairman
of the National Defense Commission (government), and supreme commander of the armed forces. His birthplace has been made a national
shrine, and statues all over North Korea commemorate his glorious deeds.
A popular hymn proclaims that his "love for the people is warmer than the
sun and deeper than the sea."

His whole family is included in the cult. Brothers, cousins, uncles on his
own and his wife's side hold prestigious positions. Five generations of his

relatives are identified with legendary or contemporary achievements, thus giving the party and the government the aura of a family affair. Until recently, Kim's younger brother was signaled out for particular attention, but in the past few years, the place of honor has been assigned to Kim Chong Il, Kim's son by his first wife.

The son, until 1980, was always anonymously referred to as the Party Center or the Glorious Party Center. He was made responsible around 1973 for administrative and managerial tasks connected with organization, propaganda, and agitation. Between 1976 and 1979, he dropped out of the headlines for two and a half years. It was variously speculated that he had been disgraced for his handling of the ax-murder affair in the DMZ (in which North Korean soldiers killed two American officers attempting to clear trees from the DMZ; the North later apologized to the United States after the U.S. army entered the area in force and removed the trees in question) or that he had been seriously wounded in an attempted coup d'etat. When restored to the limelight in North Korea, he was extravagantly hailed as "the greatest Marxist-Leninist of our time—the great leader of the World Revolution whose sun spreads its light over Africa, Asia, and Latin America."

At the Sixth KWP Congress in October 1980, Kim Chong Il emerged as his father's anointed successor. For the first time he was officially referred to by name, giving him a prestige unattainable by anonymity. He ranked second after his father in the Party Secretariat, fourth in the newly established five-member Permanent Committee of the party Politburo, and third in the party's Military Committee. Only the father and son hold posts in both the Politburo, which determines party policies, and the Secretariat, which controls party personnel. If any official—military, bureaucratic, or technical—entertained notions of opposition to Kim Il Sung, his policies, or his plans for dynastic succession, it could not be detected in the public record of the congress.

The intertwined structure of party and government in North Korea resembles the Soviet model. The constitution lodges the highest authority in the Supreme People's Assembly, which elects the president, nominally the head of state. When the assembly is not in session, its prerogatives are exercised by its standing committee. The Central People's Committee determines policy, and the State Administrative Council (the cabinet) carries it out.

The actual power center in North Korea is not in the government structure at all, but the KWP, with its two million members. The party's highest decision-making apparatus is the National Party Congress, which is supposed to meet every four years and elect the Central Committee and the Politburo. The elaborate party apparatus, directed by the General Secretariat, reaches into every phase of life in all parts of the country. The basic mechanism of control is the interlocking structure of government and party at all levels of society.

The ideology of the North resembles a religious creed far more than a political dogma. Passionately hostile to the ROK, the North is intensely security conscious. The state is an armed camp. Guards are stationed at warehouse doors and factory gates. Posters call for vigilance against spies. Frequent roadblocks stop the traveler, although all vehicles are publicly owned. Thought control is entrusted to the Party Organization and Guidance Committee and to two government bodies, the Public Security and the Political Security committees.

Fired with pride and a deep sense of national purpose, the regimented society has achieved considerable success in agricultural mechanization, industrialization, public health, and education. Four and a half million students attend school, wrestling with a curriculum closely geared to the needs of modernization and public service. Thought control of the students is achieved by the classic methods of indoctrination and endless meetings for self-criticism.

The radio blares a constant barrage of propaganda from the single official news agency. Books, magazines, and newspapers are told what stories to print and what pictures to show. The subject matter of the media is exclusively Marxism-Leninism; hostility to the ROK, the United States, Japan, and the West; and the inspiration and accomplishments of Our Beloved and Respected Leader. Although the seal of the DPRK shows the hammer, the sickle, and the pen, the people of the country are totally cut off from other communist states, knowing nothing, thinking nothing—except as dictated by the great father-government.

The constitution charges the Central People's Committee with eliminating the way of life inherited from the old society and introducing the new social way of life. Even marriage and divorce require official approval, and sexual dallying receives severe punishment if detected. In the view of the ROK, this de-Koreanization is a tremendous obstacle to unification. While the DPRK is dedicated to the elimination of the Confucian tradition, the ROK is devoted to its preservation and enrichment.

Compared with the North, the South is a relatively open society. The ideology and value system of the North are anathema to the South. Yet in the view of the ROK, Kim Il Sung is obsessed with imposing his ideology by force on the whole of the Korean Peninsula. As Kim grows older (he was 70 in 1981), he may be driven to desperation by the thought that for him so little time is left. And the ROK finds no consolation in the prospect of Kim Chong Il's succession. If the son were to see a need to strengthen his own position in Pyongyang or to acquire the recognition in the international sphere that he does not yet possess, he could possibly act more irresponsibly than his father.

Antagonistic Economic Systems

The ideological tension between North and South is aggravated by economic differences. Progress in the North has been accomplished by means of a totally controlled, socialist system geared to the welfare of the state, whereas development in the South has been engineered by a combination of private and public enterprise based on the profit motive and a competitive free market system. Because of the ROK's great pride in its achievements, it regards preservation of this economic system as an integral element of national security.

While the ROK pursued a strategy of economic growth linking the nation with the world trading community, the DPRK concentrated its efforts on indigenous heavy industry, particularly the military-related sector. Like the South, the North had to start from practically nothing after the Korean War. Although the North contained most of the peninsula's mineral reserves and power resources after the division of Korea, Pyongyang and other urban centers were destroyed by American bombing during the war. North Korean cities were rebuilt and modernized with impressive public buildings, broad avenues, and apartment complexes suggestive of Singapore, Hong Kong, or Japan. A North Korean pays only about $5.00 per month in rent.

In the 1950s, the DPRK rapidly outdistanced the ROK in economic progress. The government socialized the ownership of land and productive capital and adopted five-year plans, which were the responsibility of the State Planning Commission. The USSR and the PRC provided economic assistance, but in keeping with the North Koreans chiefly relied on their own savings, raw materials, and labor. Basic materials for food and shelter came from their own fields, forests, mines, and quarries.

Development of agriculture and industry proceeded in tandem. In agriculture, farms were nationalized or operated as collectives and heavily mechanized, and nearly half of the five million plus labor force was assigned to the fields. Farmlands were enriched with generous applications of fertilizers and helped by extensive irrigation and rural electrification projects. Farmers were stirred by *Chollima* (Flying Horse), a production drive not unlike the *Saemaul Undong* in the South. The North became self-sufficient in grain before the end of the 1970s. Wages were low, but so were costs—rice going for two cents per pound with ration coupons. On the farm, as in the factories, the government adopted material incentive programs that rewarded worthy workers with extra bonuses and fringe benefits.

Although DPRK statistics are notoriously unreliable, either treated as state secrets or distorted for propaganda purposes,[1] they are adequate to interpret the general course of industrial development. The DPRK possesses coal, iron ore, and nonferrous metals in sufficient quantities to support heavy industry. On the foundation of metallurgical and chemical plants left behind by the Japanese, the North Koreans built a compact, efficient industrial establishment able to turn out machinery, machine tools, tractors, and all but the most sophisticated of military weapons. Depending on coal and hydroelectric power, they escaped the great need for petroleum products that handicaps the ROK. Their steel output has always compared favorably with that of the South.

The overall economic advantage of the North began to disappear in the mid-1960s when the ROK addressed itself seriously to its own economic development. For diverse reasons, the ROK reversed the tables and quickly outdistanced its northern neighbor. Labor in the South proved to be more adept and productive, and the profit motive was perhaps more effective than the centralized control machinery operating in the North.

Clearly industry in the North was handicapped by the defense burdens placed on it. From 15 to 20 percent of GNP in the North was diverted to defense as compared with 5 to 10 percent in the South. In the North, 12 percent of males ages 17 to 49 were tapped for the armed services—the highest proportion of persons under arms in any country in the world except Israel. High-cost underground construction was required to protect industrial and military installations. Kim Il Sung ordered the conversion of the whole country into a fortress. The DPRK secretly developed a massive military capability for a nation its size, including domestically produced tanks, armored vehicles, long-range self-propelled artillery, and a wide range of ships and submarines.

In the mid-1970s economic strains became all too evident. For too long the government had regarded foreign investment with suspicion and had ignored the necessity of high technology for industrial progress. In a hurry to catch up, it went into debt for plants and equipment, owing $700 million to the USSR and $1.5 billion to Western nations, primarily Japan. When production continued to lag and export income dropped, the DPRK was forced to default. Its debts were not that massive, but the country could not pay and it had no credit.

A new seven-year plan, emphasizing development of export industries, went into effect in 1978. Belatedly the DPRK took a leaf from the book of the ROK. New quotas were established for cement, coal, fish, metals, and products of light industries. Extraordinary efforts were to be devoted to transport and port facilities. High-ranking positions were given to economic experts, and technical missions were exchanged, particularly with the

USSR and the communist bloc nations of Eastern Europe. Kim Il Sung made eleven "guidance visits" throughout the country to pep up flagging spirits and to overcome bottlenecks. His command economy had taken his country to an impasse.

The ROK had good reason to sense the jealousy of the North and to feel satisfied with its economic accomplishments. The GNP of the South reached $61 billion in 1979 against $17 billion for the North. The annual growth rate of the South exceeded 10 percent annually, compared with 7 percent for the North, and the gap was widening. The South in 1980 posted $17.2 billion in exports and $21.9 billion in imports against the North's record of less than $1 billion in foreign trade in each direction. While the North was unable to cover a foreign debt of $2.2 billion, the South was able to fund five times that much. As sources of international credit for the North dried up completely, the world's money markets were disposed to assent to the ROK's requests.[2]

Without doubt, the standard of living had risen in the North as well as in the South, but the disparity between the two increased the concerns of the ROK with its own security. Would jealousy and envy drive the North to military action? Comparative economic success also raised new doubts in the minds of many South Koreans about the desirability of unification. If North and South were to unify, would the North become a millstone around the neck of the South?

In the early 1980s, the economic gap between North and South heightened existing tensions. The outlook for the South was for a GNP four times greater and a per capita GNP one-third greater than those of the North. While the North floundered in economic doldrums, the South was booming. In the South the consumer goods cramming department stores were within reach of more and more workers despite galloping inflation. Having convincingly demonstrated its ability to compete in the tough world of the free market, the South was inclined to skepticism of any proposal involving economic compromise with the drab and less prosperous North. To the South, economic competition with the North was a game that was already over—and the South had won. Its victory had to be protected.

The Military Threat

Without a doubt, the greatest source of tension in Korea lies in the confrontation of two powerful armies. Fearful that the DPRK might resort to force as the only means of imposing its political and economic systems on the ROK, the ROK recognized from the outset that it had to rely on its own strength, with support and assistance from the United States, to deter military aggression from the North and to defeat an invasion should deterrence fail. This policy requires accurate assessment of the capability of the North, constant alertness in probing its intentions, and unstinted effort in matching its strength. All of these factors enter into the analysis of the military equation in North-South relations.[3]

The capability of the North depends in the first instance on the composition of its armed forces. According to intelligence estimates made public in 1979, North Korea has the fifth largest army in the world. Its ground forces were reportedly composed of 600,000 to 700,000 active duty personnel, organized into 35–40 combat divisions and brigades, including three motorized divisions, two armored divisions, and five separate armored regiments. This complement gives the North substantial superiority in armor, firepower, and mobility. The ground forces were thought to contain 50,000–100,000 commando personnel, 500–600 combat maneuver battalions, and 2.5 million reserves. Weapons systems included 2,500 medium tanks, 100 light/amphibious tanks, 1,000 armored personnel carriers, 3,500–4,000 field artillery weapons, 1,500–2,000 multiple rocket launchers, 9,000 mortars, 24,000 infantry antitank weapons, and 8,000–9,000 antiaircraft weapons.

The naval forces consisted of 31,000 personnel, manning 450 combat ships (mostly coastal patrol boats), including 15–20 submarines. The air force was said to have 45,000–50,000 personnel, with 1,100–1,150 aircraft. Most of its 650 MiG jet fighters were obsolete, and neither the DPRK's 20 fighter/bombers nor its 85 light bombers were Russia's best models. Support craft, including 250 transports, 65 helicopters, and 100 trainers round out a rather weak air arm.

The numbers tell only part of the story. The military threat from the North remains serious, and there has been no change in Pyongyang's military posture. Legitimate questions may be asked concerning the North's ability to continue its steady buildup, given its own industrial difficulties and the possible reluctance of the USSR and the PRC to supply all that the DPRK believes that it requires. Such variables as quality of leadership and weapons, morale, deployment, and logistical skills must be taken into consideration in any estimate of the existing military balance between the North and the South.

Evidence of aggressive intention on the part of the North cannot be discounted. Laboriously dug tunnels under the DMZ have been built, apparently to facilitate invasion. Infiltrators have been dispatched to the South, not only by the obvious way of Japan, but stealthily across the DMZ or by spy boats along the coast. In 1968 a daring commando team penetrated to the gates of the Blue House in a vain attempt to take the life of the president. In hundreds of incidents marring the history of the DMZ, more than a thousand people have lost their lives, including 49 Americans.

The rate of infiltration increased significantly after the death of President Park.

Military advantage would probably accrue to the aggressor should the North launch another attack. The ROK remembers that it was the DPRK, under the same Kim Il Sung, that took the initiative in 1950. It is a common thought that what he tried once, he might try again. Seoul is so close to the DMZ that a successful blitzkrieg is a tempting prospect. (The road is heavily fortified, but the fear is that Kim might be victorious if he discovers and concentrates on a single weak spot along the invasion route at a time when weather conditions would hamper air operations by both the United States and the ROK.) Understandably, a surprise attack is the nightmare of the authorities and the citizens of Seoul.

They do not intend, however, to be caught napping. They have prepared formidable defense positions on terrain generally favoring the defense. They maintain a constant alert, and they have built up their armed forces to the point that, in their opinion, they are very nearly a match for the North. The capability of the ROK is probably equal to that of the DPRK in some respects and actually superior in others. The North has greater tank capability, but the South is superior in antitank power. The North has more aircraft, but the South's air arm is more advanced. The South is no match for the North in firepower, mobility, or naval craft; but the North is no match for the South in electronics, close air support, military communications, and combat intelligence.

The ROK numbers its ground forces at 560,000 soldiers; more than a third of them had combat experience in Vietnam, but they are getting older and fewer. The ROK army is organized into 23 infantry divisions, two armored brigades, 40 artillery battalions, one surface-to-surface missile battalion operating Honest John missiles and two surface-to-surface missile battalions, each with two Hawk and two Nike Hercules batteries. The army's inventory, primarily of American manufacture, includes armored personnel carriers, tanks, missiles, mortars, and recoilless rifles in unpublicized numbers.

The ROK navy, with 20,000 sailors and 20,000 marines, operates ten aging destroyers, seven destroyer escorts, nine missile patrol craft, 48 patrol boats, and some minesweepers, but no submarines. The air force, with 25,000 personnel, has over 500 U.S.-built aircraft, including 360 fighters, mostly F-4's and F'5's. The South has more reserves than the North, with 2.5–2.8 million in various paramilitary militia and 338,000 to 1,240,000 in organized reserve forces.

The South is gaining rapidly in the race for parity with the North. Since 1975, the ROK has conducted a Forces Improvement Program (FIP), aiming at the complete modernization of the defense establishment. Calling for a total allotment of $7.6 billion to be paid for by special tax levies, the government set about acquiring missiles, patrol boats, aircraft, artillery, and sophisticated or advanced weapons systems that could not be produced domestically. In addition, it sought and obtained advice and assistance in expanding its own industrial capacity to produce military hardware and munitions. Already manufacturing rifles, machine guns, and tactical radios, it moved to rebuild older tanks; produce artillery and air-defense weapons; to coproduce light helicopters, infantry weapons, and some patrol craft; and to construct better storage and maintenance facilities for U.S. aircraft and other materiel in Korea.

Most of the projects under FIP were successfully completed by 1981. The ROK hopes that a follow-up program (FIP II, 1982–1986) will result in parity with the North by the date of its completion and provide deterrence even in the absence of American forces.

In tangible military assets, the North seems to have a clear advantage over the South. On the basis of that superiority, spokesmen for the South insist that the United States must not diminish its support to any degree in the near future. But intangible factors also must be considered in assessing the military balance. Here the South has undeniable assets. Its government is stable and solidly based. The standard of living is improving. Anticommunist sentiment is so pervasive that a fifth column or a guerrilla movement is highly unlikely. It is clearly gaining in the arms race with the North. Furthermore, the leadership of the armed forces of the ROK is highly trained and battle tested. Its soldiers are strong, tough, and patriotic. Among the intangibles, geography, economics, and psychology tend to tip the balance toward the South.

The Korean Peninsula is probably the most militarized zone in the world. Tensions are explosive. Both North and South can defend themselves against attack, but neither has the strength to attack and defeat the other without outside help. The ROK fears, however, that either with or without Soviet support, Kim Il Sung might try to make good his threat to unify the entire country by force.

But the South Koreans have gained increasing confidence in their ability to take care of themselves. In June 1981 President Chun Doo Hwan told a news conference in Djakarta that his country was powerful enough to reduce the North to ashes if dangerously provoked. His remarks triggered speculation that the ROK may have developed the capability to build an atom bomb. Although the ROK signed the Nuclear Nonproliferation Treaty, the recent deal with the French company Framatome to build the ninth and tenth reactors in South Korea could conceivably contain a secret agreement to train South Koreans in reprocessing spent reactor fuel, a process that can be used to obtain plutonium, the essential ingredient in nuclear weapons.

Conflicting Policies for Unification

As long as the condition of "one nation, two states" exists in Korea, the ROK must treat the problem of unification as its chief concern in foreign policy. If tensions between North and South could be erased, both sides could reduce their enormous expenditures for national defense. The ROK could then afford to take a more relaxed attitude toward security. But as it is, the problem of unification is the major variable for the ROK in its relations with the outside world. In dealing with the North, the sole objective of the ROK is *peaceful* unification.

Kim Il Sung claims that "reunifying our country is the greatest national duty, and the most important task for our party and our people is to take back the territory robbed from us by the imperialists." The South takes such statements seriously. Kim alternates belligerence ("the most glorious victory would come through armed struggle") with pacifism ("peaceful reunification is the long-cherished dream of our whole nation"). His speeches probably portray his mood of the moment and reveal no consistent pattern. He made perhaps his most extreme statement in 1968: "Only when we use force of arms can we gain power . . . the most decisive and positive of all forms of struggle is the struggle with arms for the liberation of our people."

The consensus of opinion in the ROK is that Kim Il Sung would not hesitate to attack if he thought he had a reasonable chance for victory. He is confident that the North excels the South in morale, discipline, economic control, and patriotism. Kim takes the position that his is the only sovereign state on the Korean Peninsula and the ROK is nothing more than a U.S. puppet. He looks on North-South relations not as a struggle between communism and democracy but as a contest between nationalism and imperialism.

Kim Il Sung's strategy for conquering the South consists of several parts. First, he would make his home base impregnable; then create a revolutionary base in the South by "united front" tactics, using infiltrators as organizers and agents provocateurs; and finally, create solidarity with the revolutionary world forces by seeking favors abroad, particularly with the Third World's nonaligned, and weakening the United States and the ROK wherever possible. In the South it is generally believed that this revolutionary strategy and Kim's preference for armed action reveal his true intentions. It is thought that he consents to dialogue only when he feels that some specific purpose can be served.

The South approaches dialogue with the North from a different perspective. The South, too, appreciates the theoretical power and prestige of a united Korea. With a combined population of 54 million (among the top fifteen in the world), armed forces of over one million, and a manufacturing and trading capacity to match its strategic value, a united nation would be the leading force of Northeast Asia. Such a formidable union would enjoy tremendous leverage in dealing with Japan and even with the PRC and the USSR.

Realizing that "one Korean nation, one Korean state" is a distant dream, the ROK views dialogue with the DPRK as a step-by-step approach toward greater security, gradual reintegration, and eventual unification. To the South, unification is a process, not an event. It realizes that the North does not reciprocate this patience. The North wants immediate unification on its own terms, by force if necessary, and accepts dialogue only to confuse the South and loosen its ties with the United States. For its part, the South feels that even a modest though hopeless effort to reach some kind of accommodation is worthwhile if it helps to lessen tensions and thus reduce the threat of invasion.

The history of North-South relations contains little promise for an optimistic future. As long as President Rhee held office, he was as eager to march northward as Kim Il Sung was to march southward. Unification except by force was out of the question. When Rhee was overthrown and the ROK plunged into chaos, Kim might have risked an attack had he been ready. Kim's opportunity passed with the restoration of order in 1961. Moving quickly to overcome the danger of invasion, Park took to the offense. He set up a Ministry of National Unification specifically to handle negotiations with the North, but made it emphatically plain that a willingness to talk was no signal that he or any of his ministers would in the slightest be soft on communism.

During those years, 1961–1965, Kim Il Sung took a soft line toward his new, hard-boiled counterpart. Kim did not denounce Park's military government and faulted the U.S. and U.N. troops for the lack of peace and unification. Kim suggested that he would open discussions with the South if U.S. troops left Korea, if ROK soldiers pulled out of Vietnam, and if the ROK abrogated its recent peace treaty with Japan.

From 1966 to 1968, Kim Il Sung shifted to a hard line. He strengthened his home base by replacing Marxism-Leninism with his own personal philosophy and stepped up commando activities in the South. His propaganda echoed the fanaticism of the Cultural Revolution in the PRC. His hard-line tactics included the capture of the American spy ship *Pueblo* and the holding of its 82 crew members captive for eleven months and the shooting down of an EC-121 reconnaissance plane. He infiltrated a host of subversives across the DMZ and sent his commandos to assassinate President Park in the Blue House. This futile activism led to increased costs for the North, deepened antagonism to communism in the outside world, and decidedly stiffened the backbone of the South.

In the 1970s, the record of North-South relations was spotty. Just after the Nixon Doctrine was announced in 1969, both sides sparred for advantage following the withdrawal of the 7th Division, one of the two then in the ROK. On August 15, 1970, President Park urged the North to compete peacefully to see which system could provide the better society. He took the initiative in arranging discussions between Red Cross delegates from both sides of the DMZ to facilitate personal and family contacts between separated relatives and friends.

In a joint communiqué issued on July 4, 1972, and released simultaneously in Seoul and Pyongyang, the two sides agreed to pursue through joint independent Korean efforts, *without outside interference,* a great unity that would transcend (but not eliminate) differences in ideas and ideologies. Ruling out the use of force, they agreed to stop slandering one another. They set up a "hot line" between the two capitals and inaugurated a Joint North-South Coordinating Committee (JNSCC) to follow up on their agreement.

Even before this agreement, in another shift of propaganda line, the North had relaxed its personal attacks on President Park, reduced the frequency of armed incidents along the frontier, halted the infiltration of communist guerrillas, and abandoned its insistence on further withdrawal of American forces and elimination of the UNC as preconditions for North-South negotiations. These signs made it seem possible for Park to continue rather than to curb liberalization trends in the South, but Park chose this moment to declare martial law and adopt the *Yushin* Constitution. He explained that domestic reforms were needed to marshal the nation's entire strength in confronting the North.

Park's toughness generated toughness in the North. Again Kim Il Sung swung from soft to hard. He renewed his demands for immediate withdrawal of all U.S. troops from the ROK and for dissolution of the UNC. He proposed the joint reduction of DPRK and ROK forces to 100,000 each and formation of a political consultative conference, comprising all political parties and social organizations, that would lead to a confederation leaving both systems intact. For good measure, he demanded that President Park legalize all activities of Communists in the South and immediately release all his jailed political opponents.

President Park bent a little, not out of a desire to appease Kim, but because of the ripple effect of Nixon's push for détente with the USSR and the Nixon visit to China. In 1973, Park issued what he called a historic statement of policy. He declared that henceforth he would not object to membership in the United Nations for both the ROK and the DPRK, and he would open the doors of the ROK to all friendly countries and nonhostile communist countries for trade and other contacts on the basis of the principles of peaceful coexistence. Rejecting the idea of a grand conference and confederation, Park suggested further meetings of the JNSCC. Failing a meeting of minds, the two sides let the negotiations lapse.

In 1974, President Park called for a nonaggression pact between the South and the North, leaving the U.N. armistice system intact. Sensing the U.S. congressional dissatisfaction with events in Indochina, Kim sent an open letter to U.S. congressmen suggesting that for the sake of peace the United States should remove its troops from Asia. He proposed bilateral peace negotiations between the DPRK and the United States—*without Seoul.* He argued that the ROK had not signed the armistice agreement and was therefore not properly a party to negotiations aimed at a peace treaty to replace the armistice. Peace and unification were separate matters: the former was of concern only to the DPRK, the PRC, and the United States; the latter was the exclusive concern of the two Koreas.

On August 15, 1974, President Park responded with his principles for unification, which were definitive as long as he lived. As a step toward peace, he advocated a mutual nonaggression pact. The North and the South should open their doors to one another for exchanges. Free, internationally supervised general elections should be held in the North and the South, with representatives to be elected in direct proportion to population. In the midst of the speech proclaiming these principles, an allegedly communist-trained assassin shot at the president. The bullet missed its intended victim, but hit and killed Mrs. Park. President Park finished the speech.

After this incident, counterproposals for unification from the North had a hollow ring, especially after discovery of tunnels under the DMZ—a discovery that alarmed the South. On one occasion, the minister of defense remarked: "In regular warfare North Korea can dispatch division-strength forces through the largest tunnel in a single hour, capture strategic positions behind the forward defense line, and completely isolate the advance defense contingent." He patently exaggerated, but he was justified in two conclusions: the tunnels would be useful in infiltrating enemy commandos in ROK uniforms behind the forward line, and the tunnels were, presumably, evidence of the North's continuing aggressive intentions. Only three tunnels were announced at the time, but as many as twenty more were suspected. The tunnels afforded plenty of grist for South Korea's propaganda mill.

Kim's persistently belligerent stance kept the ROK on a psychological edge. The DPRK news agency frequently referred to President Park in such terms as "a puppet of imperialism, a fascist hangman, and a war maniac." Kim consistently rejected every one of Park's overtures, particularly his call for a supervised national election. Kim saw the advantage of the ROK's 37 million population (compared with 17 million in the DPRK) in a "one man, one vote" situation. Kim accentuated his bellicosity by dispatching infiltrators to the South and by stepping up radio and leaflet campaigns.

Immediately after the American exodus from Indochina, Kim visited the PRC and Eastern Europe (the USSR refused to receive him) on vain missions for added help and assistance. At this time, Kim went on record as saying: "If another war is fought in Korea, the only thing we lose in war will be the military demarcation line, and the only thing we gain will be the unification of the fatherland."

Kim's activities did not escape the notice of President Park. In response, Park issued Emergency Decree no. 9, accentuated defense preparations in his economic development program, and launched FIP. To many of his countrymen, including the liberal opposition, Park appeared a leader with ice in his veins and steel in his soul. Driving ahead with all his strength and will, he concentrated on facing the threat from the North.

The hostile impasse between North and South persisted through the last year of the Ford administration and the first two years of the Carter administration. In January 1979, after President Park regained his composure following the announcement of U.S. troop withdrawal from the ROK, he publicly proposed that North and South hold talks anywhere, anytime, at any level, to achieve unification and pursue prosperity. Kim accepted, and during the next two months the two sides held meetings in an unaccustomed atmosphere of courtesy and civility.

The negotiating climate deteriorated when new intelligence estimates of the military strength of the North were made public and the United States announced the postponement of any further withdrawal of American forces. The show of U.S.-ROK military cooperation, evident in the first annual exercise (named "Team Spirit") might also have had an effect. At any rate, the North resurrected its old demands: cease mutual calumnies and slanders immediately, halt hostile military actions—including the acquisition of foreign weapons—withdraw all U.S. troops, dissolve the UNC, and convene a grand national conference as a preparation for confederation. Further negotiations on this kind of agenda were useless.

Following the assassination of President Park and the military coup of

December 12, 1979, North Korea sought an opportunity to make a new survey of the situation in the ROK. Shortly after New Year, 1980, Lee Chong Ok, prime minister of the DPRK, invited the prime minister of the ROK to reopen the suspended dialogue. For the first time, the North used the title "Republic of Korea" in the invitation, implying a recognition of the existence of a separate state rather than of a mere puppet regime. When the South accepted the invitation, delegations representing the two prime ministers met to arrange procedural matters. Their bickering had led to a complete stalemate at the time President Chun assumed office.

The Delicate Power Balance in Northeast Asia

The ROK's quest for national security is not confined to the Korean Peninsula. The pursuit of its major objective, peaceful unification, requires careful handling of relations with adversaries, neutrals, and friends—all of whom are vitally concerned with the outcome of the North-South confrontation. The ROK has shown a conciliatory attitude toward communist nations other than the DPRK, a policy of active cooperation with the United Nations and the Third World, and an earnest desire to strengthen its ties with allies and friends. All three are vital elements in its foreign policy activities.

On June 23, 1973, President Park declared that the ROK would open its doors to all friendly countries and nonhostile communist countries for trade and other contacts on the basis of the principles of coexistence. He told the world that he, as well as President Nixon, could live with détente with the USSR and the PRC.

As long as the USSR and the PRC were bound together in a solid communist bloc, they were treaty-bound allies of the DPRK and closed to any overtures from the ROK. The Sino-Soviet split opened the door for modest initiatives to the USSR, Eastern Europe, and the PRC. Making clear that it had no ideological objections to dealing with any of them, the ROK indicated its willingness to enter into trade relations and cultural exchanges. None made any response, and no such response can be anticipated until there is an improvement in ROK-DPRK relations. Communist as well as noncommunist states seem disposed to accept the status quo on the Korean Peninsula as the best alternative available.

Perhaps in response to the PRC's normalization of relations with the United States and Japan and events following the invasion of Afghanistan, the ROK noted a stiffening in Soviet attitudes. The Soviet press became more critical of the ROK government and supported more noisily the DPRK's demand for the total withdrawal of American troops. Despite the dangers inherent in an aggressive Soviet policy in Asia, the ROK, much against its own desires, followed the American lead in boycotting the Moscow Olympics. The ROK felt that the Soviet invitation was a diplomatic breakthrough, and South Koreans had high hopes of winning the soccer championship. Seoul watched the flow of arms from Moscow to Pyongyang carefully, trying to determine if the USSR was restraining the jingoistic Kim Il Sung or laying a foundation should it ever desire to use the DPRK as a surrogate to penetrate Northeast Asia more deeply.

In dealing with China, the ROK shows surprisingly little racial prejudice or psychological bitterness in spite of the Chinese "volunteers" in the Korean War. Both the PRC and the ROK keep a low profile toward one another. The ROK is similarly cautious in its relations with Taiwan. Until the advent of Deng Xiaoping, Taiwan and South Korea were unusually close because of their anticommunism and their alliances with the United States. Although they were both pushed backstage by the PRC's normalization of relations with the United States and Japan, they demonstrated remarkable resilience and independence of spirit. The ROK cannot be totally indifferent to the unification of Taiwan and the mainland because of possible conflicts of jurisdiction over offshore oil reserves.

In the words of a ROK official, "We extend the hand of friendship to the PRC, but it is Beijing that refuses to grasp it." The ROK benefits from mail and telegraph service with the PRC and would like to bid on contracts for construction of highways, public buildings, and hotels in China. South Koreans have money to invest and could build at lower prices than could the Japanese or the Americans. The ROK-U.S. aviation agreement of 1980 permits both PRC and U.S. commercial aircraft to fly over South Korean territory.

The ROK looks upon the PRC as a substantial hedge against the more dangerous USSR in Pyongyang, where the greater cultural and lesser economic influence of the Chinese is pitted against the lesser military and greater economic power of the Russians. The ROK is convinced that the PRC is more committed to the Korean status quo than is the USSR despite the extravagant statements of visiting Chinese officials praising Kim Il Sung and calling for the total and immediate withdrawal of American forces. South Koreans point out that the Chinese member of the Military Armistice Commission in Panmunjom acts independently and at times in direct opposition to his North Korean counterpart. To them, it is significant that in off-the-record conversations, Chinese Communists have let it be known that they do not want the Americans to leave. The Chinese admit candidly, but discreetly, that in their opinion, the Americans—as a counterbalance to Russian power—represent the single greatest stabilizing factor in Northeast Asia.

Although the ROK treats the USSR and the PRC gingerly for fear of upsetting the delicate balance of power in the region, it exhibits more confidence in its policy clashes with the DPRK in the global arena. The DPRK has diplomatic relations with 90 countries, the ROK with more than 100. The most significant area of confrontation is the United Nations, toward which the ROK has always been favorably disposed. A resolution of the General Assembly of December 1948 recognized the ROK as "a lawful State with effective control and jurisdiction" over its territory and said categorically, "this is the only such state on the Korean Peninsula." The United Nations fought the Korean War on the side of the ROK, and the UNC concluded the armistice and is to remain the implementing agency until replaced by some other peacekeeping arrangement. The ROK has consistently suggested U.N.-supervised national elections as the best means of accomplishing unification.

The ROK has repeatedly tried to join the United Nations, but has been blocked by a Russian veto. As an alternative, it has proposed that both Koreas be admitted. Due to prolonged and unproductive debate, the Korean question has been taken off the U.N. agenda. Nevertheless, the ROK participates in practically all important specialized agencies, including the World Bank, the International Monetary Fund, the United Nations Educational, Scientific, and Cultural Organization, the United Nations Children's Fund, the World Health Organization, the Food and Agriculture Organization, the United Nations Conference on Trade and Development, and the General Agreement on Tariffs and Trade. It has cordial relations with such regional organizations as the Asia Development Bank and the Association of Southeast Asian Nations (ASEAN).

Like all nations, the ROK formulates its international policies in the light of its own national interests. It is not willing to entrust either its security or welfare to international decisions. Believing that it has more to gain than to lose, it opposes a nuclear-free zone involving Korea without firm four-power guarantees and opposes any multilateral agreement that would ban arms deliveries to both Koreas. It has taken no unshakable position on the proposals for cross-recognition of the two Koreas and a multilateral conference for Korea's future.

The ROK desires to identify itself more closely with the Third World, especially the nonaligned nations, and wants cooperation with other developing states. As a former colony, it cannot stand by while other nations suffer from unjust treatment by the big powers or their proxies. The ROK declares that it supports the just causes of the Third World, including independence, national sovereignty, territorial integrity, and elimination of racial discrimination. Taking such a strong stand serves two purposes: it challenges the Communists in their own advertised creed and provides an opportunity to take initiatives independently of the United States.

Given its experience in adapting Western techniques to non-Western societies, the ROK feels that it has much to teach LDCs. Rural development, public health, and family planning, and industrial management are conspicuous examples. The ROK wants to export capital, labor, and manufactured products and offers technical training, grants-in-aid, and loans to needy and willing recipient nations. At reasonable costs and without political strings, South Korean workers have built roads, harbors, and housing in the Middle East; a department store in Gabon; and a textile plant in the Sudan. Such activities as these expand the market for Korean goods and earn the money to pay for imports of oil and other needed raw materials.

The ROK is especially eager to befriend the nonaligned nations. It smarts from the admission of the DPRK to nonaligned conferences and its own exclusion. Supporting the basic principles of the Bandung, Cairo, Belgrade, Lima, and Colombo conferences, the ROK has regular relations with more than fifty nonaligned nations. It is clear that South Korea can offer more by way of economic assistance than can the North, and the South confidently asserts that it opposes the counterproductive time-consuming behavior of the North Korean regime in using nonaligned meetings as forums for emotion-charged, ideological confrontation.

Finally, the ROK makes every effort to strengthen its ties with friends and allies, primarily Japan and the United States. These efforts are multichanneled and include security interests, economic cooperation, and the broader areas of cultural contacts.

Relations with Japan suffer from a heritage of prejudice, accentuated by the scars of colonialism. Some South Koreans say frankly: "We have two biases: first against the Communists, and second against Japan." It was fifteen years after the Korean War before ROK-Japanese relations, with American prodding, could be guided into a normal peacetime pattern. There is a great deal of jealousy and envy behind South Korean attitudes toward Japan; above all, South Koreans do not want to be considered pawns in U.S.-Japanese relations. It offends and angers a South Korean to be told that his country is important only because of its role in the defense of Japan.

The ROK resents the priority given Japan in American policy, thinking it ridiculous, for example, that history and geography should be ignored in favor of economics in identifying Japan with the United States and Western Europe in the Trilateral Commission. The ROK appreciates the value of Japanese economic assistance in security and national development, but insists that it pays well for every yen received. The "grubby chase for profit" underlies not only Japanese trade and investments in the ROK, but also the fisheries, trade, and shipping arrangements between Japan and North Korea. The ROK accuses Japan of utter lack of principle in seeking equidistance or symmetrical treatment in its policies toward the ROK and the DPRK. A tinge of jealousy enters into the South Korean assessment of Japan's trade with the PRC, especially since many Japanese firms shut up shop in Seoul in response to the PRC's edict that no enterprise could do business with the ROK and the PRC at the same time.

The ROK looks with ambivalence on the rapidly shifting Japanese attitudes toward rearmament. It galls Seoul that Tokyo spends so little of its GNP and its government budget on defense. The Japanese contribution to regional security is appreciated, but South Koreans do not hesitate to criticize Japan's reluctance to put its bases automatically and completely at American disposal in the event of renewed hostilities in Korea. South Koreans want Japan to become stronger, but not too strong. Above all, they do not want a Japan with nuclear arms. They resist any multilateral agreement that would reduce U.S. and increase Japanese responsibility for the defense of the ROK. It required a great amount of soul-searching on the part of the South Koreans to allow the Japanese to participate in joint planning and joint exercises and to permit the official visit to South Korea of an officer on active duty with the Japanese Self-Defense Forces. It would be a terrible nightmare for South Korea if the Japanese military juggernaut of World War II were to be recreated.

Proud of its own military establishment, the ROK thinks wistfully of the consequences, if Korean unification could be brought about satisfactorily, of utilizing the combined strength of the North and South for national all-Korean purposes. Such an eventuality is as disturbing to Japan as a reborn aggressive Japanese military machine is to South Korea.

Strains and tensions between the ROK and Japan are not one-sided. The Japanese have their own prejudices and complaints against the Koreans. The Japanese have been particularly displeased with the activities of the KCIA on Japanese soil (particularly the 1973 kidnapping of Kim Dae Jung), and they have expressed disapproval of the excessively harsh measures under the ROK's martial law regime. On the other hand, the South Koreans have accused the Japanese of participating in plots to overthrow the government of the ROK and of discriminating against South Korean residents in Japan.

This recital of differences of opinion and clashes of interest must not distort the commonality of purpose and degree of cooperation between the two countries. As neighbors have their quarrels, so they learn to live together. It is entirely possible that Japanese and Koreans understand one another better than either understands the Americans and perhaps better than Americans understand either of them. South Korean–Japanese ties are strong; by mutual desire, the ties will become stronger. Perennial issues between the ROK and Japan are dealt with in annual ministerial-level conferences held alternately in Seoul and Tokyo. Nothing influences them more toward mutual accommodation than the awareness of their stake in the continued support and goodwill of the United States.

The ROK and the United States

Although the cornerstone of South Korean policy is its relationship with the United States, Americans must not overlook one fact: the ROK is sovereign, independent, and growing in strength and will. Although a former client, it is now entitled to be treated as an equal partner. South Korea must be prepared to rely entirely on itself should the United States ever abandon its perceived role as protector and guaranto..

President Rhee was never persuaded that the United States understood the gravity of his situation or would give the support needed to prevail over the North. He was profoundly convinced that the Korean War was unfinished business, dooming him to a precarious future. To him, the armistice was acceptable only because it was sustained by the American commitment—the Mutual Defense Treaty, the presence of ground troops, military assistance, and the nuclear umbrella. It was an article of faith that the United States was the protector of the ROK, despite the limiting clause in the treaty: "take action [only] in accordance with its constitutional processes." The ROK assumed that in the event of trouble, the United States would automatically and immediately come to the rescue of the ROK. No matter how unwarranted, these were the perceptions that underlay the ROK's great confidence in, and great expectations from, the United States.

The ROK perceived no lessening of the danger to itself from either the Sino-Soviet split or the Nixon Doctrine. What was regarded as a source of relaxation in the United States was interpreted as an aggravation in the ROK. The lowering of the American military profile meant the pullout of the 7th Division, half the American contingent in Korea; this entailed a monstrous increase in the burdens of the ROK. President Park, to strengthen his own position, proclaimed martial law and adopted the *Yushin* Constitution. He felt that the United States failed to understand that his suspension of human rights stemmed exclusively from his concern for security. Even his fruitless efforts to reach an understanding with the North were not appreciated in the United States, causing him to resort to the awkward Koreagate efforts to counteract the adverse opinion held by many Americans about the ROK's internal situation.

After the ignominious U.S. pullout from Indochina, the ROK received more sympathetic consideration from the Americans. The United States, in an effort to bolster its own credibility, ardently wooed the ROK and

Japan. It became appropriate to reduce criticism of Park and to stress the renewed interest of the United States in the security of Northeast Asia. President Park was reassured by Secretary of Defense James Schlesinger's visit in 1975 and the later announcement of President Ford that "the present administration has no present intention of reducing the level of American forces in Korea."

The fear that troop withdrawal was tantamount to abandonment of the U.S. interest in Korea, thus forcing the ROK into a single-handed, perhaps even a nuclear, arms race with the North was genuine. President Park did not shy away from his new problem. He declared that his country would do everything possible to ensure its survival, including the development of nuclear arms if the U.S. troops were withdrawn. The ROK already had the know-how to produce nuclear weapons and possessed atomic reactors capable of producing plutonium. Park had taken steps to acquire a reprocessing plant from France when he was effectively blocked by President Ford. Park acquiesced because of his confidence that American forces would stay in Korea—at least in the immediate future. Perhaps he also anticipated that Ford would win re-election.

The attitude of the ROK took a 180-degree turn with the advent of the Carter administration and its announcement of phased withdrawal of the American ground forces. A shock wave of dismay and anger swept South Korean society. Not that the idea of withdrawal was new—it had been a source of continuing irritation since the 7th Division left South Korea in 1971. It was, rather, that the announcement was so abrupt. The South Koreans found it incomprehensible that a policy that had worked for 30 years should be changed without providing a substitute or insisting on a quid pro quo from the Communists. They were absolutely convinced that the United States *had* to keep its troops in the ROK until the modernization of Korean forces had been completed or until some other method had been adopted for keeping the peace. They were disconcerted that such a momentous policy decision should be formulated in the heat of a political campaign and announced without adequate consultation. Many South Koreans reached the easy conclusion that this was the American way of punishing Korea for Koreagate and the repressive actions taken under the emergency decrees.

Koreans of every bent—government officials, the political opposition, the intelligentsia, whether conservative or liberal—disapproved of the withdrawal policy. The United States lost in a moment much of the goodwill that it had taken a quarter of a century to win. The government and the populace reacted differently. Although President Park and his loyal supporters tried to make the best of a difficult situation by a spirited call for "self-reliance now," they felt deserted. The opposition, fearing a take-over of the political process by the army, saw its hopes for democratic progress shattered. Liberals, particularly students and those who had felt the sting of the authoritarian lash, felt that the last restraint preventing Park from becoming as ruthless as his northern counterpart had been removed.

The fundamental psychological shock to the South Koreans was their perception that American withdrawal might tempt Kim Il Sung to strike. The 2d Division, with its contingent along the DMZ, was a certain check to the North's schemes. The power to deter was infinitely more precious to the South Koreans than the power to defend or retaliate. An adviser in the Blue House expressed his emphatic opinion that the U.S. must get used to the idea that its soldiers were in Korea permanently. Letters to the *New York Times* advocating withdrawal only add to the trouble, he said, since the United States cannot walk away from a situation it helped to create.

In a letter to the *Korea Times* (May 27, 1977) epitomizing the sentiments of many thoughtful South Koreans, the distinguished historian Dr. Kim Jun Yop worried about the discontinuity and the confusion in American policy. In his view, the United States vacillated between the desire to remain involved in Asia and the desire to get out of Asia. Over the long range he perceived an ad hoc, on-again, off-again quality to American actions rather than any constant pursuit of permanent interests. He was concerned about the motives behind the withdrawal policy: Was it to save money, to improve security, to support democracy, to promote détente, to appease Pyongyang, to please Korea's critics? It was unnerving to him to see the United States take actions that would affect the allies' perceptions of America's maturity, prudence, reliability, and steadfastness.

He put into words typical Korean reactions to the rather stern Carter policies on human rights. He noted that perhaps the United States had a psychic need for morality after Vietnam and Watergate and suggested that morality degenerates into moralism, a posture of moral superiority as distinct from morally superior behavior. He thought that America could become an immense moral force by behaving morally and not by preaching or pressuring its friends and allies. Pointing out that leverage—economic, military, or diplomatic—even when employed for moral ends, can never quite avoid the stigma of power politics, he concluded: "The advocacy of morality or human rights or political democracy is always in danger of being perceived as indicating arrogance of power."

The immediate reactions to the withdrawal policy gave rise to deeper questions about the credibility of the American alliance. The government was cautioned not to depend exclusively on the United States because of what happened to Chiang Kai-shek, two presidents of South Vietnam, and the shah of Iran. It was a general sentiment, however, that the continued viability of the alliance should be accepted. The ROK requires arms, air and naval support, intelligence and strategic assistance, and these things are obtainable only from the United States. Trade will also be important. The ROK will be an important element in the U.S. global strategic posture and will be a good market for U.S. products, arms exports, and investments. In addition to all the material relationships that can be developed, the ROK wants as many American soldiers as possible to stay. No amount of weaponry can take the place of bodies as evidence of goodwill and helpful intent.

Even by the end of the Carter administration the ROK had given no clear indication of the road it intended to pursue in implementing its foreign policy. Changes in the world power structure, such as the relative decline of U.S. power, the apparent erosion of American will, the rising challenge of the USSR, the uncertain developments in Sino-Soviet relations, the increasing power of Japan and Western Europe, the emergence of a new China, and the world-shaking events in the Persian Gulf region, cause the ROK to reappraise its own interests and objectives continually. In its view, the time has come for Korea to look beyond its allies and participate in the global effort to meet human needs and improve the quality of life. The ROK is quietly resolved to play a positive role, not as anybody's satellite, but as the equal of any other sovereign state in this interdependent world.

3 | U.S. INTERESTS AND POLICIES
BEFORE 1969

The U.S. interest in the Korean Peninsula predates Korea's absorption into the Japanese empire. As long as Japan was paramount in East Asia, the United States acquiesced in Korea's status as a Japanese colony. In the eyes of many American officials, it was better to have Korea in the hands of Japan than under the control of expansionist Russia. With the destruction of Japanese power and the shattering of the Asian status quo by World War II, the U.S. interest in Korea inevitably revived. That interest was expressed at Cairo and pursued in the postwar military and diplomatic arrangements of the victorious Allies.

The American and Russian inability to reach agreement on methods to achieve a united, democratic Korean nation deliberately or unwittingly contributed to the gradual solidification of divided Korea. As the division at the 38th parallel, originally a temporary military convenience for accepting the surrender of the Japanese, continued, differences between north and south grew more irreconcilable and prospects for unification more remote. The focus of American policy narrowed from the future of the entire Korean Peninsula to the fate of the ROK, its southern half. In 1950, after five years of fruitless international negotiations and increasing bitterness between North and South Korea, a bloody war to halt the combined aggression of North Korea, the USSR, and the PRC against the U.S.-assisted, newly established independent ROK erupted. The hostilities ended with an indecisive armistice under which the United States accepted specific obligations for the preservation of peace on the Korean Peninsula.

With the international situation stabilized after a fashion, the United States, in its own interest, made commitments to the ROK intended to make it a stronger ally in the worldwide confrontation with the communist powers. These commitments consisted of statements of policy by American officials; a treaty of mutual assistance; stationing of U.S. military forces in the ROK; and provision of substantial amounts of military and economic aid. Since both the United States and the ROK were convinced that their national interests demanded the fullest cooperation, the two nations carried out their respective policies in an atmosphere of mutual trust and reciprocal goodwill.

Toward the end of the 1960s, the approaching debacle in Indochina caused the U.S. government to reassess its global position, particularly in East Asia. In 1969, the new administration of President Nixon made it clear that the realities of American capabilities necessitated a realignment of all American commitments, including those to Korea. The Nixon Doctrine was a watershed in U.S.-ROK relations.

The Historical U.S. Interest in Korea

The ROK is heir to the historical position assigned to the entire Korean Peninsula by American policymakers in the late nineteenth and early twentieth centuries. Toward the end of the nineteenth century, with China shedding its skin of empire, Japan unfolding its schemes for hegemony on the Asian continent, and Russia expanding toward a warm-water port on the Pacific, these three powers were predestined to clash on the Korean Peninsula. America conceived its security interest to be to preserve, as far as possible, a balance of power in Northeast Asia by encouraging an independent Korea, free from outright control by China, Russia, or Japan.

Korea did not receive nearly as much American attention as either China or Japan, for obvious reasons. American missionaries and merchants were eager to penetrate Korea, but the U.S. government did not perceive the same advantage in opening Korea as it had seen in participating in the opening of China and Japan. The American government pursued a policy of noninterference in response to the Japanese opening of Korea and its dismantling of the Chinese overlordship, which had persisted in Korea for more than a millennium.

The Americans were neither indifferent to the welfare of Koreans nor blinded to the God-given ideals of freedom and independence, which were always the oratorical cornerstones of American policy. The pragmatic Americans stated their idealistic position in forceful terms, but limited their actions to insisting on equal commercial rights for Americans, whatever the political consequences of the Japanese advance in Korea.

When Japan proclaimed its protectorate over Korea in 1905, the U.S. interest was not to undo the patent absorption of Korea into the Japanese empire (which was, in any case, beyond American strength), but to prevent the Japanese action from harming the American position elsewhere in Asia. The United States extracted an assurance from Japan that in exchange for U.S. noninterference with Japan in Korea, Japan would not interfere with American purposes in the Philippines. Many Korean critics of U.S. policy interpret this as the first American sellout of Korea.

Japan had its own way in Korea for nearly half a century. First, it eliminated the challenge of Russia by a successful war and a series of alliances. Then Japan assured itself of the diplomatic acceptance of its Korean program by understandings with Great Britain and France similar to that with the United States. Furthermore, Japan destroyed whatever hopes China might have had for the recovery of its former rights in Korea by an aggressive continental policy establishing Japan's military supremacy over Korea's neighbors—Manchuria, Mongolia, and China itself.

The mild U.S. Open Door policy—territorial integrity of the remains of China and equal rights for American citizens—gave no encouragement to Koreans like Syngman Rhee who fought for Korean independence from exile in the United States or China. The self-determination policy of Woodrow Wilson gave Koreans a glimmer of hope, but the practical politics of the Versailles conference crushed these hopes for an end to Japanese rule. Critical Koreans frequently call this rejection of the Korean appeal at Paris America's second sellout.

No challenge to Japan in Korea came from the United States or anyone else until World War II reignited Korean hopes for independence. The freedom fighters in exile turned to President Roosevelt, as the heir to Wilsonian philosophy and architect of the Four Freedoms, to champion their cause. At Cairo he persuaded Churchill and Chiang Kai-shek that "mindful of the enslavement of the people of Korea, we are determined that in due course, Korea shall become free and independent."

The fundamental American interest in a free and united Korea was not compromised by the military order in 1945 that the USSR would accept the surrender of Japanese troops north of the 38th parallel and the United States to the south of it. The division was to be temporary, for military purposes only. Immediately after the surrender, the Russians began to dig in for a permanent stay, giving every evidence that if Korea were to become united and independent, or free and democratic, it would have to be according to the Russian definition of these idealistic terms. Such an eventuality would have been detrimental to the American interest.

The Soviet, British, and American foreign ministers discussed the problem of whose interest should be paramount—no one gave much thought to the interests of the Koreans, which at best would have been difficult to determine—at the Moscow Conference (December 16–26, 1945). The conference agreed to set up a provisional democratic government, which would take all necessary steps to develop industry, transport, agriculture, and the national culture of the Korean people. Pending the establishment of this government, representatives of the U.S. and Soviet commands in Korea would work out an agreement concerning a four-power (American, British, Soviet, and Nationalist Chinese) trusteeship of Korea for a period of up to five years.[1]

Again, Koreans in the south felt cheated. Convinced that their fight for independence had earned them the right of self-government, they were insulted by the prospect of a foreign trusteeship under selfish great powers. In the Korean view, none of the trustees, not even the United States, was in any way familiar with the aspirations of Koreans or disposed to subordinate its own interests to those of Korea.

The frustrations of the three years 1945–1948 were inescapable. The USSR in the north was absorbed in creating a communist state in its own image. The United States in the south endeavored to preserve at as little cost as possible the impregnable security position that it had won in Northeast Asia by the victory over Japan. While the occupying powers argued, Koreans on both sides of the parallel kept themselves alive by hard work and the assistance granted by their increasingly antagonistic patrons.

From Unified Korea to Divided Korea

The ideal of a democratic, unified Korea was the climactic victim of the cold-hot war between the communist powers led by the USSR and the anticommunists led by the United States. Confrontation in Iran, the Balkans, and Berlin preceded the division of Korea in 1948. With the establishment of the ROK in the south and the DPRK in the north, the interests of the United States and the Soviet Union became totally identified with those of their client states. For the long term, the United States would cling to its ideal of a single, united, democratic Korea serving as a rock of stability in Northeast Asia and a buffer state for Japan. But for the immediate future, the United States would accept the reality of the ROK—one state, but half a nation—as the entity with which it had to deal in assessing its interests and formulating its policies.

The United States conceived its interests in the ROK as the maintenance of peace and stability in the Korean Peninsula and Northeast Asia. The objectives of American policy were to preserve the ROK as an independent state, to assist in the establishment of a stable government, and to contribute to its growth and development. Essential was the promotion of a sufficient degree of democracy and social justice to keep the ROK from succumbing to a totalitarian system like that of the North.

The primary concern of the United States was to prevent war and to give the U.N. system of collective security a reasonable chance to grow. Immediately after World War II, the task was not too difficult in East Asia because of the preponderant power of the United States. China was in the throes of civil war, Japan was in ruins, and Russia was engrossed in the reconstruction of its shattered homeland. Russia under Stalin, however, made it clear that it had no intention of abandoning either its political or ideological ambitions. Once Russia recovered its strength and acquired nuclear know-how, it could be expected to assert itself in Northeast Asia either directly or through its proxy, North Korea. The containment of communism, by means short of war, became a prime objective of American diplomacy.

In the accomplishment of this objective, the security of the ROK assumed increasing importance. Given the rapidly diminishing power of Chiang Kai-shek in China, the ROK loomed as the last U.S. foothold on the Asian mainland. The unassailable position of the United States in Japan, achieved primarily by General Douglas MacArthur during the occupation, appeared temporarily immune to any threat from the USSR. But the security of the ROK was essential for the maintenance of that privileged position. A Japanese proverb proclaims: "When the wind blows from the west, the leaves settle in the east." The United States, as the occupying power, accepted and adopted as its own the Japanese conviction that the security and welfare of Japan itself depended on the security of Korea. Korea in the hands of a hostile nation or group of nations would menace the very survival of Japan.

The United States also saw the need to strengthen the ROK to resist a possible attack from the north. Beyond North Korea lay the USSR and Communist China. The security forces of the ROK, including police, militia, and regular army, had to be built from the ground up. A certain amount of caution was needed, however, not to make the ROK too strong, lest some hotheaded leader set forth on a reckless drive to the north. When the Americans withdrew from South Korea in 1949,[2] they left behind a substantial amount of equipment and the Military Assistance Group to administer subsequent training and assistance programs.

In the political sphere, the United States sought to protect its interests by helping to stabilize the government of the ROK. The departure of the Japanese deprived Korea of the skills of governors, administrators, and bureaucrats. In colonial days, Japanese had filled all responsible jobs. The American occupation forces had to rely on interpreters, clever ex-collaborators, and returned exiles to administer political affairs. The Koreans were totally without experience in self-government, and the proliferating political parties made a shamble of the newly created legislature. Politicians, loudly proclaiming their devotion to democracy, operated with the only tools they knew how to use—nepotism, vote buying, bribery, intimidation, and brutality. The country slipped too close to anarchy for American comfort. Law and order were preserved only by permitting compromises with human rights and providing support for an authoritarian regime whose ruthless methods were genuinely abhorred.

The U.S. interest in strengthening the ROK necessitated generous amounts of economic aid. The ROK began its existence as an independent state as an economic basket case. On separation, the northern half of the country got the metals, minerals, and industrial base; the southern half received most of the agricultural land. The local population of the south, swelled by refugees from the north and from Japan, lacked sufficient food and raw materials to meet the needs of its people. Stark poverty was everywhere. Such things as GNP and per capita income were too low for practical measurement.

The United States provided food and other goods and assisted the ROK in creating the infrastructure necessary for modernization. The United States believed that such economic help as was extended was in its enlightened interest since the greater the prosperity, or the stronger the hope for a higher standard of living, the brighter would be the chances for the development of an independent, communism-resistant nation.

The United States did not neglect such intangible interests as encouragement of democracy, social justice, and respect for human rights. Although living conditions were primitive and a military organization exercised the American fiat, Americans on the spot never passed up an opportunity to talk or write about the contributions of American missionaries and their educational institutions in Korea. The United States constantly extolled the ideals of democracy and made possible opportunities for hundreds, perhaps thousands, of Koreans to pursue their studies in the United States or to make a new life for themselves abroad.

Between World War II and the Korean War, the Joint Chiefs of Staff (Admirals William Leahy and Chester Nimitz, Generals Dwight D. Eisenhower and Carl Spaatz) advised President Truman that "from the standpoint of military security, the U.S. has little strategic interest in maintaining the present troops and bases in Korea."[3]

American policymakers simply considered Korea less vital than other areas in Asia. The most earthshaking event of the period was the ascent of Mao Zedong and the founding on October 1, 1949, of the People's Republic of China. The creeping spread of communism in Europe and Asia stimulated a serious debate in Washington and throughout the United States about where and how to cope with a situation that seemed to call for military confrontation with the communist powers and assistance to nations eager to preserve their freedom. The problems of Asia, however, were no less crucial than those of Western Europe.

In a January 12, 1950, address on Asia, Secretary of State Dean Acheson described the defense perimeter of the United States as extending from Japan to the Ryukyus and thence to the Philippines. Many Koreans refer to this speech as another American sellout and an open invitation to the Communists to launch their invasion. Should an attack occur beyond our defense perimeter, said Acheson, resistance would initially have to come from the people attacked and only then from the commitments of the entire civilized world under the Charter of the United Nations. He thought it a mistake to become obsessed with military considerations because too many problems did not admit of military solutions.

Specifically referring to Korea, he pointed out: "We have taken great steps which have ended our military occupation, and in cooperation with the United Nations, have established an independent and sovereign country recognized by nearly all the rest of the world."⁴ To him, the idea that the United States should stop halfway through the achievement of the establishment of this country was defeatism and utter madness for our interests in Asia.

Far from abandoning the ROK, Secretary Acheson called for a much broader defense than that the United States could provide on its own. In directing attention to the nonmilitary factors in security and to the need for nonmilitary measures to solve problems stemming from the expansion of communism, he voiced ideas, which if heeded, might have avoided many of the most bitter consequences of Korea—and Vietnam. Within a month of the secretary's address, the free debate on U.S. policy in Asia was temporarily suspended by Senator Joseph McCarthy's attack on the Department of State, the Department of Defense, the media, and the universities for their alleged connection with the international communist conspiracy.

On June 25, 1950, President Truman decided that U.S. interests in the ROK were sufficiently vital to justify a police action—in reality, a war—which cost 50,000 U.S. lives, hundreds of thousands wounded, and billions of dollars. To be sure, the United States was concerned with the survival of the ROK, but primarily it was ensuring its own survival in the face of communist expansion. The alternatives, as perceived in the United States, were retreat before the growing menace of communism (symbolized by the USSR, aided and abetted by the PRC and their client, the DPRK) or confronting the enemy in Korea, the immediate point of contact.

The fate of the ROK was only part of the reason for the American action. In the official American view, the battleline was drawn in Korea to defend the ROK; beyond that, the American objective was to defend Japan, Chiang Kai-shek's dwindling power in China, the free world's position in Southeast Asia, the future of Western Europe, and ultimately the United States and its chosen way of life.

South Koreans are quick to argue that in fighting for the ROK, Americans assumed responsibility for guaranteeing the future of the ROK, against all threats, all enemies—forever. This argument distorts the nature of the American concept of its security interest in the Korean Peninsula. The American objective is to preserve peace and stability not only because this benefits the ROK, Japan, or other friendly nations but also because Korea is the place most crucial in East Asia and the western Pacific to the security of the United States in its worldwide confrontation with the Soviet Union.

It is not easy to distinguish the interests of the ROK and those of the United States, and ordinarily such distinctions are unnecessary. It is conceivable, however, that the priorities of Washington and Seoul may differ. For example, in the view of Washington, a "swing" strategy (that is, swinging units of the American armed forces temporarily from the western Pacific to the NATO theater or the Persian Gulf) may appear essential. In Seoul, and even in Tokyo, such a strategy seems an unwarranted risk. It is, however, neither immoral nor amoral for Washington to concern itself primarily with its own needs. It is the obligation of any government to ensure the security and welfare of its own people.

Neither the U.S. government nor any other government in this sophisticated, complex modern world is likely to be so tunnel-visioned about its own selfish needs that it foolishly offends allies or alienates friends. Nor can long-range interests be jeopardized by the prospect of some transitory tactical advantage. Concern for the immediate security of the ROK must be tempered by equal, or perhaps greater, considerations—the ultimate value of a unified Korea, the avoidance of hostilities threatening the global involvement of the superpowers.

From the beginning the United States perceived its interests in the ROK as peace, progress, and justice. As ends of policy, these ideals are constant; the means of pursuing them must vary as the situation demands. These objectives derive from the historical involvement of the United States in the affairs of the Korean Peninsula and, since 1945, have been identified with the security and welfare of the ROK, first as an American client and subsequently as an American ally. When the "cynical, brutal, and naked aggression" (Secretary Acheson) of North Korea threatened these interests, President Truman took a stand: the line against communist expansionism would be drawn in Korea.

The Police Action and the Armistice

President Truman told the American people that they were engaged not in a war but in a police action under U.N. auspices. In the view of the president, successful resistance to communist aggression was imperative—

(a) To demonstrate that aggression will not be accepted by us or by the United Nations and to provide a rallying point around which the spirits and energies of the free world can be mobilized to meet the worldwide threat which the Soviet Union now poses.

(b) To deflate the dangerously exaggerated political and military prestige of Communist China, which now threatens to undermine the resistance of non-Communist Asia and to consolidate the hold of Communism on China itself.

(c) To afford more time for and to give direct assistance to the organization of non-Communist resistance in Asia, both outside and inside China.

(d) To carry out our commitments of honor to the South Koreans and to demonstrate to the world that the friendship of the United States is of inestimable value in time of adversity.

(e) To make possible a far more satisfactory peace settlement for Japan and to contribute greatly to the post-treaty security position of Japan in relation to the continent.

(f) To lend resolution to many countries not only in Asia but also in Europe and the Middle East who are now living within the shadow of Communist power and to let them know that they need not now rush to come to terms with Communism on whatever terms they can get, meaning complete submission.

(g) To inspire those who may be called upon to fight against great odds if subjected to sudden onslaught by the Soviet Union or by Communist China.

(h) To lend point and urgency to the rapid buildup of the defenses of the western world.

(i) To bring the United Nations through its first great effort on collective security and to produce a free-world coalition of incalculable value to the national security interests of the United States.

(j) To alert the peoples behind the Iron Curtain that their masters are bent upon wars of aggression and that this crime will be resisted by the free world.[5]

This list of expected benefits reveals the local and global considerations behind the decisions of the president and his advisers.

Because the United Nations had played a leading role in Korean affairs since 1947, the United States proceeded to act in closest cooperation with that organization. Five days after the North Korean invasion on June 25, 1950, President Truman sent American air and naval forces into action to assist the ROK. Within a few days, he authorized the bombing of specified targets in North Korea, approved the use of ground forces in the fighting, and ordered a naval blockade of the entire Korean coast.

On July 7, the U.N. Security Council asked the president to establish a unified command for all U.N. forces in Korea and to appoint a commander in chief (CINCUNC, or commander in chief, United Nations' Command). This action was possible only because the Soviet delegation was boycotting sessions of the Security Council. The U.N. command structure in Korea still exists.

Under General MacArthur, the first commanding general appointed (later dismissed) by President Truman, sixteen member-nations of the United Nations (Australia, Belgium, Canada, Colombia, Ethiopia, France, Greece, Luxembourg, the Netherlands, New Zealand, the Philippines, Thailand, Turkey, South Africa, Great Britain, and the United States dispatched ground troops, naval units, and aircraft. A dozen others contributed food, clothing, and medical supplies and personnel.

During the entire period of hostilities in Korea, and since, the United States has technically been only first among equals, although its contribution to the war and its assistance to the ROK far outweigh those of other U.N. members. Diplomatic decisions and military contributions were based on free will and independent judgment.

The effects of Security Council and General Assembly actions during the war lasted long beyond the conclusion of the armistice. Depending on their country's policy, some delegates spoke for North Korea and some for the South. The General Assembly set up a United Nations Commission on Unification and Rehabilitation of Korea (UNCURK) to implement its objective of a unified, independent, democratic Korea and a United Nations Korean Reconstruction Agency (UNKRA) for purposes indicated in its title. It also explored methods to bring about a cease-fire and proposed a conference to shift the Korean question from the battlefield to the conference table. It also passed two resolutions in 1951 condemning Communist China for its aggression and recommending that every state should embargo the sale of arms, munitions, and implements of war to North Korea and Communist China. These two resolutions caused resentment and deep anger in Beijing, making it difficult for the PRC to accept membership in the United Nations even twenty years later.

It took a little over two years—July 10, 1951, to July 27, 1953—to negotiate an armistice. During that time the fighting continued and casualties mounted. In the United States, President Eisenhower succeeded President Truman, but scarcely a ripple disturbed U.S. policy toward the ROK as John Foster Dulles, an influential adviser to Truman and Acheson, became Eisenhower's secretary of state.

On the day the armistice was signed, a joint statement of the sixteen nations with troops in Korea promised that they would continue to support efforts to bring about a unified, independent, and democratic Korea and would work with the United Nations in assisting the people of Korea to repair the ravages of war. They affirmed that "if there is a renewal of the armed attack . . . we should be united and prompt to resist. The consequences of such a breach of the armistice would be so grave that in all probability it would not be possible to confine hostilities within the frontiers of Korea."

The armistice agreement, which will remain effective until specifically modified or replaced by a peace treaty or its equivalent, provided for: (1) a demilitarized zone (the DMZ) extending two kilometers on either side of a demarcation line corresponding roughly to the battlefront near the 38th parallel; (2) arrangements for a cease-fire; (3) mutual withdrawal of forces from designated coastal islands and waters off Korea; (4) cessation of introduction into Korea of military reinforcements; (5) establishment of (1) the Military Armistice Commission (MAC), composed of five officers from each side, to supervise the armistice and settle through regulations any violations, (b) the Neutral Nations Supervisory Commission (NNSC), composed of officers from Sweden, Switzerland, Poland, and Czechoslovakia, to carry out specified functions of supervision, observation, inspection, and investigation, and (c) the Neutral Nations Repatriation Commission, composed of officers of the NNSC plus India, for repatriation of prisoners of war; and (6) the convening within three months of a political conference of representatives of both sides to negotiate the withdrawal of foreign forces from Korea and the peaceful settlement of the Korean question. This agreement was to be *temporary,* pending the conclusion of lasting peace.

The Repatriation Commission disbanded after the completion of its work. The conference for "the peaceful settlement of the Korean question" met in Geneva in the spring of 1954, but ended in total disagreement. Secretary of State Dulles flatly opposed any settlement that would surrender at Geneva the freedom for which so many fought and died in Korea.

The continuing implementation of the armistice is very much in the American interest. The DMZ, although heavily guarded and patrolled, provides a joint security area where the two sides can meet to air differences. Despite the thousands of incidents along the military demarcation line, all-out hostilities have been avoided. The MAC still meets regularly, observing strict military protocol and investigating grievances reported by either side. The NNSC, although stripped of its intended functions, remains on the job at Panmunjom, acting as interested observers, its good offices available to all concerned for consultation.

The Mutual Defense Treaty

While negotiations for the armistice were under way, President Rhee was afraid of being deserted by the United States and the United Nations. As prerequisites for the armistice agreement, he demanded a defense pact with the United States, a positive commitment of American aid, guarantees of Korean unification, and the withdrawal of Chinese troops. President Eisenhower's philosophy was the armistice first, then the defense pact and negotiations over such political matters as unification and the withdrawal of Chinese troops.

Rhee was concerned more about a unified nation than the survival of the ROK. To him, an armistice without the guarantees he wanted would be a death warrant for the Korean nation. "He was apprehensive about those whom he considered appeasers in the United States and the United Nations who would perch upon the branches of the tree of freedom and constantly hack away at its trunk."⁶ He was as angry over the armistice's sacrifice of Korean national interests as was President Thieu, later, over the neglect of South Vietnam's interests in the cease-fire agreements that sealed the fate of his country.

On October 1, 1953, the United States and Korea signed the Mutual Defense Treaty, which Secretary of State Dulles said would prevent a renewal of communist aggression in Korea. Earlier American treaties in the Pacific area (the ANZUS pact with Australia and New Zealand and the treaty with the Republic of the Philippines) were designed primarily with the menace of a resurgent Japan in mind. Together with similar agreements with the Republic of China (ROC) on Taiwan, Japan, and the Southeast Asian Treaty Organization (SEATO), the Korean treaty was intended to create a defense system to contain communism.

After a preamble affirming the desire of the two parties to strengthen efforts for collective defense, the first of six articles in the U.S.-ROK Mutual Defense Treaty pledges adherence to peaceful purposes of the United Nations. Article II provides joint consultation if the security of either is threatened by armed attack and calls on both to employ self-help and mutual aid to develop means to deter armed attack. Article III, which is the heart of the treaty, recognizes that an armed attack on one of the parties would be dangerous to the other's peace and safety and declares that both signatories would act, in accordance with each state's constitutional processes, to meet the common danger. Article IV states that the ROK and the United States accept the right to dispose U.S. land, air, and sea forces in and about the territory of the ROK as determined by mutual agreement.

In the course of hearings before the Senate Foreign Relations Committee, Secretary Dulles explained the purposes of the treaty and gave his views on the implications of the American commitment.[7] In his opinion, the primary purpose of the treaty was to state clearly and unequivocally the common determination of the United States and the ROK to defend themselves against external armed attack, thus dispelling any illusion that either nation stood alone in the Pacific area. Convinced that the Communists would not have attacked in 1950 had they known what the United States and the United Nations would do, Dulles wanted no similar miscalculation in the future.

Another purpose of the treaty was to give the ROK formal assurance of continued U.S. concern for its security. The South Koreans knew that the Communists remained poised in the north, ready to strike again. They wanted a U.S. deterrent to that threat. The United States, for its part, wanted to secure the ROK against that threat and to advance the cause of independence and unity for all Koreans.

The secretary was asked to respond to three questions: To what kinds of action does the treaty commit our government? Under what conditions do we bind ourselves to come to the support of Korea? What are some of the hazards, as well as the advantages, for us in this treaty? In his defense of the treaty, he was joined by General Matthew Ridgway, then army chief of staff and formerly in command of U.S. forces in the Far East.

According to the witnesses before the Senate committee, the treaty would maintain the will of the South Korean people to resist communist aggression and develop their strength and capacity to defeat it. The treaty would provide the South Koreans with the vital element of confidence necessary to their struggle for survival.

In discussing the relationship between the treaty and possible insurrection within the ROK, Secretary Dulles explained the limitations inherent in the treaty commitment. In South Korea, a large, well-trained, well-equipped, well-disciplined, and loyal force was at the disposal of the government. To him, there seemed to be no need for the United States to indicate any willingness, disposition, or obligation to participate in the internal security of the ROK. In his view, the United States would be under no obligation to interfere in an armed insurrection or coup d'etat or to take any military measures as a result of the violent overthrow of the government. If it seemed wise, the United States could withdraw its forces from Korea. The United States had the right but not the obligation, in accordance with the treaty, to dispose forces in and about Korea. Although the United States would not necessarily be involved in internal insurrection, it was clear that for Dulles aggression from North Korea would be treated not as internal insurrection, but as a hostile, external attack.

When asked if the ROK was necessary for the defense of the United States in the Pacific, General Ridgway replied: "Positively. Yes, Sir." He maintained that the ROK could contribute to the security of the United States in the event of general war or renewal of hostilities in Northeast Asia. If communist forces were to overrun the Korean Peninsula, they would directly and seriously threaten an area of vital strategic importance to the United States: namely, the offshore island chain in the Far East and, above all, the key element in the chain—the main Japanese islands.

In reply to a direct question, General Ridgway expressed his opinion that the United States would not keep its forces in South Korea indefinitely. Anticipating the position of Defense Secretary Harold Brown in the Carter administration, General Ridgway said that joint resistance to an armed attack could take various forms. The ROK was but one of the locations where U.S. forces, to be effective, could be placed in the Far East.

When Secretary Dulles was asked if the United States was overextending itself in making this treaty commitment to the ROK and whether it had the military power to fulfill all its commitments, he replied: "Affirmative," assuming that the United States would meet the enemy at places and by means of its own choosing. If the United States had to maintain ground forces at any place where the enemy might choose to attack, it would become subservient to the enemy.

Dulles explained that if there were a breach of the armistice, the U.S. reaction would not necessarily be confined to Korea, but determination of means and places would be in accordance with the constitutional processes of the United States. No privileged sanctuaries would be granted across the Yalu if that area were being used as a base for attack. If the enemy struck across the 38th parallel, the United States would choose whether to hit Pyongyang, Beijing, or Moscow. By making it clear, the secretary concluded, that the choice would be American whether Korea, Indochina, or some other area of the Pacific were to be involved, it would be possible for the United States to protect its vital interests without overextension.

Even with the data in the hearings on the Mutual Defense Treaty, it is impossible to determine precisely either the South Korean or the American perception of the American commitment. The wording of the treaty was sufficiently ambiguous to permit both sides to make their respective interpretations of obligations and limitations. On the American side, it was unanimously agreed that if President Rhee attempted to unify Korea by force without the sanction of the United Nations, the United States would be under no obligation to assist him. If a threat to American interests developed in Korea, it would have to be met with appropriate American action whatever the treaty obligation. The United States was committing itself, not only because of the terms of the treaty, but also because of the disposition of U.S. forces in Korea and the very nature of the American commitment to the integrity of the ROK. Senator Hubert Humphrey later pointed out that "all this is within this whole area of the indefinite and the imponderable, but once you have made an agreement you are tied in pretty definitely."[8]

Before ratifying the Mutual Defense Treaty, the Senate made clear its understanding that the United States was not obligated under the treaty to participate in the internal security of the Korean Republic or to take any military measures as a result of the violent overthrow of the government or a coup d'etat. There was, in fact, no obligation for the United States to maintain any armed forces whatsoever in Korea. At the insistence of the Senate and with the agreement of the ROK, the following understanding was added to the text of the treaty:

> It is the understanding of the United States that neither party is obligated, under Article III of the above treaty, to come to the aid of the other except in case of an external armed attack against such party; nor shall anything in the present Treaty be construed as requiring the United States to give assistance to Korea except in the event of an armed attack against territory which has been recognized by the United States as lawfully brought under the administrative control of the Republic of Korea.[9]

When the treaty took force on November 17, 1954, the discussion of its implications and the extent of the U.S. commitment temporarily halted. American attention in East Asia shifted to Indochina and the offshore islands of the ROC. The armistice and the U.S.-ROK Mutual Defense Treaty contributed to the continuance of peace on the Korean Peninsula, but the effectiveness of the documents without the concurrent presence of U.S. forces in Korea and the programs of military and economic assistance launched by the United States to strengthen the ROK is uncertain.

Military and Economic Assistance

The armistice agreement did not envision that the Korean Peninsula would become the center of a heavily rearmed Northeast Asia. Both sides agreed to cease introducing military reinforcements into Korea and supplying combat aircraft, armored vehicles, weapons, and ammunition. Rotation of troops and replacement of equipment was to be effected only through specified ports of entry and subject to inspection by the NNSC. These provisions, however, were ignored as a military buildup took place both north and south of the demarcation line.

In view of the continuing threat to the ROK from the USSR, the PRC, and North Korea, the United States backed its treaty commitment by leaving American troops in the ROK and expediting the strengthening of the armed forces of the ROK. Two American divisions, with sophisticated equipment and substantial support units in and about Korea, remained on station in the ROK after 1955. These American forces not only provided military muscle and imparted a sense of confidence to the ROK, but also constituted an effective deterrent against further communist adventures. The political and psychological impact of the American presence was at least as meaningful as its military potential.

The costs of the American troops were charged to the United States, not to the ROK. The troops were under the command of a single officer who wore three hats. He was at once CINCUNC reporting to the U.S. Joint Chiefs of Staff as the executive agent of the United Nations; commanding general, U.S. Forces/Korea, with planning and coordinating staff only, reporting to the commander in chief, Pacific; and commanding general, 8th Army, reporting to the commander in chief, U.S. Army, Pacific. As war clouds gathered over the Taiwan Strait and Indochina in the late 1950s, the American military presence in the ROK effectively prevented the spread of hostilities from Southeast to Northeast Asia.

In addition to maintaining troops and bases in the ROK, the United States energetically pushed a program to strengthen the Korean armed forces. President Truman began the process of transferring essential military items to the ROK, training ROK military personnel, and generally increasing the capacity of the ROK to defend itself. On a trip to Korea between his election and inauguration, President Eisenhower inspected the front. As a matter of interest, he observed North Korea's use of tunnels as an infallible way of protecting its own men while harassing ROK positions with artillery fire. The North Koreans would push their guns to the mouth of a tunnel, fire once, and immediately withdraw.[10] What he saw convinced him of the need for massive military assistance to the ROK. The United States was to provide more than $3 billion worth of equipment, supplies, and services to the ROK between 1953 and 1969.[11]

After the armistice, the size of the Korean armed forces leveled off at approximately 650,000. The ROK forces remained totally dependent on U.S. support for weapons, ammunition, vehicles, fuels, and replacement parts. The United States turned over to the ROK all its inventory after the war except for the portion needed for its own residual forces. Supplies— including food, clothing, and other consumables—were likewise given to the Koreans.

The ROK military establishment proved much too costly to sustain without continuing U.S. assistance. American expenditures in Korea for troop maintenance—including the hiring of Korean nationals, local procurement, and purchases by American personnel—amounted to an estimated $3 billion during the 1950s and the 1960s. A large part of the U.S. Military Assistance Program (MAP) expenditures went directly to meet the budgetary needs of the ROK, providing money for the ROK defense forces and building up the ROK's defense-related infrastructure. The economic impact of such assistance could not be isolated or quantified.[12]

The army developed into the most powerful and effective organization in the nation. As training improved, service academies were established, and opportunities for education multiplied. The armed forces became thoroughly Americanized in organization and procedures, but they were ridden with military factionalism and corruption. Their influence extended far beyond military affairs, into the political, economic, and social life of the nation. Thanks to skills developed by American teachers, leaders, and commanders, Korean military personnel assumed an important role in civic action programs, assisting local farmers in rice planting and harvesting; building and repairing roads, constructing dams and schools; and providing transport and construction equipment. The armed forces operated technical schools where servicemen were taught trades that proved lucrative in civilian life. A large number of Korean mechanics, communications technicians, repairmen, and clerks received their basic training in the service schools. On a more exalted level, many of the nation's political and economic elite either came from the armed forces or owed their positions to skills displayed in working with the military.

The ability of Syngman Rhee to manipulate the army kept him in power until he was toppled by the mass uprising of 1960. During the ensuing year of popular democracy, plots within the army command led to the coup d'etat of May 16, 1961. A group of young officers organized by Kim Jong Pil overthrew the government of John M. Chang (Chang Myun) and placed Major General Park Chung Hee in the presidency. This was followed by a mass purge of the older military leaders.

Ten days after the coup d'etat, the ROK army was placed under the command of the American general who was then CINCUNC for operational control against communist aggression. The Americans were concerned more with a possible invasion from the North than with internal rivalries for political power. The UNC was made responsible for training and preparedness against the Communists, but not to control appointments or to mediate the jealousies and intrigues that plagued the ROK high command.

Under Park, the army assumed even more influence over the national development of the ROK. By the late 1960s, army men occupied one-fifth to one-half of all cabinet posts and headed three-fourths of the large, publicly financed industrial establishments. They dominated the National Assembly and filled the majority of influential ambassadorial posts. The army mentality permeated the *Yushin* Constitution and furnished the driving power behind the five-year plans. The experience of the ROK military, inspired and fueled largely by the United States in the formative years of the ROK, accounted for the decidedly authoritarian bias of the new bureaucrats and technocrats toward efficient administration, forced economic growth, and technical and scientific approaches to problem solving.

The economic commitment of the United States to the future of the ROK was as important as its military commitment. The two were complementary, and often indistinguishable. Both the military and economic assistance programs were undeniable evidence that the United States recognized the importance of the ROK to U.S. security. The United States was willing to pay whatever price seemed justified and required for effective fulfillment of the Mutual Defense Treaty.

Even before the Korean War, Americans saw and acted on Korea's need for economic help. Plummeted into a situation of incredible anarchy and poverty by the departure of the Japanese, Korea required a tremendous supply of food, goods, and raw materials to become a stable, strong, and prosperous country. Funds under Government Appropriations for Relief in Occupied Areas provided $502 million from 1945 to 1949. The first civilian organization, the Economic Cooperation Administration, spent a further $100 million during 1949 and 1950.[13]

American economic assistance before the outbreak of the Korean war aimed primarily at preventing starvation and disease. Imports into the ROK consisted of food, fertilizers, coal, oil, blankets, clothing, and textiles. The American occupation authorities carried out a land distribution program (mostly Japanese-held lands) to former tenants and turned many former Japanese-owned industries over to the Korean government. Land reform helped reduce rural instability and undermined communist influence among the peasants. The program for disposal of industries was less successful because the political elite had neither the ability nor the will to make the most of this economic windfall.

In the two years of hostilities, more than a million civilians died, and five million were made destitute. Among the casualties were 500,000 war widows, 15,000 amputees, and 100,000 orphans. Of 5,000 villages, 1,200 were destroyed. In the course of changing hands four times, Seoul suffered the loss of 300,000 houses and damage to 100,000 more. Farms, irrigation systems, forests, mines, factories, and fishing fleets were destroyed. No wonder President Eisenhower, on surveying the wreckage, was moved to assure President Rhee that the United States would continue economic aid to help restore the devastated land.

During the war, the UNC established the Civilian Relief Agency to provide food, medicine, shelter, and other essentials of life. The UNKRA, created in 1950 and operational in 1952, set up its own machinery and used its own assets to alleviate misery and prevent unrest. The ordinary activities of an army at war brought some permanent benefits to the suffering country. Roads and bridges were built, railroads repaired, telephone and telegraph lines installed, and vehicles imported, thus boosting the civilian economy. The relief afforded by buildings set aside for schools, hospitals, and orphanages was more than a temporary blessing.

As soon as the armistice was signed, the United States inaugurated an economic assistance program under a single agency, successively called the Foreign Operations Administration, the International Cooperation Agency, and the Agency for International Development (AID). Congress's rationale for foreign economic aid was that such assistance strengthened the recipient against the blandishments of communist enemies, thus contributing significantly to mutual security. The benefits to the recipient nation were secondary to the prime purpose of promoting the American part of mutual security.

Between 1954 and 1974, economic aid to the ROK totaled about $5 billion (pre-inflation dollars). The exact amount depends on the method of accounting. An AID publication of December 1974 shows $4.7 billion as the total amount. Of this 39 percent went for industry and mining, 38 percent for agriculture and natural resources, 9 percent for general and miscellaneous purposes, 7 percent for social development, 5 percent for transport, and the remainder for public administration, education, public health, and sanitation.[14]

For U.S. bookkeeping purposes, the report noted that the sum total of $4.7 billion consisted primarily of $2.6 billion in support assistance, technical assistance, and development grants for specific projects to cover raw materials, equipment for industry, oil, and lubricants for transport; $900 million for relief funds immediately following the war; $500 million in development loans; and $1.6 billion in Food for Peace shipments. The last item represents transactions where the U.S. government buys grain, tobacco, fibers, or other agricultural products from American farmers, paying them in dollars. Then it ships and sells the commodities to the government of the ROK, which in turn sells the imports to Korean consumers who pay the dollar equivalent in *won* at a fixed exchange rate. The *won* thus received are known as counterpart funds and are deposited to the credit of the Korean government. During the 1950s, they kept the government of the ROK economically alive.

The specific objectives of U.S. assistance programs were always couched in such attractive terms as rebuilding the war-ruined country; revitalizing the economic life of the nation; assisting the ROK to improve resource mobilization and allocation; developing the rural economy; accelerating the growth and efficiency of domestic and export industries; or improving the government's organization, administrative capacities, and social policies. [15] In the administration of such an ambitious program, however, it was inevitable that bureaucratism, delay, red tape, favoritism, illegal commissions, bribery, kickbacks, and other irregularities would arise. Koreans spent most of their time defeating the red tape and made most of their profits outwitting the bureaucrats. Since practically no consumer goods were available in the ROK except those imported from the United States, import or foreign exchange licenses were worth a small fortune. Such simple things as copper wire, nails, radios, truck tires, powdered milk—or even the boxes they were shipped in—were precious luxuries.

Every imported item, whether sold on the legitimate or the black market, added to the counterpart funds on which the government depended. In 1957, one of the most critical years, U.S. aid shipments accounted for 86 percent of all imports and imports for 14 percent of the GNP. Given the size of the U.S. interest in the ROK economy, it was certain that Americans were involved at every bureaucratic level of the decision-making process. Friends and enemies were made across desks and in corridors and lobbies.

Weighed down by mounting political responsibilities elsewhere in the world and haunted by increasing signs of the exhaustibility of its own limited resources, the United States by the end of the 1950s was embarrassed by stories of Korean abuses of aid. In the ROK at least, drastic changes were needed in the economic assistance program. Many Americans grew more critical of the doughty old anticommunist freedom fighter, President Rhee. They accused him of using U.S. aid for the aggrandizement of his personal power and for the immediate rather than the long-run benefit of his nation. He preferred tourist resorts, swank hotels, and a civilian airline to a solid infrastructure.

President Rhee was slow to realize that the Americans were determined to end the aid program or perhaps to revise it. His failure to restructure U.S.-ROK economic relations contributed to his downfall. The Park government's five-year plans for economic development adopted a strategy of industrial growth based on production for export rather than mere import substitution. The government offered subsidies for exports, devalued the inflated currency, and liberalized the laws to attract more foreign capital. As the U.S. aid program came to an end, the leadership of the ROK geared itself to increase exports; the policy was to earn the money to pay for all the goods previously received for nothing. Any future U.S. aid would be a loan, not a grant, and would, therefore, have to be repaid.

From the standpoint of the American commitment of economic assistance to the ROK, the first decade after the war, 1953–1963, was crucial.

Under the regime of President Rhee, the nation scarcely survived. Beginning with the infusion of new blood under Park Chung Hee, the ROK took off on the road to economic recovery. Between 1961 and 1967, per capita GNP increased by 29 percent, from $108 million to $139 million; industrial production doubled; exports rose from $33 million to $350 million; and gold and foreign exchange reserves grew from $146 million to $356 million. Much of this rate of growth and development can be credited to the hard work of the Koreans themselves, but at least two new elements entered the picture: normalization of relations with Japan (described later) and the payment of substantial sums to the ROK as a reward for its participation in the hostilities in Vietnam.

U.S. Policy Statements

An unusually close relationship developed in the early days of the Park regime because of the intense U.S. desire for Asian support in Vietnam. High American officials rewarded the ROK for its dispatch of troops to Vietnam with assurances that had no basis in the Mutual Defense Treaty. The activities of the ROK in Vietnam and the concomitant American statements of policy are often interpreted as committing the United States morally to the destiny of the ROK.

Just after Park rose to power, President Kennedy entered the White House. He was far too engrossed in Laos, the Cuban missile crisis, the Congo, Khrushchev in Europe, and the perennial China problem to give more than passing attention to the travails of the ROK. As the U.S. entanglement in Vietnam made increasing demands on the president's time and the nation's pocketbook, Korean affairs faded deeper into the background. Meanwhile, the Park regime in Seoul gradually consolidated its political power base and successfully launched the First Five-Year Plan.

After President Johnson succeeded Kennedy, the United States and the ROK both perceived new ways to be of greater value to each other. State visits became annual affairs, usually commemorated by joint communiqués. In January 1964, Secretary of State Dean Rusk and President Park cosigned a statement arguing that "powerful Korean and United States Forces adequate to the defense of the Republic of Korea would be maintained in order to meet the continuing Communist menace in the Far East."[16] At that time, the Sino-Soviet split had not been convincingly demonstrated, and there was genuine concern that a combined communist juggernaut might choose to strike anywhere between Korea in the north and Vietnam in the south.

In May 1965, after hostilities had begun in Vietnam, President Johnson in a meeting with Park:

reaffirmed the determination and readiness of the United States to render forthwith and effectively all possible assistance including the use of armed forces, in accordance with the Mutual Defense Treaty of 1954, to meet the common danger occasioned by an armed attack on the Republic of Korea. He said that the United States will continue to maintain powerful forces in Korea at the request of the Korean Government, and will assist in maintaining Korean Forces at levels sufficient, in conjunction with United States Forces, to ensure Korea's security.[17]

Johnson already had initiated conversations regarding the display of an Asian flag at the side of the U.S. flag in Vietnam and recognized the necessity of assuring the ROK that its security would not suffer by deploying part of its forces in Vietnam. Johnson's unilateral promise could be considered binding only during *his* term of office. It did not possess the authority of law.

As the desire for assistance from the ROK in Vietnam increased during the optimistic year 1966, Vice-President Humphrey, in an extemporaneous address on February 23, told the Koreans during a visit in Seoul:

The United States Government and the people of the United States have a firm commitment to the defense of Korea. As long as there is one American soldier on the line of the border, the demarcation line, the whole and entire power of the United States of America is committed to the security and defense of Korea. Korea today is as strong as the United States and Korea put together. America today is as strong as the United States and Korea put together. We are allies, we are friends, you should have no questions, no doubts.[18]

The Koreans could scarcely be blamed if such statements raised their hopes and expectations. They were not disposed to raise questions about the legality and the limitations inherent in the vice-president's speech. At about the same time, U.S. Ambassador to the ROK Winthrop Brown made public his own assurance that "the United States will continue to maintain powerful forces in Korea at the request of the Korean Government, and will assist in maintaining Korean Forces at levels sufficient, in conjunction with United States Forces, to insure Korea's security."[19]

In November 1966, President Johnson, on his way through Seoul en route home from a conference in Manila, issued another joint communiqué with President Park:

The two Presidents acknowledged the need to ensure that the forces of aggression do not again menace the peace and tranquility of the Republic of Korea. They agreed that the growing strength of the Communist forces in the northern part of Korea and of the Chinese Communists remained a major threat to the security of the Republic of Korea and neighboring areas.

President Johnson reaffirmed the readiness and determination of the United States to render prompt and effective assistance to defeat an armed attack against the Republic of Korea in accordance with the Mutual Defense Treaty of 1954. President Johnson assured President Park that the United States has no plan to reduce the present level of United States Forces in Korea, and would continue to support Korean Armed Forces at levels adequate to ensure Korea's security. They agreed that their two governments would continue to consult closely to ensure that the Korean Forces are strengthened and modernized within the limitations imposed by legislative and budgetary considerations.[20]

Remarkably this statement specifies the Chinese Communists, together with the communist forces in North Korea, as the major threat to the ROK. The year witnessed the start of the Great Proletarian Cultural Revolution in China when the PRC considered the United States, not the USSR, as Enemy Number One. At that time the PRC feared encirclement by a hostile United States supporting the Republic of Vietnam to the south and the ROK to the north. The key words in the statement, so far as the ROK was concerned, were "prompt and effective assistance to *defeat.*" These words, although not in the text of the Mutual Defense Treaty or even implied by it, were much more reassuring than the cold promise to "take action in accordance with their constitutional processes." President Park would have liked Johnson's promise "to take automatic and instantaneous action" rather than the mere reaffirmation of "the readiness and determination to render prompt and effective assistance," but Johnson was unwilling to go that far.

The phrase "prompt and effective assistance to defeat an armed attack" was repeated in 1967, but it was modified slightly in the Johnson-Park joint communiqué at Honolulu on April 18, 1968. This communiqué followed on the heels of President Johnson's announcement of his decision not to run again. It also reflected the sobering effects of the Tet offensive in Vietnam and the increasingly belligerent and aggressive actions of the North Korean Communists during the preceding eighteen months. These actions included the attack on the Blue House and the seizure of the *U.S.S. Pueblo* in international waters. In this statement, the two Presidents agreed that

Further aggressive actions from the North would constitute a grave threat to peace and in that event, the two governments would immediately determine the action to be taken to meet this threat under the Mutual Defense Treaty between the United States and the Republic of Korea. In accordance with this Treaty, President Johnson reaffirmed the readiness and determination of the United States to render prompt and effective assistance to repel armed attacks against the Republic of Korea.[21]

Previously President Johnson had committed the United States to *de-feat* an armed attack; now the commitment was to *repel* armed attacks. Experience in Vietnam by April 1968 had shown the vast difference between defeating and repelling an enemy. At the Honolulu meeting, the American president reaffirmed his adherence to the joint policy declaration of July 7, 1953, of the sixteen United Nations participants in the Korean War. In further recognition of the need to bolster Korean faith in the American commitment to the security of the ROK, Johnson agreed to periodic cabinet-level meetings to discuss military assistance and to counter infiltration and sabotage.

When President Nixon met with Park in San Francisco, August 21-22, 1969, their joint communiqué was more cautious in tone. It stated that Korean forces and American troops stationed in Korea must remain strong and alert and reaffirmed the determination to counter armed attacks against the Republic of Korea in accordance with the Mutual Defense Treaty.[22] The more restrained rhetoric reflected the views of the new administration and its circumspect response to the rapidly changing strategic environment in East Asia and the western Pacific.

The Vietnam War

The tenor of the verbal assurances entered on the public record for the benefit of the ROK between 1964 and 1969 are understandable only in light of the vicissitudes of the United States in the Vietnam war. The United States needed allies, particularly Asian allies, in Vietnam. Recognizing this need, the ROK quite naturally pressed the United States for the most ample reward in words and dollars that could be extracted for its assistance.

As noted, President Johnson probed for Asian help before actual hostilities got underway. The Koreans were the first to be approached because of the skills and morale of their soldiers. The ROK government, for its part, signaled that it would welcome the chance to repay the free world for its contribution to Korea's struggle for survival. Regarding the Vietnam front as a second front for the ROK, President Park conceived of his country's participation as a further guarantee of the security of his own country and as a contribution to the strengthening of the anticommunist front in Asia. Too, he saw all the incidents and brushfire wars in Asia, indeed throughout the world, as episodes in a single crusade to contain communist aggression.

The Koreans first sent a hospital unit to Vietnam, then an engineering battalion with support troops, and finally one and then another combat division. At the peak, almost 50,000 Koreans were stationed in Vietnam; with rotation, almost 300,000 ROK soldiers received combat experience. As of February 7, 1970, Korean casualties included 3,094 killed, 3,051 wounded, and four missing in action.[23] In addition to fighting men, the Korean contingent in Vietnam included technicians, contractors, and stevedores. It was fundamental to the United States that the ROK's assistance should not degrade its capacity to defend itself against the North or slow economic development. Therefore, the United States agreed to meet all the extra costs, both in *won* and foreign exchange, of the ROK contingent in Vietnam.

Before the first combat group, the Tiger Division, left for Vietnam in 1965, the United States agreed not to reduce its forces in the ROK significantly without prior consultation with the government of the ROK; to amend MAP to Korea's benefit; to modernize Korean forces in the ROK in firepower, communications, and mobility; to provide equipment, logistical support, construction, training, transportation, subsistence, overseas allowances, and funds for legitimate noncombatant claims that might be brought against the ROK forces in Vietnam; to make restitution for cash losses by Korean forces in Vietnam that did not result from negligence.[24]

The publication of the letter of Ambassador Brown to Tong Won Lee, minister of foreign affairs, quoting policy statements by Rusk, Johnson, and Humphrey was timed to coincide with the dispatch of the second combat group, the White Horse Division, in March 1966. Simultaneously, the U.S. ambassador negotiated an agreement on support to be provided the ROK to "see to it that the integrity of Korea's defense is maintained and strengthened, and that Korea's economic progress is further promoted." According to the extremely illuminating details of this agreement, the United States agreed:

1. To provide over the next few years substantial items of equipment for the modernization of Republic of Korea forces in Korea.

2. To equip as necessary, and finance all additional *won* costs of the additional forces deployed to the Republic of Vietnam.

3. To equip, provide for the training and finance complete replacement of the additional forces deployed to the Republic of Vietnam.

4. To contribute to filling the requirements determined by our two governments to be necessary, following completion of a joint United States–Republic of Korea study, for the improvement of the Republic of Korea anti-infiltration capability.

5. To provide equipment to expand the Republic of Korea arsenal for increased ammunition production in Korea.

6. To provide communications facilities for exclusive Republic of Korea

use, the character of which is to be agreed between United States and Republic of Korea officials in Seoul and Saigon. These facilities will meet requirements for communication with your forces in the Republic of Vietnam.

7. To provide four C-54 aircraft to the Republic of Korea Air Force for support of Republic of Korea forces in the Republic of Vietnam.

8. To provide for the improvement of military barracks and bachelor officers' quarters and related facilities for troop welfare such as cooking, messing, sanitation, and recreational facilities from proceeds of the Military Assistance Program (MAP) excess sales.

9. To assume the costs of overseas allowances to these forces at the scale agreed between General Beach and Minister of National Defense Kim Sung Eun on March 4, 1966.

10. To provide death and disability gratuities resulting from casualties in Vietnam at double the rates recently agreed to by the joint United States–Republic of Korea Military Committee.[25]

In additional agreements for economic assistance, the United States agreed to pay all of the net additional costs of deploying these extra forces and of activating and maintaining in Korea a reserve division and brigade and support elements. It also dropped a contemplated change requiring the ROK to pay for certain MAP items. The United States further consented to procure in Korea, as far as practical, supplies, services, and equipment for ROK forces in Vietnam and to direct to Korea selected types of procurement for U.S. and Republic of Vietnam forces when the ROK had the productive capability and could meet specifications and delivery schedules at reasonably competitive prices. Finally, it was agreed that the AID would procure in Korea as much as could be supplied for rural construction, pacification, relief, and logistics programs in the Republic of Vietnam. Korean contractors would be given expanded opportunities to participate in construction projects in Vietnam; increased technical assistance would be given the ROK in the general field of export promotion; additional loans (amounts not specified) over and above the $150 million already committed would be made available to the ROK for development purposes; and, if justified by performance, $15 million in program loans would be provided to the ROK to support exports to the Republic of Vietnam and for other development needs.[26]

Other agreements obligated the United States to underwrite special *kimchi* (a pickled cabbage, fish, and garlic concoction highly prized by Koreans) rations and permitted Korean contractors to use the Military Sea Transport Service to ship goods to Vietnam. The United States paid overseas allowances of $1.25 per day to private soldiers, whose regular pay was $1.60 per month, and doubled or tripled the pay of officers. In addition, Korean soldiers enthusiastically took advantage of PX privileges. Although the Korean soldiers in no way considered themselves mercenaries, they sent back home millions of dollars through official channels.

The total cost of U.S. support from 1965 to 1970 was $928 million.[27] Each Korean soldier cost the United States between $5,000 and $8,000 annually. Korean earnings from Vietnam from 1965 to 1969 were estimated at $546 million.[28] The ROK government benefited from the Vietnam experience; so did the individual soldiers, contractors, and companies, so did a lot of under-the-table experts. Despite the sums accruing to the ROK, however, the ROK probably earned less than Japan and only a little more than Taiwan—neither of which participated in the war.

After listening to a recitation of these facts during the course of the Symington hearings on U.S. security arrangements abroad, Senator James Fulbright observed that he could not see that the ROK's participation in Vietnam was such a high and mighty action. It looked to him less like a gesture of self-sacrifice and more like a good business deal, at the request and urging of the United States. For value received, the ROK gained nearly $1 billion in subsidies. This was the real foundation of the export industries on which the Korean economic miracle was constructed. Senator Symington felt that the American people had been deceived about the ROK's desire to participate in the South Vietnam venture, and he hoped the exposure of past circumstances would prevent involvement in a similar situation in the future.

U.S.-ROK Relations in 1969

When President Nixon assumed office in 1969, it looked as if the ROK was the staunchest ally of the United States in East Asia and would remain so whatever might develop after Vietnam. Glancing backward, Ambassador Brown described the ROK as a country once totally devastated, full of refugees, land—homes—schools destroyed, but now a vigorous country participating responsibly in the affairs of Asia. In his view and that of his colleagues, this transformation would have been impossible without the treaty, the presence of U.S. forces, and the program of military and economic assistance, which assured South Koreans that they were reasonably safe from North Korean attacks. As Brown extolled the accomplishments of U.S. aid in building the economy and assisting the Koreans in meeting their social and economic needs, Fulbright commented that the ROK sounded like a glowing paradise. "It ought to be," he added icily. "We have almost paved it with gold."[29]

The conflicts of opinion regarding the future of U.S.-ROK relations, exposed in some detail by the Symington hearings, began to crystallize on the eve of the announcement of the Nixon Doctrine. Before the final denouement in Indochina, spokesmen for the Johnson administration had expressed the belief that a visible U.S. presence in the ROK would, for some time, be a very useful deterrent to the North and a morale builder for the South. In their judgment, the American military detachment made the South Koreans feel that they had an ally that was visible, present, and committed to protect the country from attack. The U.S. forces were considered the prime factor in the preservation of peace and stability; without them the North and South Koreans would have been at one another's throats at the drop of a hat.

According to William Porter, who succeeded Winthrop Brown as ambassador to the ROK, a commitment to the defense of Korea was in the American interest because it gave a sense of confidence, not only to the ROK, but to others far beyond the Korean border.[30] It represented a commitment to the freedom and development of the Korean people and attracted the attention and admiration of a large part of Asia and other parts of the world. He felt that the United States needed soldiers as well as diplomats to deter aggression, to prevent the kind of attack that happened in 1950. Because of the treaty, a recurrence of such an attack would involve the United States in a major hostility.

The necessity for an American commitment, its nature, extent, limitations, and duration, were the subject of sharp controversy. In negotiations with the Koreans, Americans followed policies of caution and restraint. Despite the ROK's efforts to persuade the United States to agree to automatic and instantaneous response in the event of an armed attack, the United States deliberately limited itself to the obligation to take action in accordance with constitutional processes. This allowed the United States to consider a wide range of options in retaliating against any armed attack from the outside.

The American negotiators repeatedly told the Koreans that the United States had made no commitments either in connection with the dispatch of ROK troops to Vietnam or otherwise, to keep any U.S. forces in the peninsula for any specified period of time. The United States, however, agreed to consult with the ROK before substantially reducing its forces in Korea. When Ambassador Porter was asked under what circumstances the United States might be able to remove its ground forces, he suggested that some adjustment in its posture might be possible as the ROK developed its economy and implemented an adequate program of modernization—that is, provided the United States did not intend to change its basic commitment to the Koreans radically. Porter admitted that although the Koreans anticipated an end to dependence on the United States, they probably would always desire some kind of visible evidence of American companionship, given their proximity to the Soviet Union and China.[31]

In 1969, U.S.-ROK relations were, in a word, "excellent." Korea was one of the few countries in which demonstrations called for Americans not to go home. But the same questions persisted throughout the ensuing decade: Exactly what was the U.S. commitment—Survival of the ROK? Survival of the ROK as a democratic state? Reunification of the Korean Peninsula? Did commitment to the ROK mean the same thing as the commitment to safeguard the U.S. interest in Northeast Asia? Did the commitment require the continued presence of a given number of American troops? What did the United States want the Koreans to believe— That the United States was committed to the Mutual Defense Treaty or to inferences derived from the perceived meaning of the contractual obligations? On what would the judgment of credibility depend? Was it in the American interest to leave these questions deliberately vague or to seek precise answers?

In 1969, Senator Symington suggested that the changing international environment might make it advisable at some future time to re-examine past commitments—implying that in the case of the ROK, Americans should be free to follow the commitment of 1950, or to divest themselves of it, or to modify it to suit the changing times. The suggestion was as appropriate at the beginning of the 1980s as it had been a decade earlier.

4 | THE CHANGING STRATEGIC ENVIRONMENT

Until 1969, American policy toward the ROK was rooted in the cold war and conditioned by circumstances primarily shaped and controlled by American power and American will. The era of U.S. dominance in the western Pacific and East Asia, which had existed since World War II, ended in the jungles of Vietnam. In the 1970s shifts in superpower relationships and perceived differences in the intentions and capabilities of other nations whose decisions and actions directly affected the United States and the ROK, particularly the USSR, Japan, and the two Chinas, profoundly changed the global environment. The fundamental shift in world affairs between Vietnam and the end of the Carter administration is sometimes described as the passing of the bipolar world, or the transformation of the bipolar world into a multipolar world. In fact, it was a diffusion of the concept of polarity. Although the superpowers' geopolitical and ideological rivalry continued, other nations felt less compelled, or less inclined, to entrust their security and welfare to one or the other.

The United States remained as dedicated as ever to the protection of its own land and people and to the preservation of its capitalist way of life. Behind its policies lay principles and ideals that it conceived of as peculiarly American. To safeguard those principles and ideals, the United States persistently sought a doctrine or strategy that would guarantee peace and stability, within which all nations could work out their own preferred destiny. Since the preponderance enjoyed by the United States at the end of World War II was severely eroded, the conflicting goals of the United

States and the USSR were in constant confrontation, always straining diplomacy and sometimes threatening war.

Similarly, the USSR was devoted to the security of Mother Russia, and to its ideology. While the United States clung to its hope for peace as an attainable ideal, the USSR looked on it as a condition achievable only after a worldwide communist victory. To the United States, peace and stability were acceptable ends of policy; the the USSR, peaceful coexistence and armed struggle were alternate means of pursuing its ultimate goals. The global struggle of the superpowers, supported by their allies, clients, surrogates, and well-wishers, was still the name of the game. Lesser states were little more than pawns.

This assumption of the overriding importance of the U.S.-USSR rivalry as the dominant external influence on U.S.-ROK relations is not intended to minimize the influence of less powerful nations on U.S. policy. Every nation has its own significant role to play. Every U.S. response to a situation central to the ROK must result from careful calculation not only of the reaction of the USSR, but of the rights and interests of third parties.

The changing strategic environment of the 1970s accounts for changing U.S. attitudes toward the ROK and for the growing number of questions raised by Americans about their defense commitments to the ROK. Such problems as the level and nature of troops stationed in the ROK and the amount of material made available at any one time for its defense must be determined in the light of demands on U.S. resources by other nations in the world. The positioning and deployment of aircraft carriers, ships of the line, missiles, and manpower depends on continuous reappraisal of the comparative needs of competing trouble spots.

During the 1970s, economic problems magnified conflicts between the United States and third parties affected by U.S.-ROK relations. With the end of the U.S. grant-in-aid military assistance program, both military and commercial sales to the ROK had to be consummated in keeping with practices of the international market system. The United States was obliged to compete with other suppliers (notably Japan) of material goods, and the ROK lost much of its privileged position as a favored American client. With the oil crisis of 1973, the ROK, along with everybody else, scrambled to find new ways to meet its energy demands. The competition stiffened as prices skyrocketed. Then, as the United States and the ROK sought to regulate their import-export relationship on a mutually beneficial basis, they encountered the politico-economic opposition of such rivals as Japan, Taiwan, and the Philippines.

Both the United States and the ROK discovered that they were less independent in their economic policies than they cared to admit and that their welfare depended not only on themselves, but on the smooth working of a thoroughly integrated global economic system. The ROK needed other sources of capital besides the United States and access to markets beyond the United States where it could sell its products and services. The more the ROK developed, the more it challenged the United States as an economic competitor. It became increasingly clear to both nations, however, that the stabilizing influence of the American dollar and the continued prosperity of the American economic system were as essential to world peace as the strength of the American armed forces—especially in Northeast Asia.

Even a cursory study of the rights and interests of third parties affecting and affected by U.S.-ROK relations shows the impossibility of satisfying everybody all the time. What favors one offends another. Decisions must be made on the hardheaded determination of what is best for the American national interest, bearing in mind that fundamental parts of that interest are the military support, economic cooperation, goodwill, and trust of friends and allies. Presumably all nations have a vital interest in preventing the ultimate nuclear war; most do accept the premise that continued peace on the Korean Peninsula is a desired step in the right direction.

The Changing U.S. Role in East Asia

The United States and the Soviet Union both played leading roles in shaping the post–World War II system. But it was the power of the United States that dominated the skies and the seas from Tokyo to Singapore. General MacArthur was supreme commander in occupied Japan; the Americans and Russians shared responsibility in Korea; American support seemed to guarantee the future of Nationalist China; and American policies in the Philippines seemed to point the way for former colonies to emerge as nations deserving independence and capable of political democracy.

American power was at its peak not only in Asia, but throughout the world. The United States had built the mightiest fighting machine the world had ever seen; its scientists had produced the atom bomb. While other nations were damaged or destroyed, the United States alone enjoyed the prosperity and productive capacity that made possible the Marshall Plan for Europe and a worldwide assistance program for the LDCs of the Third World. The spiritual convictions of the Americans were the heart of the war aims of the World War II Allies and were embodied in the Charter of the United Nations. The idealism of Woodrow Wilson and Franklin D. Roosevelt gave a distinctive character to the brave new world in the Pacific, which was, in fact, a Pax Americana.

The American position was no sooner established than it was challenged. The American people had no appetite for that much power, no faith in its permanence, and no desire for its maintenance. Choosing again to return to normalcy, they were content to assist others in the process of rehabilitation and reconstruction. The defeated enemies—Japan in the Pacific and Germany in Europe—sustained by their inner qualities and aided by benevolent victors, took the lead on the path to recovery.

The USSR launched a fundamental challenge to the American position of world leadership. The Soviets could not accept the ideology of capitalist democracy or tolerate American hegemony in Europe and Asia. The descent of the iron curtain in Europe ushered in the cold war. The USSR militantly opposed the United States in Iran, the Balkans, and Eastern Europe. The Soviets supported revolutions everywhere against capitalistic, democratic governments. Gaining an important ally with the victory of Mao Zedong in China, Stalin launched (or at least acceded to) the hot war in Korea.

The Korean armistice and the Geneva Conference afforded the United States the opportunity to reappraise its global position, especially in East Asia. The conclusions of Eisenhower and Dulles regarding the worldwide monolithic communist menace did not differ substantially from those of Truman and Acheson. Fundamentally, it was an accepted article of faith that the United States could not contain communist aggression alone. Sixteen nations had participated in the action in Korea, and their continued cooperation was deemed essential. Furthermore, of the nonmembers of the United Nations, the spectacular rebirth of Germany and Japan from the ashes clearly indicated their coming importance in confronting the communist monolith.

As the leader of the free world, the United States constructed an alliance system comprising the Rio Pact with Latin American nations, NATO with Western Europe, and, in the Asia-Pacific region, pacts of mutual defense with Australia and New Zealand, the Philippines, Japan, the ROK, the ROC on Taiwan, and the nations joined in the Southeast Asia Treaty Organization (Great Britain, France, Australia, New Zealand, Pakistan, Thailand, and the Philippines). The treaties covering the Asian nations committed the United States to act in accordance with its constitutional processes in the event of outside aggression. These alliances were strengthened by American programs of military, economic, and technical assistance and were made more credible by the then current doctrine of massive retaliation.

By virtue of the American interpretation of obligations arising from its commitments, the United States automatically responded to any threat in East Asia. It was assumed that U.S. interests were involved in, for example, a change of government in the ROK, a demonstration in Japan, an attack on the islands off the China coast, or insurgency in Southeast Asia.

The real or alleged communist connection was sufficient to trigger American action, although it became quite obvious that the communist world was no more monolithic than the free world. Moscow factions, Beijing factions, and assorted local factions gave the lie to the pretense of unity even within a local communist party in any Asian country. No matter how deeply local insurgencies were rooted in economic disparities and social inequities, American policy treated them as products of communist deviltry.

The long war in Vietnam exposed the inadequacy of anticommunism as the sole rationale for U.S. action and revealed the futility of reliance on superior conventional military power as the most effective method of accomplishing national objectives. These lessons neither dimmed Americans' faith in their own ideals nor cast doubts on their good intentions. Vietnam showed the necessity for the United States to reappraise its real interests—global and regional—and to reassess the course that had followed for nearly two decades. This was the first order of business for the Nixon administration.

The Nixon Doctrine

Six months after his inauguration in 1969, President Nixon announced new guiding principles for U.S. foreign policy:

> First, the United States will keep all of its treaty commitments ... Second, we shall provide a shield if a nuclear power threatens the freedom of a nation allied with us, or of a nation whose survival we consider vital to our security ... Third, in cases involving other types of aggression we shall furnish military and economic assistance when requested in accordance with our treaty commitments. But we shall look to the nation directly threatened to assume the primary responsibilities for providing the manpower for its defense.[1]

Without abandoning Asia, the Nixon Doctrine provided that the United States would systematically and deliberately lower its military profile in East Asia and the western Pacific. Nixon made it clear that the United States would make a greater effort for peaceful coexistence with its communist adversaries, but would not bear the responsibility for stability and peace alone.

In the four years from 1969 to 1973, while continuing hostilities and inconclusive peace negotiations characterized the situation in Indochina, the Nixon Doctrine was honored or ignored, as deemed expedient. Thousands of American troops came home—from Thailand, Vietnam, the Philippines, and Korea—but the war was widened in Laos and Cambodia in the interest of peace with honor.

Americans were sharply divided over the best means of meeting the continuing challenge to the United States in Asia. They generally agreed that the danger originated with the remnants of the communist bloc, fueled and driven by the Soviet Union. The Sino-Soviet split, although not necessarily permanent, afforded an opportunity for the United States and its allies to redefine their goals and to forge a strategy for their accomplishment. No responsible American contemplated the abandonment of the national interest or the scrapping of commitments for the protection of that interest in East Asia and the western Pacific. The dilemmas of policy lay in the choice of tactics to be pursued to achieve agreed goals.

In spite of Vietnam, convinced "cold warriors," both inside and outside the government, retained their faith in old philosophies and old methods. They believed a satisfactory future could be guaranteed by more of the same—greater power, greater strength in confrontation, and uncompromising cooperation with all anti-communists regardless of past performance or form of government. The old Nixonites treated the doctrine of the new Nixon not as a statement of a new faith, but as an untried tactic that might work if backed by adequate power. They would never accept any real or apparent reduction of U.S. military might except as the perceived mandate of the American people and the American Congress.

Those who supported the Nixon doctrine at its face value believed that the old methods of naked force had been tried and found wanting. They were under no illusions about the intentions of the Soviet Union and were not about to consent to any compromise jeopardizing national survival or reducing the credibility of the power of the United States to deter war with the USSR. They felt that under the Nixon Doctrine, détente—the preferred path to peace—was at least possible. President Nixon could reasonably have placed himself in either camp.

The fate of the Nixon Doctrine under its own architect will never be known. The defeat in Indochina deprived the president of the power to determine the nation's destiny. In the ensuing atmosphere of bitterness and disillusionment, Watergate denied the hapless Nixon of the opportunity to rally his people and lead them along new paths to peace.

President Ford was in office too briefly to put a definitive stamp on U.S. foreign policy. Soon after his accession to office he journeyed through much of East Asia after meeting Brezhnev in Vladivostok in an effort to revive the American spirit and to renew the faith of Asians in the U.S. commitment to their future. In a speech in Honolulu on Pearl Harbor Day, 1975, he proclaimed the high-sounding Pacific Doctrine. He attempted to shift the emphasis in American policy from the Nixon Doctrine to end war to the Pacific Doctrine to keep peace. He announced that he would handle specific problems with the Philippines, Taiwan, the ROK, and Japan not in any spirit of retreat, but in a spirit of confidence. In accord with the realities of détent, he would dedicate U.S. strength to solving universal problems of security and prosperity. In the hope that his words would have a ring of sincerity, he took advantage of two opportunities to provide local demonstrations of American military power. Following the seizure of the United States merchant vessel *Mayaguez* by Cambodian naval forces on May 12, 1975, he ordered air, marine, and naval units into action to secure the release of the ship and its 40 crew members. Then in August 1976 after the brutal slaying of two American officers by North Korean guards in the DMZ, the United States dispatched a carrier task force to Korea, placed all U.S. and ROK troops along the DMZ on full alert status, deployed an F-lll squadron from the United States, and brought in aerial reinforcements from Okinawa.

The Carter Tilt

President Carter's election in 1976 seemed to herald a new look in foreign affairs. In his campaign, Carter promised to reduce the size of the federal establishment and balance the budget. He would concentrate less on opposition to the Communists and more on cooperation with America's democratic allies. He would make Christian principles and such American ideals as human rights the core of his foreign policy. He took a studied antimilitary stance despite his apprenticeship to Admiral Hyman Rickover, the famed sponsor of the nuclear submarine and proponent of military preparedness.

Admittedly, Carter had a hard act to follow. For the implementation of his policies, he inherited a military and civil bureaucracy that had mushroomed into a massive establishment after World War II. It was not about to be whittled away by a well-meaning amateur from Georgia. Carter appointed cronies and recognized experts in sympathy with his own views to top political jobs. In foreign affairs, his team consisted of such disparate individuals as Cyrus Vance, Zbigniew Brzezinski, and Andrew Young. He added a sprinkling of McGovern liberals to the veteran policymaking corps in the State Department and handed out assorted ambassadorships to his most deserving political supporters. For the most part, President Carter was well served in Asia by seasoned diplomats in the ROK and Taiwan and by Senator Mike Mansfield in Japan and Leonard Woodcock in Beijing.

Once in office, the president discovered that it was far easier to make campaign promises than to formulate and execute effective policies. A "new look" eluded him. He had to whittle down his hopes and ideals to fit the demands of domestic politics and the responsible use of power.

Without the backing of a majority, a president is helpless. President Carter experienced difficulty retaining support. Respected for his personal integrity but criticized for his political naiveté, he was opposed by many old Washington hands in his own party as well as by independents and a solid bloc of Republicans. Many business leaders and intellectuals and many segments of the media—which seemed to go gunning for him—regarded him with skepticism. Even the two groups that supported him most strongly—blacks and organized labor—increasingly deserted him. His rating in the opinion polls dropped because of the gnawing effects of unemployment, a stagnant economic growth rate, and galloping inflation.

President Carter attracted even more criticism for his conduct of foreign policy. He could not be faulted for his priorities: "to provide for our nation's strength and safety, to stand by our allies and friends, to support national independence and integrity, and to work diligently for peace."[2] According to his critics, however, he lacked consistency and showed an excessive willingness to compromise with his adversaries. He was, therefore, held responsible for a monumental decline in the power, prestige, and credibility of the United States. His defenders argued that a consistent line, a grand strategy, or a magic formula, however attractive in theory, is never possible in practice. Crises are solved as they arise. Compromises are always described as a surrender by all parties involved, but mutual concession is the only possible method of preserving peace.

President Carter had to weather more than his share of crises in foreign policy: disputes with the European members of NATO; the B-1 bomber, the MX missile system, and the neutron bomb; the Russian brigade in Cuba; the Russians and their Cuban surrogates in Ethiopia, Yemen, and Angola; the Panama Canal Treaty; Middle East peace and the Camp David accords; the Strategic Arms Limitations Talks; the Chinese war to teach the Vietnamese a lesson over Cambodia; civil unrest with anti-American overtones in the Caribbean; hostages in Iran; and a Soviet advance that obliged President Carter to make decisions about policy toward the ROK. Naturally, the president had to trim his sails to ride out the storms. Where necessary, he backed away from his campaign rhetoric and tailored his foreign policy decisions to conform to his reading of the domestic political situation. He reneged on his promises to cut the military budget. In his own way he tried to convince his own people, his friends, and his adversaries that he possessed toughness and an iron will to go with his Christian heart.

In summarizing the changing U.S. role in East Asia in the 1980s, we can readily discern the basic differences in the strategic environment affecting U.S.-ROK relations. By 1980, the preponderance of military and economic power enjoyed by the United States in 1945 had given way to a new equilibrium of forces. Having lost its nuclear monopoly and its massive superiority in conventional arms, the United States was hard pressed to maintain parity with the rapidly growing military strength of the USSR.

The economic predominance of the United States had likewise disappeared. At the end of World War II, the United States accounted for 50 percent of the world's GNP, compared with 20 percent in 1980, and the industrial and technological leadership of the United States was unchallenged. In 1945, a favorable balance of trade made possible generous American gifts to underdeveloped and suffering nations. The United States was creditor to the world, and the dollar was as good as gold, but by 1980 it was hopelessly in the throes of economic recession.

The strategic story of the 1970s was only partially attributable to the decline of the United States. The gains of the rest of the world were equally important. While the United States maintained levels of military power judged adequate by successive administrations, the USSR dedicated its efforts to advancement. While the United States rested on its economic laurels, Japan, the ROK, Taiwan, Hong Kong, and Singapore in Asia alone hurled new challenges at the American giant. Even such LDCs as the Philippines, Thailand, Malaysia, and Indonesia began to stir with new economic life.

These changes in the strategic environment exerted a strong influence on U.S. policy toward the ROK. The United States was obliged to give new and changing weight to the Soviet Union, Japan, China, and other nations with rights and interests in the Korean Peninsula. The United States was only one of many nations concerned with the future of Korea. Perhaps more importantly, Korea was only one of the many places in the world where the vital interests of the major powers clashed.

At the end of the Carter administration, the international prestige of the United States was at a low ebb. But it was still highly regarded as a superpower, respected for its devotion to universally recognized human ideals, and esteemed as the mainstay of international peace and stability.

The Mounting Soviet Challenge

Of all the external influences of U.S.-ROK relations at the beginning of the Reagan administration, the most crucial was that exerted by the USSR. Like the United States, the Soviet Union is a superpower. Since its interests are global, it views the Korean Peninsula as a distant but important square on the international chessboard. An American-Soviet conflict anywhere on earth produces repercussions on both sides of the DMZ in Korea. Conversely, any clash of interests anywhere in Korea must be treated with extreme gravity because of the possibility of its expanding into a wider war involving both superpowers.

The fundamental clash between the United States and the Soviet Union involves ideology. To the Russians, the USSR is the champion of ideals. In the Soviet value system, revolution for social justice is to be prized more highly than political stability. A just war is better than an unjust peace. Prosperity is to be measured not by the privileges of the elite, but by the condition of the masses. To the USSR, communism is the wave of the future. Acts of subversion and war are justified if they push mankind toward the communist utopia. In international relations, the USSR lives by a double standard: one set of laws for ordinary nations and one for the communist. According to Henry Kissinger, the Russians feel that they have an insight into the forces of history. The Russians alone understand that class struggle and economic determinism make inevitable the revolution that will end in communist victory.

Permanent coexistence is impossible when Communists use goodwill as a cover for hypocrisy, deception, and propaganda. The basic policy of the Soviets is that they must be free to fill every vacuum and exploit every opportunity to advance the interests of the Russian state. For them there is no such thing as noninterference in internal affairs. Rather than risk nuclear suicide, they may make tactical compromises. But they cannot be expected to waver in their undeviating support for their own form of government: the philosophy of democratic centralism, the doctrine of national liberation, and the ultimate victory of communism.

The possession of adequate power is an indispensable part of ideological confrontation. The Russians do not underestimate American power, but they are not overawed by it. They understand the reluctance of Americans to resort to the use of force. Apparently, the Russians feel that they have achieved a nuclear deterrence and, perhaps, parity in conventional arms. Confidence in their own military might has been at the core of their innate expansionism. Brezhnev, like Stalin and Khrushchev before him, has not shied away from risk taking in testing his adversaries.

The USSR seeks to advance its power and prestige throughout the world by various means: doctrinal affinity, military strength, diplomatic statecraft, trade, aid, and propaganda. Every device familiar to the United States is part of the equipment of the USSR. The Soviets also use all overt and covert means to bolster friendly regimes or to seduce those cooperative with the United States. Where the Russians cannot control events or go on the initiative, they concentrate on taking advantage of American mistakes. The successor to Brezhnev will have the same grandiose goals and will pursue the same opportunistic tactics as his predecessors.[3]

Just as the United States has friends and allies, so has the USSR. The economic power of the East European bloc adds substantially to the Russian clout, as do the Soviet military surrogates of Cuba in Latin America and Vietnam in Southeast Asia. Indians and North Koreans are valuable allies. But the communist world is not monolithic. For all their unity of purpose, Communists outside the USSR have been unable to overcome differences in dogma; nor have they been willing to permit the label "communist" to be used as a cover for promotion of the interests of the Russian state.

The vital interests of the Russian state are the driving forces in Soviet foreign policy. The major concerns of the USSR in world affairs are a secure homeland, a satisfactory national economy, safe borders, a balance of power with the United States, and a voice in world affairs commensurate with its international status. Korea is important to the USSR only as it fits within this framework.

From Moscow's perspective, East Asia is more remote and less vital than Europe or the Middle East. But neither Asia nor Europe can be neglected. Russia always has wanted warm-water ports in Asia, and it must guard its 4,500-mile border with China. At one time in history, Russia extended across Siberia, stretched north of Japan through the Kuriles and the Aleutians, and reached into Alaska and down the North American coast to the environs of San Francisco. The Russian frontier was pushed back when the United States purchased Alaska and Japan drove the Russians out of Sakhalin, Korea, Manchuria, and Inner Mongolia. Russia's southward expansion was halted by the Chinese, who were obliged in the process to accept unequal treaties surrendering nearly a million square miles of Chinese territory. The Russian drive into Iran, Afghanistan, and Tibet was stopped by British power in South Asia.

Contemporary Soviet concepts of security in Asia do not demand recreation of tsarist grandeur. The Soviets are concerned primarily with meeting the triple threat of the United States, Japan, and, especially, the PRC. Fundamentally they must, of course, avoid nationalistic or religious uprisings of minority elements within their own body politic. Beyond their borders they seek an unassailable power position in the arc extending from the Red Sea to Vladivostok. They have adopted India as a base of operations in the subcontinent and the Indian Ocean. They have allied themselves with Vietnam in Southeast Asia and with the DPRK in Northeast Asia.

The Chinese view all these measures as manifestations of Soviet hegemonism. The strong Soviet military contingent on the Russo-Chinese border, the naval buildup in the Pacific, the struggle for influence in North Korea, the consolidation of power in Mongolia and Turkestan, and the generous aid to India have long provided the Chinese with incontrovertible evidence of the Soviet stranglehold.

To the Chinese, the Soviet alliance with Vietnam established Vietnam as a Trojan horse in Southeast Asia and gave the Soviets a base to threaten the United States in the Philippines and to disrupt the sea-lanes to Japan. The Chinese believe that the Soviet move into Afghanistan toward the

Persian Gulf, with Iran and Pakistan as possibly the next objectives, is in keeping with Soviet determination to extend its influence deeper into Asia and Africa, to edge the United States out of Asia, to blackmail Japan, and thus to dominate the future of the globe.

The Russians deny any ambition for world domination or hegemonism of any type. They say that they have no wish to encircle China, it is the Chinese who want to encircle the Soviet Union. To the Soviets, the Chinese are threatening them in Turkestan (where China and Russia meet), Afghanistan, and Pakistan and are challenging them in Vietnam and North Korea. Periodically, the Chinese take aggressive action in border territories (according to the Russians) and make ominous statements about the rectification of unequal treaties. Most maliciously, the PRC encourages Japan to rearm and endeavors to play the American card against the Soviet Union. The Russian position is that the USSR wants peace, trade, and a collective defense system that will permit the ASEAN nations, the ROK, Taiwan, and every other nation in Asia to pursue its own destiny, free from outside interference.

To guarantee its ideology and to protect its national interests, the USSR has engaged in a massive military buildup, approaching—some say surpassing—the United States in quality and quantity. In conservative U.S. opinion, the Soviet Union's reach is global, its ambition without limit.[4] Led by a highly skilled group of leaders whose grand strategy includes military, political, and economic factors, the USSR has developed a military capability far beyond the needs of defense or retaliation. In all areas—strategic, conventional, naval, air, and ground—the Soviets allegedly have reached levels equal to or exceeding those of the United States.

It is impossible to substantiate perceptions of equality or superiority in total military capability. The number of planes, ships, or tanks reported in intelligence estimates or professional journals cannot provide a reliable comparison of striking power or survivability. Measuring capability by totaling numbers of weapons is like adding apples and oranges. The value of any item in an inventory depends on such immeasurable factors as geography, climate, human dependability, and the will and intention of policymakers. The rapid development of weapons technology quickly outdates any estimate of the military balance. Policymakers on both sides of the iron curtain can select and interpret statistics to affirm or deny any contentions—particularly at budget time.

The Soviet military buildup in East Asia and the western Pacific is undeniable. Fifty-one well-equipped divisions, made up of a million men, are poised along the Russo-Chinese border. Soviet forces in the Kurile Islands off northern Japan reportedly have been augmented to 12,000 troops armed with tanks, heavy artillery, and helicopters. The air inventory has been beefed up with Backfire bombers. In 1978, the Soviet navy, operating out of Vladivostok and Sovetskaya Gavan on the Sea of Japan and Petropavlovsk on the Kamchatka Peninsula, had 113 submarines (some with ballistic missile–launching capability), 67 major surface combatant ships, and 466 auxiliary surface ships, representing 22–32 percent of all Soviet naval assets. Also in the area were 355 naval aircraft, or 27 percent of Soviet assets in this category.[5] In 1980, the Soviet Pacific fleet was strengthened by the addition of the V/STOL ASW (vertical/short takeoff and landing, antisubmarine warfare) aircraft carrier *Minsk* and its amphibious escort ship, the *Ivan Rogov*.

The Russians have frequently engaged in menacing military exercises off Japan and the Korean coast. The forces in the Kuriles have openly practiced amphibious landings in terrain remarkably similar to that of Hokkaido, the northernmost of Japan's main islands. Air sorties from Soviet bases, previously twice a week, but more recently twice a day, approach Japanese ports so closely as to send Japanese fighters scrambling into the air. Attack and ballistic missile submarines cruise ominously on the surface as they head in and out of ports to remind Japan, Korea, and the PRC of their presence. Covert submarine patrols and overt naval visits and exercises constantly demonstrate the naval power available to support Russian policy. The Russians constantly monitor movements of American ships, particularly when any unusual military exercise or concentration of naval units is involved.

The obvious increase in the Soviet naval capability in the western Pacific has by no means given the USSR command of the sea. With its augmented power, the Russian fleet provides the USSR with an effective nuclear deterrent. Undoubtedly, it can cut lines of communication and protect its own coastline. But the Russians are far from the point where they can challenge the Americans in the open ocean. The Americans retain respected strength in their carriers, surface combat units, nuclear-powered ballistic missile–launching submarines of the Polaris and Trident class, and sophisticated ASW capability.

Neither the relative decline of U.S. power nor the spectacular manifestation of growing Soviet power is necessarily an index of intentions. It is sometimes asserted that the shift in the power balance indicates either a warning of further aggressiveness on the part of the USSR or further unwillingness on the part of the United States to defend its commitments and vital interests in Europe and Asia. Neither assumption is true. The Americans are not that weak, and the Russians are not that strong. The Russians do build and deploy their forces to serve national interests to best advantage, but so do the Americans. The Russians engage in exercises to maintain military efficiency, but so do the Americans.

Furthermore, the Russians, like the Americans, encounter problems in executing policies. They, too, are subject to mistakes and miscalculations. They cannot fix a timetable for action or set up an inflexible strategy for achieving their objectives. They, too, must respond to the countermoves of their adversaries. They must establish priorities in the determination of their own interests that are sometimes incompatible. The Russians might want to edge the Americans out of Asia and dismantle the U.S. alliance system and forward bases, but they do not want to turn Asia over to the Chinese. Since they cannot have it both ways, they must choose whether it is better to oppose the Americans or to counter the Chinese.

Both Russian and American leaders seem to prefer peace to war. They shy away from confrontation that promises destruction rather than victory, and they appreciate the horror that would accompany total war. Although the Russians have been less hesitant than the Americans to assume risks, they have no appetite for testing the ultimate American determination to use force if necessary to protect a vital rather than a peripheral national interest. Neither the Russians nor the Americans appear willing to take responsibility for an initiative that could lead to nuclear suicide.

Such considerations as these have a direct relevance to U.S. policy toward the ROK. The Americans must always take the power of the Soviets and their willingness to use it into account. The Americans must also realistically estimate their own power and the possibility that at some point they might have to resort to military force to protect a vital interest. Nevertheless, the Russians probably view the American presence in the ROK as a stabilizing factor, tempering the actions of both North and South Korea. Since both the Soviet Union and the United States are reasonably satisfied with the status quo on the Korean Peninsula and since both share a fundamental desire not to antagonize Japan, it would seem mutually advantageous to seek a peaceful solution to whatever differences might arise between them.

The Sino-Soviet Split

Of the legitimate interests of the USSR in Asia that cannot be denied or overlooked, the first is the need to protect itself against the consequences of the Sino-Soviet split. The historical record shows alternating periods of friendship and enmity between Russia and China. Stalin cooperated with Chiang Kai-shek's Kuomintang and then deserted them for the Communists. The alliance of 1950 produced joint Soviet-Chinese opposition to the United States in Korea and Vietnam, but it was shattered in the 1960s and 1970s by bitter ideological disputes and clashes of national interests. The alliance expired formally in April 1980.

The Russians look on the Chinese with a sense of ideological contempt and political antagonism that is thoroughly reciprocated and feel that their stern policies and strong military force prevent Chinese encirclement. They perceive a Chinese threat in Korea, on the Manchurian border, in Mongolia and Central Asia, in Afghanistan, and in Vietnam. The Russians are rivals of the Chinese in seeking influence with insurgents in capitalist-ruled states and with factions in socialist or nonaligned states. Nowhere is the Soviet-Chinese rivalry more bitter than in the Korean Peninsula.

Both the USSR and the PRC have treaties of mutual assistance with North Korea. Both have supplied military and economic assistance to the DPRK, but the USSR was less generous than the PRC in spilling blood for their socialist ally. The Soviets fear that memories of the Korean War, plus the common cultural background of Chinese and Koreans, tend to tie the PRC and the DPRK more closely together than Russians and Koreans could ever be joined. Consequently, the USSR does not want any development in Korea to lend support to the PRC's anti-Soviet domestic and foreign policies. The Russian-Chinese competition for favor in the Korean Peninsula has a dual effect on American policy: it allows for greater freedom of maneuver in dealing with the ROK, and it consumes Russian energies, tying down Russian forces that might otherwise be released to oppose Americans in other parts of the world.

The USSR is concerned about the future potential of the PRC. It would be a nightmare for the Soviets if the PRC developed the economic and technological skills of Japan and if the modernization programs of the PRC provided hundreds of Chinese divisions with the weaponry to match the military machine of the USSR. It is easy to understand why Russian literary fancies often recall the scourge of the Mongols and speculate on wiping out the Chinese military capability—atomic or otherwise—before the PRC becomes too strong for the Russians to destroy.

The USSR hates, perhaps fears, the Chinese drive for modernization. It also dislikes the increasing closeness of the PRC with Japan and the United States, with all the technology transfers that might be accomplished. The USSR fears U.S.-Japan-PRC hegemonism as much as the PRC fears Soviet hegemonism. A U.S.-Japan-PRC alliance (with the possible addition of the ROK) would make the USSR feel genuinely encircled on the Asian rim of its vast territory.

The USSR hopes that present trends in U.S.-PRC relations are impermanent. It reasons that the United States and the USSR have more in common than either has with the PRC. Both are Western in cultural background; both are conservative; and both are more closely wedded to the maintenance of peace and stability in Asia than is the PRC. The USSR also is aware that at some future time it might be mutually advantageous to revive the sometime USSR-PRC spirit of friendship. Both nations keep a dialogue alive. Their diplomats and trade representatives often toast one another at public functions. They carry on endless if fruitless discussions about the possibility of compromising on their perennial conflicts. Although in the early 1980s the Russians and the Chinese appeared to take opposite sides of any issue automatically, their hostility could conceivably soften at some future date.

In May 1980, the annual trade agreement between the USSR and the PRC provided for an exchange of goods in 1980 amounting to $375 million (compared with $500 million in 1979). Although the total sum represents a substantial decline, it is remarkable that any trade at all continues in the midst of all the political fuss and fury. The USSR sells industrial machinery, parts for Soviet aircraft, and autos and spare auto parts and buys foodstuffs and mining products. The potential for greater trade relations exists, if political obstacles would disappear. It will be interesting to see what differences, if any, will occur in USSR-PRC relations when a new leader succeeds Brezhnev in Moscow.

The USSR and Japan

The Soviet interest in Japan is scarcely less important than the Sino-Soviet split as an external influence on U.S.-ROK relations. Japan has extended the USSR about $1.5 billion in credit for some half-dozen projects in Siberia and Sakhalin involving oil, natural gas, coal, timber, pulpwood, and wood chips. New projects, under negotiation in early 1981, include petroleum development, copper and other mineral development, large-diameter steel pipes, and sizable harbor construction. The building of major railway lines may come in the future.

The Japanese are wary of creating a Frankenstein's monster, and they want American cooperation as a condition for further ventures in Siberian development. The PRC naturally condemns the entire Siberian operation, and the USSR pretends indifference to Japan's program of assistance. The expressed Russian attitude is that Siberia will be developed, with or without the help of Japan. The resources of Siberia will always have a ready market. The longer Japan holds back from joining the process of exploitation, the more it will have to pay for Siberia's products in the long run.

The USSR can be unyielding or flexible, tough or conciliatory—as the case demands—toward Japan. The Soviet naval maneuvers and refusal to discuss the northern islands issue represent the tough side; the exchange of diplomatic visits shows the USSR in its softer moods. When Japan boycotted the Moscow Olympics in 1980 and joined in the sanctions against Iran, the Soviet ambassador to Japan left no doubt about Russian sternness. "Economic sanctions usually backfire," he said, "and Russian troops will be withdrawn from Afghanistan only when aggression against Afghanistan is stopped and peaceful relations between Afghanistan and Pakistan [are] established."

Peaceful understanding with Japan ranks high on the scale of Russian interests in Northeast Asia. It is a safe guess that the USSR ranks Japan (and the PRC) higher than Korea in its priorities. To retain the goodwill of Japan and to avoid exacerbating the Sino-Soviet split, the USSR would, in all likelihood, be disposed to make whatever compromises seemed necessary to preserve peace and stability on the Korean Peninsula.

The Soviet Union and North Korea

The tangible interests of the Soviet Union in the Korean Peninsula are lodged in its ally, the DPRK. For Moscow, Pyongyang is distant but important. The geographic location of Korea makes it far too vital to be in the hands of an unsympathetic power. Since the liberation of Korea from Japan, the USSR has assumed a patron-client relationship with the North, similar to that between the United States and the South. The USSR is handicapped, however, by the presence of the PRC in the North. As long as the Communists were friendly and opposed to the United States during the cold war, the servant did not mind having two masters. But when the Communists reached the parting of the ways, the USSR and the PRC became rivals in Pyongyang.

With the defeat of Japan in 1945, the Russians had a ready-made puppet regime complete with army, party, and government organizations poised to take over all of Korea. When the Americans stood firm in the South, the Russians were far too busy with their own reconstruction and with Western Europe to push their advantage in Korea. China, which was in the midst of its own civil war, neither aided nor resisted the Soviet moves.

When the actual division of Korea took place, the Russians supported Kim Il Sung with substantial military and economic aid. They supplied the advisers, officers, and technicians—along with the tanks, trucks, planes, and artillery—with which the Communists began the Korean War. When the battle turned against the Communists, the Chinese poured human waves of volunteers across the Yalu. After the armistice, the Russians discovered they had to share influence in Pyongyang with their Chinese ally. Sharing influence implied sharing the obligation to rebuild war-torn North Korea. Overburdened with its own problems of rehabilitation and reconstruction, China had little to offer. Russia provided most of the assistance and enjoyed most of the influence.

This relationship changed with the advent of Khrushchev. Idolatrously following the cult of their beloved leader, North Koreans disliked Khrushchev's de-Stalinization crusade, his détente with the United States, and his adventurism and capitulationism in Cuba. Perceiving the cooling of the USSR-DPRK relations, Zhou Enlai quietly stepped up China's program of military and economic assistance to the DPRK. A subdued but unmistakable contest for primacy was under way in Pyongyang.

Kim Il Sung was quick to play the Russians off against the Chinese to strengthen his own independent grip on the military, government, and party power. He purged rivals suspected of being too close either to Beijing or Moscow. He developed his *juche* ideology of self-reliance, criticizing both the USSR and the PRC—then locked in bitter debate—for their leftist opportunism, ideological revisionism, and great-power chauvinism. Seeing the ROK wallowing in political and economic helplessness, he fixed national development as his highest priority. He determined to use both the PRC and the USSR—giants though they were—as instruments to serve his nationalistic purposes.

In 1961, the DPRK negotiated trade agreements and treaties of mutual assistance with both the PRC and the USSR. Each treaty prohibited the DPRK from taking hostile action against its cosigner. The irony of these agreements is that they were intended to prevent the DPRK from cooperating with the United States, Japan, or the ROK; instead, they operated after the Sino-Soviet split to keep the DPRK from cooperating with either the USSR or the PRC against the other. If the USSR and the PRC should come to blows, the DPRK is legally and technically prohibited from taking part on either side. Following the signing of these agreements, both China and Russia accelerated their aid to North Korea.

The course of USSR-DPRK relations has never been smooth. The Brezhnev doctrine, which claims for the USSR the right to intervene in any fraternal state to protect its socialist structure, is unacceptable to the DPRK. Nor did the DPRK endorse Brezhnev's proposal for a collective security pact for the Pacific that would renounce the use of force, reject interference in internal affairs, guarantee frontiers, and promise cooperation in economic and other fields.

The Russians found the North Koreans much too independent. Too often the North Koreans seemed to take the Chinese side in Sino-Russian disputes (the India-China border affair, the Vietnamese incursion into Cambodia, and the Sino-Vietnamese border war) and to acquiesce without a murmur in Deng Xiaoping's diplomatic initiatives toward Japan and the United States. The Russians were exasperated by the DPRK's aspirations for leadership in the nonaligned movement, and they resented its failure to applaud the USSR's armed advance into Afghanistan. The Russians felt that the DPRK's handling of the *Pueblo* incident, the shooting down of an EC-121 reconnaissance plane, and the ax-murders of the American officers in the DMZ approached recklessness.

Nonetheless, the Russians continued to supply the DPRK with planes, missiles, and gunboats and provided the know-how for North Korean production of tanks, armored cars, rockets, artillery pieces, submarines, and destroyers. Although the Russians built the DPRK into a mighty military power, they held back from supplying the latest weapons systems in aircraft, electronic air defense, amphibious landing craft, missiles, and personnel carriers. The Russians used North Korea to channel armaments to Third World countries that did not want to publicize the Russian connection, including Burundi, Egypt, Libya, Mozambique, Pakistan, Sierra Leone, Tanzania, Togoland, Syria (for the Palestine Liberation Organization), and Zaire. North Korean pilots have flown and serviced Soviet MiG-21/23's supplied to Libya, as well as some of the MiGs supplied to Syria and Egypt during the 1973 Middle East war.[6]

The Russian flow of military goods to the DPRK has been accompanied by a parallel traffic in such civilian items as petroleum products, industrial machinery, and spare parts. By the late 1970s, the negative trade balance had plunged the DPRK $700 million into debt to Russia. The entire amount was in default. A large number of economic advisers, paid by the Russians, were unable to maintain the concentration on military production that the DPRK insisted on and at the same time move the country ahead toward a higher standard of living. Much of the Russian economic activity centered near the port of Najin on the northeast coast of Korea, where, it was said, the Russians were angling for a naval base.

Official feelings between Russians and North Koreans are anything but cordial. Diplomatic visits and cultural exchanges are infrequent and formal. Kim Il Sung still smarts from the rebuff suffered in 1975 when the Russians told him they were too busy to receive him. At that time, he was in Eastern Europe seeking support for his idea that the expulsion of the Americans from Saigon gave him his golden opportunity for unifying Korea—by force if necessary. The Beloved Leader fears that the Russians will try to interfere when he mandates the succession of power to his son.

Although the Russians and the North Koreans genuinely need each other, they have significant differences of opinion on issues of direct concern to Americans. In the matter of reunification of Korea, the Russians insist on the maintenance of peace and stability, even at the cost of delaying reunification; the North Koreans want reunification at the earliest opportunity, regardless of risks or consequences. To the Russians, war would be a no-win situation—they could not afford to let their client lose; they could not contain him should he defeat the South. The North Koreans find continued frustration of their nationalist ambitions intolerable. The status quo, or at least peaceful change at a controlled pace, is as much a Russian as an American desire.

The Russians reacted mildly, but the North Koreans resolutely opposed U.S. suggestions for a four-power (U.S., USSR, Japan, and PRC) or six-power (the same four plus the DPRK and ROK) conference on Korean affairs. The DPRK also rejected proposals for cross-recognition (the USSR and the PRC recognize Seoul in exchange for U.S. recognition of Pyong-yang) and entry of the two Koreas into the United Nations. The USSR took no public stand on the DPRK's proposal for two-way talks between the United States and the DPRK.

Although the USSR openly supports the DPRK's insistence on com-plete withdrawal of American ground forces as a precondition for peace, like the PRC it has quietly signaled that it views the American presence in the ROK as a regional stabilizing force. The Americans deter North Kore-ans from warlike activities and cool hotheaded South Korean generals. The American presence effectively limits the demands for more assistance that both North and South Koreans can make to their respective suppliers.

Military stabilization in Northeast Asia has broadened the scope of in-ternational relations, auguring well for a more peaceful future. In support-ing the DPRK, neither the Russians nor the mainland Chinese have been willing to ignore the strength and the potential of the ROK completely. Aware that Chinese overtures to the United States and Japan could well be extended to include the ROK, the Russians have opened their doors, ever so slightly, to the ROK. They permitted a South Korean wrestling team to compete in the USSR and granted a South Korean cabinet mem-ber permission to attend a meeting held at Tashkent under the auspices of the United Nations. The Russians and the South Koreans regularly engage in irregular trade through Hong Kong, and occasionally fur hats and heavy woolen shirts manufactured in South Korea—with labels in Cyrillic let-ters—are offered at very cheap prices in Seoul markets. North Koreans do not like any contact between Russians and South Koreans, fearing that any concession, however small, by the USSR to South Korea will lead to even-tual recognition.

In summary, the specific local interests of the USSR in the Korean Pen-insula seem to indicate a Russian preference for peace. It is only when the analysis is extended to cover the world view of the U.S.-USSR conflicts that the dangers inherent in the Korean situation are clearly exposed.

The Influence of Japan

Next to the Soviet Union, Japan exerts the strongest influence on U.S. policies toward the ROK. Japan in the 1980s is an economic giant whose security is intimately linked with that of the United States. Since a war in

Northeast Asia would be disastrous for Japan, it wants to make sure that the United States retains the capability and the will to preserve the peace and stability of the Korean Peninsula.

The Japanese are aware that to a large extent, their future depends on the protection of their interests, not exclusively in the ROK or the DPRK, but in the entire peninsula. Therefore, they are constrained to exert maximum influence on Soviet and Chinese policies in the North and on American policies in the South—not for the sake of the Koreans, but for the sake of their own survival.

Geography and history account primarily for the vital interest of Japan in Korea. The two nations are neighbors; the waters that in peacetime provide fish for their food and commerce for their livelihood in wartime constitute the lines of communication essential between friends and vulnerable to enemies. Japan's territorial disputes over these waters are with both Koreas and involve limits of jurisdiction, fishing rights, regulation of trade, and exploitation of resources, including oil. In the event of war in Northeast Asia, either between the two Koreas or involving the great powers, naval operations in these waters would immediately threaten Japan's vital maritime lifelines.

Historically, Japan and Korea share a cultural heritage of Buddhism and Confucianism. They have a linguistic affinity that exacerbates their differences, but smooths the path to mutual understanding. Japanese and Koreans have a love-hate relationship sharpened by centuries of close political relations. Japanese attitudes toward Koreans range from indifference to contempt—only recently flavored with a modicum of respect.

Koreans criticize, but they copy the Japanese. Such fundamental patterns of social life in Korea as school curricula and uniforms, legal systems and procedures, business organization, festivals and holidays, bear the unmistakable stamp of Japan. Japanese radio blankets Korea, and Japanese television reaches the coastal regions. In a sense, the Japanese (and the Chinese) have cultural affinities with Koreans analogous to those between Anglo-Saxons and Latins in the West.

From a strategic point of view, Korea is the land bridge between Japan and the Asian continent. Before World War II the main traffic was westward. After the conquest of Korea, the armed forces of Japan planted their flag in Manchuria (Manchukuo), Mongolia, and the China mainland. Contemporary Japan is concerned that in time of turmoil the flow of traffic might be reversed. Peace is the only safe policy for Japan. It is not that the Japanese have become pacifists; it is only that their older generation has experienced firsthand the consequences of defeat.

Economically, the Japanese have a significant stake in Korea. Although prewar Japanese investments in colonial Korea, including land, homes, mines, factories, public buildings, and utilities, were entirely wiped out and all Japanese living in Korea were repatriated in 1945, Japan subsequently received from Korea the economic boost needed for its new prosperity. The factories of Japan profited from hundreds of millions of dollars in procurement orders for services, supplies, and equipment needed by the U.N. forces in Korea. After a decade of spectacular economic progress between 1955–1965, Japan again turned to Korea for trade and investment.

In 1980, Japan took about 20 percent of Korea's exports, ranking as the ROK's second-best customer after the United States. Japan provided between 35 and 40 percent of Korea's imports and was the number-one supplier for the ROK. The two-way trade approached $9 billion, with more than $3 billion in ROK exports to Japan and nearly $6 billion in ROK imports from Japan. The negative trade balance offset a large share of ROK trade earnings elsewhere in the world.

From 1962 to 1979, Japan invested more than $1 billion in the ROK—some 60 percent of all foreign investments. By 1980 the value of Japanese investments in the ROK was perhaps four times that of U.S. interests. It was estimated that the Japanese controlled over a thousand enterprises, with a net worth exceeding $1.7 billion, through equity holdings, dummy partnerships, management contracts, and licensing arrangements. Most Japanese capital (75 percent) was in mining and such manufacturing enterprises as chemicals, electronic products, textiles and garments, machinery, oil refining, metalwork, and shipbuilding. Most of the remainder (22 percent) was in tertiary industries like hotels and tourism, construction and engineering, banking, transport and warehouses, and electric power. The economic linkage between Japan and the ROK was between elites, without a broad people-to-people basis. A powerful "Korea lobby" was created in Tokyo. Naturally, the Japanese wanted the Americans to help keep the ROK safe for the Japanese *yen*.

Japanese leaders have a deep distrust for the authoritarianism existing on both sides of the 38th parallel in Korea. Japanese hate the communism of Kim Il Sung, distinct as it is from the ideological systems of China and the Soviet Union, and think that the regime of Chun Doo Hwan is likely to prove more dictatorial than those of Park Chung Hee and Syngman Rhee. With a healthy respect for human rights and a profound conviction that repression spawns revolt, the Japanese would like to see orderly progress toward democracy in both Koreas.

Another source of Japanese interest stems from the presence of Koreans in Japan. Sharply divided in loyalty between North and South, they have formed organizations to foster their viewpoint and to influence the government of Japan to favor their respective homeland. Subject to some ostracism and discrimination in Japan, these groups have not helped matters by their internecine feuds. Although the authorities have had no excessive trouble so far with these Korean residents, the Japanese do not relish the prospect of waves of refugees fleeing to Japan if Korea were again to be engulfed in hostilities.

After World War II, Japan's policies toward Korea were formulated within the framework of the political limitations imposed by defeat. Article IX of the constitution adopted during the occupation renounced war as a sovereign national right and rejected the threat or use of force as a means of settling international disputes. Japan also obligated itself never to maintain land, sea, and air forces and never to recognize the right of belligerency. Amending these restrictions would require a two-thirds vote of the Diet.

After the outbreak of hostilities in Korea in 1950, Japan was treated, particularly by the United States, as a new ally rather than a recent enemy. The U.S. peace settlement with Japan the following year removed the fetters on Japanese sovereignty and practically made Japan a ward of the United States in national security matters. The peace settlement did not solve the lingering disputes between Japan and Korea. Following a judicial decision that Article IX did not deprive Japan of the right of self-preservation, Japan created the Self-Defense Forces. In 1956, Japan and the USSR concluded an agreement, not quite a treaty of peace, ending the state of hostilities and restoring normal diplomatic relations.

Throughout the late 1950s and early 1960s Japan paid little attention to Korea. Kim Il Sung concerned himself only with his communist backers, the PRC and the USSR. President Rhee was blatantly hostile to Japan; to him unification of North Korea and South Korea under his leadership was the best guarantee that Korea would not fall into the lap of Japan.

In January 1960, Japan and the United States negotiated the Treaty of Mutual Cooperation and Security, the capstone of their relationship. By Article V of the treaty,

> . . . each party recognizes that an armed attack against either party in the territory under the administration of Japan would be dangerous to its own peace and safety and declares that it would act to meet the common danger in accordance with its constitutional provisions and processes.

Article VI stated: "For the purpose of contributing to the security of Japan and the maintenance of international peace and security in the Far East, the United States of America is granted the use by its land, air and naval forces of facilities and areas in Japan."

An Added Minute to the Treaty provided:

> ... Major changes in the deployment into Japan of United States Armed Forces, major changes in their equipment, and the use of facilities and areas in Japan as bases for military combat operations to be undertaken from Japan other than those conducted under Article V of the said Treaty, shall be the subjects of prior consultation with the Government of Japan.[7]

These key clauses defined the relative roles and responsibilities of the United States and Japan in the event renewed hostilities in Korea threatened their security.

Bolstered by this treaty and its own prosperity, Japan's interest in Korea reawakened. The collapse of the Rhee regime, the open split between China and the Soviet Union, and the neglect of Northeast Asia in the early 1960s implied in the burgeoning American involvement in Indochina strengthened this interest. Desiring to enlist Japan in the effort to develop the ROK, the United States encouraged both Japan and the ROK to normalize relations, officially nonexistent since the end of World War II. In 1965, the two nations, on a basis of equality and reciprocity, signed agreements settling their controversies over property claims, debts, fishing rights, status of Koreans in Japan, and territorial jurisdiction over islands between Korea and Japan. These agreements paved the way for economic grants and loans; the ROK needed the money and Japan eyed the ROK as a place for profitable investment. By refusing to recognize South Korea as the sole sovereign state on the Korean Peninsula, however, Japan left the door open for possible overtures to the North.

The next important development resulted from announcement of the Nixon Doctrine in July 1969. Japan was relieved that the United States had extracted itself from Vietnam, but disliked the idea of a reduction of U.S. forces in Taiwan and Korea. Japan considered that its own defense perimeter included Okinawa, Taiwan, and Korea.

Seeking to maintain stability despite the rapid and profound changes in the Far East, in November 1969 President Nixon and Japanese Prime Minister Sato Eisaku agreed that "the security of the Republic of Korea was essential to Japan's own security." Sato endeavored to remove doubts about the possible negative effects of the "prior consultation" clause by declaring that if the need should arise, the Japanese government would decide its attitude promptly and positively. It was noted, however, that a *positive* reply was not quite the same as an *affirmative* reply.

President Nixon's détente with China was quickly followed and soon outdistanced by similar moves on the part of Japan. Prime Ministers Tanaka Katuei and Zhou Enlai, meeting in Shanghai, agreed on ways to continue Japan's relations with Taiwan while normalizing diplomatic relations between Beijing and Tokyo, opening the way for expanded trade and substantial Japanese investment in the PRC. In accepting an "antihegemony" clause in the Shanghai communiqué, Tanaka and Zhou began the negotiating process that led to the Japan-China Treaty of Peace and Friendship in August 1978.

Along with the unfolding American policy of a lower military profile in Asia, a spirit of greater independence and self-reliance crept into Japan's security and diplomatic policies. Noting the initiation of reunification talks between North and South Korea, some Japanese economic interests—textiles, fishing, mining, communications, shipping, electronics, autos, and steel—sought opportunities in North Korea. They explored possibilities for credits, loans, eased travel arrangements, greater cultural contacts, and an ultimate political agreement. The government was cautious, emphasizing that it did not see Kim Il Sung as a military threat, that it did not recognize the ROK as the sole sovereign state in Korea, and that Japan was vitally interested in the stability of the entire Korean Peninsula.

The petroleum embargo of 1973 further enhanced Japan's spirit of independence. Japan determined that it had to be more pro-Arab and less pro-Israel than the United States and that it had to push ahead strenuously with its nuclear power program despite U.S. opposition. In the meantime, minicrises developed between Japan and the ROK over the KCIA's kidnapping of South Korean dissident political leader Kim Dae Jung from a Tokyo hotel room; the arrest of two Japanese youths for inciting antigovernment demonstrations in Seoul; and the Japanese implication in the murder of Mrs. Park. It was just at this juncture that President Nixon resigned and the last of the U.S. presence was forcibly ejected from Saigon.

In an atmosphere of some urgency, President Ford and Prime Minister Miki Takeo met to reassess U.S. policies toward East Asia in general and toward Japan and Korea in particular. In a joint announcement on August 6, 1975, the two leaders agreed that the security of the Republic of Korea was essential to the maintenance of peace on the Korean Peninsula, which in turn was necessary for the peace and security of East Asia, including Japan. In elaborating on the prior consultation clause, Miki said that it was inconceivable that Japan would quibble or hesitate during an actual crisis in neighboring South Korea.

Prime Minister Miki, in his brief administration (1974–1976), set the general line for Japanese policy toward Korea. He favored close economic and political ties with the South, without barring relations with the North. Since another Korean war would inevitably involve Japan, the ultimate challenge to Japanese diplomacy was to influence events away from war and toward a stable peace on the Korean Peninsula. Peaceful reunification of the two Koreas was sometimes stated to be ideal, although a unified

Korea would constitute a potential threat to Japan. Japan encouraged both Koreas to expand their dialogue, but was obviously happier with a condition of peaceful coexistence.

The Miki line would welcome the simultaneous entry of the two Koreas into the United Nations and would prefer a situation of formal peace to the post-armistice arrangement still in effect. It would support any international initiative, from two-power talks to a six-power conference, whose objective was the stabilization of the Korean situation. It would encourage Japan and the United States to undertake talks with the North, while the USSR and the PRC made parallel efforts to improve relations with the South. The desired end would be cross-recognition or any other condition tending to normalize relations between the two Koreas and outside powers. Until such ends could be achieved, the United States should maintain the deterring power of the American military presence in the South.

Late in the Ford administration, Japan was reassured by prevailing U.S. policies toward the ROK. On a trip to the Far East shortly after the fall of Saigon, Secretary of Defense Schlesinger repeated his pledge to the Koreans that the United States would stand by its treaty commitments. In a ministerial-level defense meeting in Japan with his Japanese counterparts, Schlesinger worked out satisfactory procedures and guidelines guaranteeing consultation and participation in mutual defense activities. He laid the groundwork for massive multinational military exercises. On his return to Washington, he told a congressional committee that the United States had learned that it must strike at the heart of the military power of an enemy and declared that the United States would not rule out the use of tactical nuclear weapons in Korea. To make his tough line more credible, a State Department official told Congress that the administration had no plans to reduce the U.S. force level in the ROK during 1975.

President Carter's unexpected announcement of phased withdrawal of U.S. troops from Korea upset the Japanese, who felt they were not consulted adequately in the decision-making process. To the Japanese, premature withdrawal from Korea would destabilize Northeast Asia. They feared it might trigger an arms race between North and South Korea and might give either or both an excuse to develop nuclear weapons. Prime Minister Fukuda Takeo hastened to Washington to probe the views of the new administration. In a joint statement, the president and the prime minister noted the continuing importance of peace and stability on the Korean Peninsula for the security of Japan and East Asia as a whole. They agreed on the desirability of continued efforts to reduce tension on the Korean Peninsula and strongly hoped for an early resumption of the dialogue between the North and South. Fukuda was reassured by Carter's statement that the United States, after consultation with the Republic of Korea *and Japan,* would proceed with the phaseout of ground troops in ways that would not endanger the peace on the Korean Peninsula.

Prime Minister Fukuda, like Miki before him and Ohira Masayoshi and Suzuki Zenko after him, was the spokesman for the ruling Liberal Democratic Party, which held an unshakable grip on the government. They represented a consensus that seemed to be taking shape in Japan, making new judgments about the United States, the Soviet Union, and China and advocating a far stronger defense posture and a more independent diplomatic course in world affairs. These were the key factors in shaping Japanese ideas about U.S. policies toward the ROK.

Aware of the "no more Vietnams" sentiment in the United States and the undercurrent of neo-isolationism, the Japanese increasingly felt they could not entrust their future solely to the protection of the United States. Realizing that the curtain was gradually being rung down on an age when the U.S. nuclear umbrella guaranteed safety, they were obliged to reassess the weaknesses as well as the strengths in the U.S. relationship. The two nations approached their problems with different emphases, the Americans being more concerned about defense and the Japanese about economic survival. They ascribed different values to such issues as the relative cost of their respective contributions to mutual security, the trade imbalance, and fair or unfair competition in marketing steel, autos, color televisions, or citrus fruits. Even in defense matters, many Japanese expressed doubts about the credibility of the United States. They were not sure that the United States continued to possess the will or the capability to act as peacekeeper in Asia.

The Japanese lost nothing in respect for actual American military power or for individual Americans living in their midst. They admitted that it would be unrealistic to sever the massive U.S.-Japanese ties in mutual security, trade, and investment. They knew that without the United States, they could not preserve themselves against the armed attacks of an outside aggressor. In contrast to Vietnam days when anti-American riots were bitter and frequent, in 1980 the city mayor headed the welcoming committee when the American carrier *Midway* returned to station in Yokosuka. To some Japanese, however, the security treaty with the United States had become like an old family Bible—nice to have around and refer to nostalgically, but no longer useful for guidance.

The Japanese consensus in formation of policies toward the USSR was that détente was preferable to confrontation, conciliation to irritation, and peace to war. Without admitting any linkage to the ideas of Brezhnev, the Japanese favored a nonaggression pact for the Pacific. The northern islands issue was annoying, and the prospect of profit from participation in the development of eastern Siberia was inviting, but the fact of the growth of

Soviet military and naval strength was undeniable. The Japanese were concerned, but not alarmed. The Soviets might have ended American predominance, but they had not achieved a predominance of their own. The nearer the superpowers were to balance, the greater the opportunity for Japan to maneuver.

The Japanese were not willing to concede superior Russian intelligence or strategic thinking. The Russians, too, had difficulties. Their grand design for domination, if they had one, was subject to interruptions. They, too, were limited, even in their disruptive capability. They had no grounds for confidence about their future in Korea. Obliged to take firm measures and use their power to restrain Kim Il Sung, they had little reason to believe that he would be a malleable instrument should they decide to use him at some future time for their own purposes, as they had used the local authorities in Afghanistan.

Prime Minister Tanaka, following the initiatives of President Nixon, had set Japan's course toward both Chinas. Eased by the program of the Four Modernizations, this course had led to the Treaty of Peace and Friendship concluded in August 1978. This treaty made possible the modus vivendi allowing Japan to deal with Taiwan and left to an indefinite future settlement of the triangular relationship between Japan, China, and Korea. Despite increasing trade, aid, and loans to the PRC, Japan by no means approved all elements of Chinese foreign policy. Specifically Japan disapproved of China's support for the Pol Pot regime in Cambodia and its pedagogical war in Vietnam.

Japan shows increasing concern about its problems of defense and diplomacy. The dilemma is whether to rely on traditional policies with as little change as possible or to assume increasing responsibilities in keeping with its enormous economic power. Change does not come easily, resisted as it is by an indifferent mass of the Japanese population, left-wingers, a substantial number of women, antiwar socialists, and cost-conscious taxpayers who want to keep defense costs down. Prime Minister Suzuki identifies readily with the traditionalists who have dominated the defense debate since the end of the American occupation.

The urge for change comes from a highly motivated segment of business leaders, publicists, and dedicated nationalists, particularly within the bureaucracy and the Self-Defense Forces. This new group obviously is gaining strength, but it cannot yet muster the two-thirds vote in the Diet required to change Article IX of the antiwar constitution.

At the time Prime Minister Suzuki visited Washington early in 1981, Japan and the United States held widely divergent opinions about the adequacy of their respective security policies. Japanese authorities pointed out that over the preceding decade, Japan's annual defense expenditures had increased at the rate of 10 percent per year, compared with a 2 percent increase for NATO and an annual decline of 2 percent for the United States. Japan ranked sixth among the nations of the world in defense expenditures, spending two-thirds as much as Britain and half as much as West Germany. (Although the Japanese limit defense expenditures to 0.9 percent of the GNP, the total would be 1.5 percent if the Japanese included military pensions in their accounting, as is the customary procedure in the United States and NATO nations.)

The Japanese were consistently adding new types of weapons and equipment to their inventory. They acquired the advanced F-15 fighter, P-3-c patrol planes, and early warning E2C reconnaissance craft. They were in the market for a substantial amount of advanced weapons and equipment for their fleet. They were constantly working toward standardization of arms with the United States, and they had the skill and the production facilities to build, maintain, and repair even the most sophisticated of modern armaments.

Japanese Diet members spoke openly of the army and the navy, instead of the self-defense forces. They discussed the pros and cons of cruise missiles, ASW-carriers, in-flight refueling capability, and manufacture of weapons for export. They even dared to debate the taboo subject of nuclear development.

Japanese and American military authorities conducted training exercises as though they were in command of joint forces, NATO style. In planning for regional contingencies, they coordinated such activities as command and control, joint intelligence gathering, and logistical support. Despite mutual suspicions, the Japanese took cautious steps toward closer cooperation with the South Koreans. For the first time, the chief of the Self-Defense Agency visited the ROK and suggested mutual inspection of military facilities. A retired admiral of the Maritime Self-Defense Forces, with pre–World War II experience, proposed exchanges of students, goodwill visits by naval units, and joint preparations for defense of the Sea of Japan and the straits leading to the open ocean. He was quick to deny any Japanese ambitions for regional domination or any motives for his proposals other than the defense of Japan itself.

On the American side, government officials privately and in public expressed their displeasure over Japan's unwillingness to increase its defense expenditures to levels warranted by its spectacular economic growth. The imbalance between American and Japanese contributions to mutual defense seemed no longer justifiable. Americans wanted the Japanese to assume greater obligations particularly for coastal defense and command of the Japanese straits, maritime patrols, antisubmarine warfare, and maintenance of the safety of the sea-lanes.

The dilemma of defense also appeared in the diplomatic arena. Some Japanese writers called for the end of "my home" or "kneel to the ground" diplomacy. No longer should the Japanese place a premium on placating everybody. They should assert their own views regardless of consequences. No longer should the Japanese be mere merchants of transistor radios, as de Gaulle referred to Prime Minister Ikeda Hayato. Their diplomacy should be multidirectional, smoothing out difficulties between East and West. They should not devote their efforts to the anachronistic pursuit of military power to protect their overseas investments, but relying on the good faith and sense of justice of all nations, should concentrate on solving such great global issues of the future as access to markets and raw materials, freedom of the seas, utilization of resources, prevention of pollution, conservation of energy, and reduction of the types of tensions that lead to senseless war.

Such ideas as these were reflected in the ever-changing course of U.S.-Japanese relations. The underlying sensitivity to the factor of inequality in the mutual security relationship was aggravated by the trade wars in automobiles and semiconductors on the eve of the Suzuki visit. The ill-advised use of the term "alliance" in the Reagan-Suzuki communiqué was so displeasing to some Japanese political circles that it led to the resignation of a foreign minister widely known for his pro-American sentiments. At the same time the unfortunate sinking of a Japanese fishing vessel by an American nuclear submarine and the alleged cutting of fishermen's nets by American warships on maneuver stirred up latent anti-American feelings. The diplomatic atmosphere was further clouded by the revival of a long-standing argument whether American ships with nuclear weapons aboard should be permitted to dock at Japanese ports. When the *Midway* returned to Yokosuka in 1981, it failed to attract the enthusiastic welcome it had received the previous year.

It was in light of these changing defense and diplomatic attitudes that the Japanese formulated their ideas about Korea. In the Japanese view, the primary objective of American policy should be the prevention of war. Unless required by a crisis somewhere else in the world, the United States should make no changes in the deployment of American forces in Korea that would destabilize the situation in Northeast Asia. By word and deed, the United States should carry out its commitments to the ROK and to Japan. The United States should be firm against North Korean aggression, but not unnecessarily belligerent in the tone of its pronouncements. While continuing to assist the ROK, the United States should stop short of providing it the muscle to attack the North. Americans should firmly encourage democracy and protest the excesses of authoritarian regimes North or South. Finally, the United States should support steps toward peaceful reunification and should make no changes in existing relations without prior consultation with the Japanese. It was of great consequence to both Japan and the United States that their policies toward the ROK be in basic harmony.

China and U.S.-Korean Policies

China's influence on U.S.-Korean relations is more complicated than that of the Soviet Union or Japan. Although China has the greatest and most direct national interest in the Korean Peninsula of any of the great powers due to its geographical proximity, its policies are the most amorphous because of the profound changes taking place in the post-Mao leadership and the impermanence of its perceptions of friends and enemies.

The passing of the Gang of Four in Beijing brought the pragmatists to power, with consequent modifications of the extreme attitudes and actions of the Cultural Revolution. The adoption of the Four Modernizations program shattered the old ideological attachments to the Soviet Union and the lesser socialist states of North Korea and Vietnam. Old friends became enemies, ancient enemies became new friends. Since each of these developments could possibly represent nothing more than a transient evolutionary phase in China's revolution, extreme care must be exercised in evaluating China's capabilities and intentions, as they influence U.S. policies toward the Korean Peninsula.

China's leaders make periodic reports elucidating their current line in foreign affairs to the Congress or Central Committee of the Chinese Communist Party or to the National People's Congress. Their fundamental presumptions are enlightening. In their view, both hegemonic powers, the Soviet Union and the United States, strive to dominate the world, and their continued contention will someday lead to a new world war. The Chinese are against this, but they are not afraid of it.

According to Chinese spokesmen, the two hegemonic powers are the biggest international exploiters and oppressors of today and the common enemies of the peoples of the world. The Chinese people should form the broadest possible united front within the Second and the Third World to cope with the invasion, subversion, exploitation, intervention, and oppression of the two great superpowers. The United States wants to protect its interests, and the USSR wants to expand. Soviet imperialism presents the greatest danger because it seeks to pocket all of Europe, Asia, and Africa. Massing its troops in Eastern Europe and building its military power in Asia while accelerating its plunder of strategic resources and its scramble for bases in Africa and the Middle East, the Soviet Union attempts to encircle Europe and Asia by dominating the western Pacific, seizing access routes to the Persian Gulf, thrusting around the Cape of Good Hope, and blocking the main navigation routes to the Atlantic Ocean in the West.[8]

In the Chinese view, the main enemy should be opposed by utilizing even the smallest rift among enemies, and taking advantage of every— even the smallest—opportunity of cooperating with an ally, even though the ally be temporary, vacillating, unstable, unreliable, and conditional. In spite of ideological antagonisms, China can cooperate with the United States on the basis of the Shanghai communiqué. Such cooperation signifies neither approval of U.S. policies nor any love of the American people.

For the moment it is useful for China to encourage NATO and the United States in Europe, closer U.S.-Japanese ties, Japanese rearmament, and continued U.S. military interest in Southeast Asia and the Indian Ocean. The stronger the enemies of the USSR, the greater their will to stand up against China's number-one enemy. China reserves the right to pursue alternative policies should the United States fail to fulfill Chinese expectations.

In dealing with China, the United States confronts a dilemma. Torn between its repugnance for communism and the advantage of accepting the PRC as a potential ally, the United States cannot ignore the image of China as the sworn enemy of capitalism, a closed society with a planned economy and regimented people, a fetish for secrecy, and disdain for universally recognized human rights. A remnant of loyalty to the concept of Free China, to the conviction that Taiwan at its worst is better than Communist China at its best, persists among Americans. On the other hand, Americans realize that China is the oldest political reality in the world today, representing an ancient and honorable culture. Normal relations with China are the only way to preserve stability in Asia and peaceful coexistence with all nations, regardless of ideology. Neither Democrats nor Republicans can escape this dilemma.

In light of these uncertainties and ambiguities, China has formulated its policies toward Korea, primarily North Korea, considering fully their implications for the United States. The United States, for its part, has determined its policies toward Korea, primarily South Korea, with an eye toward the influences exerted by China and the effects of U.S. policy on the PRC.

The national interest of China in the Korean Peninsula is undeniable. By sea and by air, Korea is as closely linked to China as it is to Japan. The long land frontier exposing Manchuria, the industrial heart of China, to Korea affords no protection either to Korea or to China. The rail and highway system from Seoul through Pyongyang across the Yalu River to Shenyang and eventually to Beijing, provides the access route over which Chinese volunteers poured into Korea.

Korean history has been intimately tied up with that of China. The racial origin of the Koreans is in the mountainous areas of Northeast Asia, but their cultural patterns are Chinese. Large border areas, still with a significant percentage of mixed Korean and Chinese population, have been fought over for centuries, sometimes belonging to China and sometimes to the Northern Korean kingdom of Koryo. Chinese, as well as Japanese, interfered constantly in Korea's internal affairs, giving their support to their favored Korean rivals for power. Until replaced by Japan near the end of the nineteenth century, China long enjoyed suzerainty over the ruling dynasty in Seoul.

In the 1950s, when the world was different, the PRC was an ally of the USSR, the sponsor of the DPRK in Pyongyang. In the Korean War, the Soviets gave the North Koreans advice and a certain amount of support, but the Chinese furnished the troops who fought the U.N. forces to a standstill. The Chinese regarded the stalemate as a victory that prevented an American invasion. Chinese troops remained in North Korea until 1958.

After the Korean War the Chinese shared with the Russians the costs of helping the DPRK survive and develop. They were rivals for predominant political influence in Pyongyang. Each had its stooges in the entourage of Kim Il Sung, but by playing off one group against the other, Kim established his own cult of the individual. Despite the widening Sino-Soviet split after 1961, Kim managed to lean to both sides, showing his favors sometimes to the PRC, sometimes to the USSR. He shared with both an antagonism to the purposes of the United States in Vietnam and the ROK, and he depended on both for maximum assistance. In 1966, during the Cultural Revolution in China, Kim was shocked to see himself described by fanatical Red Guards as a fat revisionist. For five years DPRK–PRC relations were strained, with the Chinese delegate even refusing to attend MAC meetings in Panmunjom.

A new atmosphere developed with the eclipse of Lin Biao and the rise of Zhou Enlai in Beijing. At the same time, the Nixon initiatives in East Asia produced the Nixon-Sato joint communiqué stressing the importance of Korea and Taiwan to the security of Japan. In response, Zhou Enlai journeyed to Pyongyang to reshuffle his cards with Kim Il Sung. In 1970, Zhou and Kim jointly announced their conviction that the presence of U.S. troops in Korea and the revival of Japanese militarism were the greatest threats to peace and security in Asia. They called on the United States to withdraw its troops and on Japan to abrogate its treaty with the United States and to abolish its military bases. As part of the deal, China agreed to provide additional military, economic, and technical assistance to North Korea, including ships, fuel, and technical advisers.

The Zhou Enlai–Kim Il Sung agreement followed closely on the heels of the Sino-Russian clash in the channel islands of the Ussuri River separating Manchuria and Siberia. Kim clearly displayed a tilt toward Beijing in the balance he endeavored to maintain between his two backers.

As Zhou redirected China's stance toward the United States, he took great pains not to alienate Kim Il Sung. When the DPRK and the ROK began reunification talks after the U.S.-China détente, Zhou Enlai gave his unequivocal support to all proposals of the DPRK. He endorsed the "just stand of the Korean people" for withdrawal of U.S. troops, the mutual reduction of the armed forces of the DPRK and the ROK, and a political consultative conference between democratic elements in North and South leading to a confederation government for a unified Korea. The PRC also advocated the disbandment of UNCURK and replacement of the armistice arrangements by a peace treaty between the appropriate parties.

While war and peace hung in uneasy balance in Indochina until the final denouement in Saigon on April 30, 1975, China manifested a cautious ambivalence in dealing with Korea. Aid continued to flow from Beijing to Pyongyang, and a petroleum pipeline was constructed linking the oil fields of China with markets in North Korea. Routine Chinese statements praised Kim Il Sung and duly recognized the DPRK as the sole sovereign state on the Korean Peninsula. Above all, China strove to ensure that the Soviet Union would not get the upper hand in shaping the policies of the DPRK.

China hedged its bets on Korea by showing a certain amount of interest in the ROK. Beijing realized that normalization of relations with Tokyo and Washington would tend to reduce tensions with Seoul, despite Beijing's closeness to Pyongyang. When the ROK let it be known that it had no objection to communication with communist nonenemies, including the PRC, Beijing softened its condemnation of the ROK as a puppet of American imperialists and inaugurated mail and telegraph service between Beijing and Seoul. The PRC allowed Korean residents in the PRC to apply for exist visas to visit relatives in the ROK. Both the Chinese and the South Koreans appreciated the possible benefits of trade and of South Korean participation in China's development. It was rumored that ROK and PRC officials met in Hong Kong and Tokyo to discuss cooperation.

After 1975, the PRC subtly modified its policies regarding Korea to accord with the basic shift in its strategic thinking. To Kim Il Sung, the United States remained the *bête noire;* to Zhou Enlai, the USSR replaced the United States as enemy number one. Zhou felt that the wedding of the USSR and the DPRK had to be prevented at all costs and that a closer union of the PRC, Japan, and the United States was required to balance the growth of Soviet power.

By 1980 the PRC acted on the assumption that China needed the DPRK far more than the DPRK needed China. In the Chinese-Russian rivalry in Pyongyang, Russia held the trump card—its ability to supply Kim Il Sung with sophisticated weaponry and technological assistance. China was handicapped by its own determination not to allow complications in Pyongyang to upset its burgeoning détente with Japan and the United States. China's only consolation was an awareness that Russia, too, wanted no war on the Korean Peninsula and shrank away from further credits to the bankrupt Kim Il Sung. The feeling of security from war gave the Chinese a greater degree of freedom in their diplomatic maneuvering.

On the one hand, the Chinese embellished their record of pro-DPRK pronouncements. Premier Hua Guofeng's first trip outside of China was to North Korea. He told a huge rally in Pyongyang that the Chinese government and people denounced the U.S. government and its policy of aggression and division. The United States should withdraw all its aggressor troops and military equipment from the ROK and enter into direct negotiations for peace. The armistice arrangements should be ended, and the UNC disbanded. The quest for unification should be accomplished by the Korean people themselves, without outside interference and under the correct leadership of Kim Il Sung.

A strong Chinese statement appeared in the *Beijing Review* (May 18, 1981) shortly after the two-day security meeting in San Francisco between Secretary of Defense Caspar Weinberger and the South Korean Defense Minister Choo Young Bok. The article alleged that the "old hoax about the security of the South being threatened by a North Korean military buildup" was trotted out again as a pretext for boosting the South Korean "dictatorship's military might." Acknowledging that tension is escalating on the peninsula, the Chinese laid the blame on the governments of South Korea and the United States. The statement concluded that there is only one way to create favorable conditions for the peaceful solution of the Korean problem, and that is for the U.S. government to end its interference in Korean internal affairs, discontinue its policy of two Koreas, cut off its military aid to South Korea's dictatorial regime, and pull all its troops and military equipment out of the South.[9]

On the other hand, the Chinese revealed their ambivalence, and probably their true sentiments, in conversations with Americans and Japanese. They dismissed the idea that Kim was a cat ready to pounce on South Korea, confessing that their real cause for concern was the possibility that the South might invade the North. In MAC meetings, their delegate referred to the "U.S. side" rather than "the enemy side." Although the Chinese could not say so openly, they intimated that they were not overly upset by the status quo. Despite overt opposition to U.S. diplomatic initiatives to ease tensions on the Korean Peninsula, they were prepared to discuss two Koreas in the United Nations, an international conference on the Korean question, and cross-recognition. They definitely did not want the United States to withdraw its troops, and they advocated greater Japanese interest in the defense of Korea. The prime interest of the PRC was not the future of the ROK, but containment of the Soviet Union.

These facets of the USSR-PRC-U.S.-Japan quadrangle must be correctly assessed in formulating an effective U.S. policy toward the ROK. Washington must be concerned more with such problems as reconciliation of nuclear policy with the PRC, the disposition of the Taiwan question, and the progress of normalization than with Beijing propaganda-like statements about relations with the DPRK.

The China factor is one of the most elusive variables in the formation of effective U.S. policies toward the ROK. The rights and interests of Taiwan are practically overlooked as the United States tries to decide how far it can safely discount routine PRC statements of allegiance to the DPRK and to what extent it can rely on China's opposition to Soviet hegemonism to keep the PRC in line with U.S. objectives in Korea. Without tilting too far toward the PRC, the United States is inclined to add the PRC cautiously to the list of powers genuinely desiring peace and stability in Northeast Asia. The options must be kept open, however, as long as the future role of the PRC in the rapidly changing strategic environment of East Asia is so unpredictable.

5 | NONMILITARY ISSUES SINCE 1969

During the Carter administration, the customary goodwill in U.S.-ROK relations was endangered by increasing differences in such nonmilitary matters as aid, trade, and investment, South Korean efforts to exert extraordinary political influence in the United States, and American insistence on making human rights a prime determinant of foreign policy. The hard feelings engendered by disputes in these areas clouded the atmosphere in which both nations addressed the more vital issue of mutual security.

Aid, Trade, and Investment

Grants and loans, supplemented by investments and steadily growing trade, may have been less spectacular than military commitments in contributing to mutual security, but they were a vital ingredient in the maintenance of confidence and goodwill in relations between the United States and the ROK. The security commitments of the United States to the ROK provided the framework within which South Korea was able to survive and to flourish. Without an atmosphere of confidence, South Koreans would scarcely have been motivated to work so hard for their own future. Moreover, foreign investments would not have been forthcoming had it not been for the presence of American soldiers along the DMZ. The American security umbrella by itself, however, was not sufficient to guarantee a safe, prosperous ROK. South Korea needed security and economic support for political stability, economic resilience, and international stature.

American economic assistance, administered by the AID and its predecessors, was so closely linked to security assistance that at times the two were indistinguishable. In the two decades following the Korean War, the United States extended to the ROK $12.5 billion in economic and military aid. At one time the AID mission in Seoul was the largest in the world, employing 550 American advisers and technicians and helping over 4,000 South Koreans receive the advanced training that enabled them to become responsible leaders in their country's major institutions.

In the early 1950s American assistance programs contributed to national recovery by providing food and raw materials. Additionally, the United States provided commodities and development loans for power plants, railways, highways, and other elements of the economic infrastructure.

The path of cooperation was not always smooth. President Rhee was interested more in political reunification and prestige than in long-term economic development. Despite differences of opinion with Americans, he depended on their support. Some Americans, in exasperation or distaste, argued that the United States was pouring millions down a rat hole. South Koreans, on the other hand, insisted that Americans were insensitive to the difficulties of the ROK and impatient to achieve American-style results in an environment that they simply did not understand. Americans accused the Koreans of being corrupt, ineffective, and unappreciative, while Koreans often felt that Americans were doing too little to ameliorate the wretched conditions for which they were partly responsible.

Under President Park, these antagonisms gradually disappeared. Americans and Koreans gained mutual confidence and respect as they sensed progress and ultimate success of the Mutual Assistance Program. In the first two five-year plans (1962–1966 and 1967–1971) Americans cooperated closely through every stage of planning and implementation. Americans could reasonably claim a share of the credit for guiding the ROK from poverty and chaos toward stability and self-reliance.

Despite recurring disagreements, both sides benefited from the extensive American assistance programs. For the South Koreans, American aid made possible growth of the GNP and an immense improvement in the quality of life. The benefits were not limited to Seoul or to the upper levels of society; they extended to the poor as well as to the rich and from one end of the country to the other.

Assistance to the ROK was also beneficial to the United States. As the preamble to the Food for Peace Statute (1955) stated, the purpose of the act was to expand international trade, to develop and expand export markets for U.S. agricultural commodities, to combat hunger and malnutrition in developing countries, and to promote in other ways the foreign policy of the United States. In shipping food and other commodities to the ROK, the U.S. government provided markets and supported prices for American producers. In helping others, the United States was helping itself.

Furthermore, in making the ROK stronger, the United States was serving its own best interests. A stable and prosperous ROK meant security for all of Northeast Asia. A strong ROK, together with a strong Japan, was a solid buffer against communist states with interests in Northeast Asia. In enabling the ROK to defend itself, the United States was saving the American taxpayer the cost of defending the ROK.

As the ROK prospered, the need for American grants-in-aid became less critical. Repayable loans were substituted for outright gifts. In the 1960s, the normalization treaty with Japan gave the ROK access to Japanese markets and sources of commercial credit, ending the ROK's dependence on the United States. The $1 billion in payments to the government of the ROK for its help in the Vietnam War also substantially reduced the continuing need for further aid. Ordinary trade became the dominant economic link between the United States and the ROK. The donor-recipient–patron-client relationship gave way to a trading partnership between equals.

The new relationship, although beneficial, also gave rise to knotty economic issues. Just as the ROK was setting forth on an independent economic course, it encountered extraordinary difficulties. The Third Five-Year Plan (1972–1976), conceived and executed by the Koreans without American advice, relied largely on the development of export industries to bring balanced prosperity to city and countryside. Precisely at this juncture, the Americans dealt the Koreans several cruel economic blows. The withdrawal of the 7th Division cut deeply into their revenues; President Nixon's decoupling of gold and the dollar weakened the *won* (which was tied to the dollar); and his imposition of a 10 percent surtax on imports hurt the ROK, as well as all other exporters in East Asia. The oil crisis climaxed the Koreans' difficulty.

Despite these problems, a healthy trade grew up between the United States and the ROK. By 1980 it approached $10 billion. In overall trade volume, the United States exceeded Japan for the first time. Japan ranked first in exports to Korea, but the United States led in imports. As of 1980, the ROK was twelfth among U.S. customers and expected to become seventh or eighth within two years, ahead of France and Italy. Some 1,500 American firms conducted business in the ROK, employing thousands of Americans who were building up strong personal and institutional ties with the ROK.

More than 125 American enterprises, a veritable Who's Who of American capitalism (including American Airlines, Bank of America, Douglas Aircraft, Exxon, Gulf Oil, Union Oil, Foremost, General Motors, 3-M,

Dow Chemical, Union Carbide, and Hyatt Hotels), had invested some $250 million in the ROK by 1980. American lending institutions had made some $6 billion available to the government of the ROK. Americans accounted for 28 percent of all foreign loans, 21 percent of foreign investments, and 25 percent of industrial licensing arrangements. Practically all American companies made good profits in the ROK, handicaps and complaints notwithstanding.

The ROK developed into a major market for such American agricultural products as rice, wheat, corn, and soybeans and for high-technology machinery. Other U.S. trade items included cotton, tobacco, hides and skins, logs and lumber, and increasing quantities of coal, rubber, chemicals, aircraft, and communications equipment. The market outlook was good for such American products as equipment for nuclear, thermal, and hydroelectric power plants, computers, heavy machinery and machine tools, metalworking and -finishing machinery, construction and mining equipment, and textile and clothing production facilities. (The U.S. Commerce Department does not include sales of arms and weapons systems in trade totals.)

To the United States, the ROK sold textiles, footwear, plywood, televisions, auto tires, bicycle tires and tubes, specialty steels, and electronic products. Although the ROK-U.S. trade balance was negative against the ROK, the difference was more than made up by U.S. government expenditures in the ROK, tourism, and capital investment. Loans from private banking consortia or such international lending institutions as the World Bank, the International Monetary Fund, or the Asia Development Bank—to which Americans were substantial contributors—usually met the ROK's shortfalls in international finance.

The generous terms of U.S. Export-Import Bank loans were absolutely essential for promoting American trade. Without financial assistance from the U.S. government, American traders could not have overcome the international competition. As worldwide exports from the ROK zoomed, economic issues sharpened not only between the ROK and the United States but between the ROK and all of its trading partners.

As the ROK's difficulties in maintaining the pace of export expansion mounted, it subsidized heavily industries unable to meet foreign competition. Korean trademarks were unknown, quality control was suspect, and rising production costs priced Korean goods out of newly acquired markets. In answer to the ROK's export-support policies, the United States adopted severe protectionist measures, subjecting one-third of all South Korean exports to some sort of trade restrictions. The United States levied import surtaxes or called for quotas, normal marketing arrangements, and voluntary export controls on a long list of products including footwear, textiles, televisions, purses, leather goods, and specialty steels. It was alleged, for example, that imports of Korean footwear caused the closure of half of America's shoe factories and the unemployment of 30 percent of that industry's workers.

The United States also called on the ROK to diversify its export markets by lessening its concentration on the United States, to reduce its high level of export subsidies, to restructure its domestic economy to de-emphasize exports, and to liberalize entry of American goods into Korean import markets. In contrast to the openness of the American market, the Korean market remained difficult for Americans to penetrate in spite of recent liberalizing regulations. American businessmen in the ROK complained of red tape and such irregular trade practices as bribes, payoffs, kickbacks, unpredictable tax and customs levies, and institutionalized corruption. Too often those who tried to resist such irregularities found themselves victims of harassment or discrimination (usually in the form of favored treatment of Japanese competitors).

American officials explained at great length that protective actions against the Koreans were temporary and transitory measures taken to stabilize home markets and maintain equilibrium in balance of payments in the face of sudden and drastic surges of exports in sensitive categories. The American ambassador warned Koreans that their government, like other successful governments in East Asia, would have to adjust its own economic policies if it wished to keep U.S. doors open to Korean imports.

Koreans and Americans treat economic issues with different degrees of seriousness. Issues peripheral to Americans are vital to Koreans. Koreans think that if Americans are genuinely committed to the survival of the ROK, they must, in their own self-interest, be prepared to make concessions. Economic livelihood is the foundation stone of national security for the ROK.

Both nations agree that they will gain globally from economic collaboration. They see that they must work together to overcome imbalances in trade and current accounts, rising oil costs, and assistance to less developed Third World nations. The ROK government has proposed combining Korean labor with American capital and know-how to support overseas projects that would expand markets and sources of raw materials for both countries. Koreans and Americans are needed to solve such worldwide problems as nuclear proliferation, environmental pollution, and access to scarce resources.

Both nations have demonstrated that they are deeply conscious of the linkage between economic understanding and mutual security. Koreans are aware that Americans feel that since the ROK has become a well-developed, modernized, industrial nation, it should bear a larger share of the costs of mutual defense. Both sides realize that as long as the United States and the ROK are commercial competitors, arguments are inevitable. But both are sufficiently sensible to recognize that it would be the height of folly to let their disagreements blind them to their interdependence in security matters.

Korean Efforts to Influence U.S. Politics

While embroiled in discussions over economics and the withdrawal issue during the Carter administration, relations between the United States and Korea were further strained by Koreagate and human rights issues. The Tongsun Park affair, which rated American headlines for three years (1976–1978), was part of a long-standing Korean campaign to soften criticism of Park and to engender stronger support for his government.

In the early days of the Park administration, Americans were so skeptical of the president that they bugged the Blue House, the Ministry of Defense, and other important government offices in Seoul. After a brief time, the practice was stopped because the gains did not warrant the risks. The American government became well informed through other means about irregular Korean political and economic practices vis-à-vis Americans, but chose not to protest openly because of the overriding concern with security.

In 1967, when President Park stood for popular election for the first time, his supporters approached American companies in the ROK for substantial campaign contributions. The process was repeated during his second campaign in 1971. Votes bought with American money may have contributed to Park's slim victory over Kim Dae Jung in 1971.

In 1971 the South Koreans were genuinely worried about the fragility of their security and the prospect of dwindling American support. At the moment, the fear was that the United States would abandon Asia. The wtihdrawal of the 7th Division only heightened this concern. On the eve of proclaiming the *Yushin* Constitution, President Park was alarmed at the apparent American indifference to mounting threats from the North and feared that Congress might refuse to approve the Nixon administration's promise of military aid to compensate for the troop withdrawal. He saw a need for a campaign to convince Americans that his authoritarian regime was justified for reasons of national security and economic development and that a strong ROK was as essential for Americans as for Koreans. Other nations, notably the ROC and Israel, conducted highly successful lobbies; why not South Korea?

President Park personally commanded the effort to influence the American administration, Congress, opinion molders, and Koreans living in the

United States. The objective was normal, but the means chosen to achieve it were questionable and often illegal. The plan was to seduce, and if possible to buy off, American leaders, especially members of Congress; to apply covert pressures on businessmen; to organize pro-ROK business groups and professional associations and societies; to conduct symposia on U.S.-ROK relations; to publish pro-Park newspapers and broadcast pro-Park programs; to infiltrate Korean communities in the United States; and to intimidate critics of the Park regime, especially Koreans with relatives in the ROK.

Government agencies in Seoul, with supplements from commissions on sales of American commodities to the ROK (primarily rice), and individuals or companies suspected of being members of Reverend Moon's organization provided the necessary funds for this effort. Among the illegalities practiced were secret contributions to congressional campaign funds; use of unregistered agents for covert operations; and attempts to implant the ROK intelligence network in the White House, the Joint Chiefs of Staff, and various congressional offices.[1]

Appointed by President Park, the key figure in the operation in the United States was Tongsun Park, a free-spending South Korean millionaire-businessman headquartered in the Georgetown Club in Washington. His reputed associates included the KCIA station chief in Washington; the director of the quasi-official Research Institute on Korean Affairs in Silver Spring, Maryland; the head of the Moon Organization's Korean Culture and Freedom Foundation in New York; the well-known Suzi Park Thomson in Speaker Carl Albert's office, and a Korean member of the staff of Congressman Cornelius Gallagher. The congressional investigation of Koreagate revealed that between 1970 and 1975, South Koreans disbursed $750,000 in political payments and covert gifts to campaign funds on the theory that a few hundred dollars, and a few girls, can convert enemies to friends. The influence of the KCIA permeated the entire lobbying operation, which was born in excessive zeal and died in counterproductivity.

Under Park, the ROK intelligence apparatus concentrated its attention on members of Congress because they voted the funds for military and economic aid to the ROK. Parties for susceptible congressmen in Washington became the order of the day, with frequent favors and discreet offers of bribes. American officials were at least as guilty as Koreans in the whole nettling and damaging performance—as Senator Jacob Javits called it. Congressmen visiting the ROK were wined and dined, and some were honored with university degrees. The hope was, of course, that the VIP treatment would bring its rewards in favorable votes.

In the category of education, information, and cultural activities, the South Koreans engaged in the types of cultural activities common between friendly countries and which Americans openly conduct abroad. They made contacts, usually through the prestigious Korean Traders Association, with American University, University of California (Berkeley), Columbia, Harvard, University of Hawaii, University of Southern California, University of Washington, and Western Michigan University, negotiating financial support for Korean studies, exchange professorships, and scholarship programs involving Koreans. In every case, the institutions insisted on local control and complete academic freedom before accepting a grant. In terminating one sequence of negotiations, a Korean representative remarked that he did not intend to let Americans slap him in the face for helping them with his own hard-earned money.

The South Koreans also approached research institutes and individual scholars directly, offering to underwrite serious studies promoting Korean causes. The ROK government sponsored a succession of conferences and symposia on such topics as Korea and the Major Powers, Strategy and Security in Northeast Asia, Reunification of the Korea Peninsula, and Communist North Korea. Travel expenses were paid and the honoraria were generous.

A coterie of Korean, American, and Japanese scholars well known for views favorable to the ROK were usually among the invitees. Scholars usually were glad to take advantage of proffered opportunities to complete and publicize their work. Practically all the participants in these conferences enjoyed impeccable reputations and were immune to any accusation of doctoring conclusions to meet the whims of the sponsors, and their papers turned out to be valuable sources of research materials. The only criticism that could be leveled against the conference device was the needless secrecy about the source of funding.

The objective of the South Korean cultural program was to inform Americans about the political, economic, and cultural accomplishments of the ROK and the strategic importance of the ROK to the free world. All information about the ROK was government inspired and tightly controlled. The ROK's Ministry of Culture and Information and its Korean Overseas Information Service (KOIS) reflected its model, the United States Information Agency, and its successor, the United States International Communication Agency. Through the Korean Information Office in Washington and Korean consulates in major American cities, KOIS disseminated press releases, policy statements, trade and tourist promotion folders, pamphlets, brochures, and books portraying the ROK positively and sympathetically.

The ROK could not be faulted for its conception or its aims. The Koreans ran into trouble only when they crudely tried to distort the content of Voice of America broadcasts; to exert pressure on Korean-language newspapers and broadcasts in the United States; to harass or intimidate nongovernment publishers, editors, and reporters; and to choke off stories originating inside the ROK critical of the ROK or its governmental system.

It is clear that the dispute between Koreans and Americans over Koreagate centered about questions of impropriety and illegality. Koreans felt their actions were no different from those of other governments, whereas Americans insisted that the Koreans had drifted too far from accepted standards of conduct. Both sides worried lest spectacular news stories would damage the commitment to mutual security.

It was impossible to divorce the scandals—the Tongsun Park affair, the crude approaches to congressmen, businessmen, scholars, and media representatives—from ordinary laudable efforts to maintain good relations. The U.S. momentum was to find, convict, and punish the American legislators who had taken improper payments. It was this resolve that kept the pot boiling so high and so long. Seoul and Washington generally agreed that it would have been better if, at the first exposure of wrongdoing, the Koreans had admitted to overzealousness, let half a dozen people resign, and trusted that the whole matter would blow over.

The climax of bitterness came when Congress threatened to cut off aid to the ROK unless Ambassador Kim Dong Jo returned to the United States to testify. A Seoul newspaper declared that Washington would never have treated the representative of an European ally so disrespectfully and reflected that Washington did not really give a damn about Korean sensibilities. The paper alleged that Washington was using the recall of the ambassador as an excuse for interfering in the internal affairs of the ROK. The intense national pride of the South Koreans swelled to the surface and threatened to explode into an anti-American crusade.

The investigation of Koreagate had the wholesome effect of clearing the air. The victims of the exposure were removed from the scene, either by dismissal, resignation, or retirement. In most cases, the publicity was sufficient to end such blatant practices as out-and-out bribery, intimidation, and manipulation. In the future, the Koreans will likely limit their efforts to exert political influence in the United States to legitimate and sophisticated means.

The best result of the investigation was to give both the United States and the ROK a better perspective on the relative importance of each aspect of their complicated relationship: military, economic, political, and psychological. The ROK was seriously worried about the American alliance in the 1970s and could scarcely be blamed for seeking to take out a little insurance on Capitol Hill. For its part, the United States could not let Korean misdeeds damage the American national interest in the ROK, the stability of Northeast Asia, and its own security.

Human Rights in the ROK

Along with trade disputes and Koreagate, the issue of human rights ruffled many tempers in the ROK and the United States during the Carter administration. Many Koreans' perceptions of human rights differ from those of Americans, and Korean leaders do not consider that their domestic policies should be subject to consultation with other governments. Koreans have been social philosophers longer than Americans have, and Korean traditionalists view individual rights as inseparable from social obligations. After the manner of Confucius, they conceive liberty as part of some larger virtue—wisdom, harmony, propriety. They are likely to conceive freedom by itself as licentiousness—a release from socially important restraints.

With boundless assurance that life in the ROK is incomparably freer than life in the communist North, the government acknowledges that rule by decree or by martial law inhibits the exercise of political rights. It would like to grant as much freedom as Americans enjoy but the necessities of security and development preclude this. The survival and prosperity of the state takes precedence over the rights and welfare of the individual. Even the political opposition admits this priority; it merely argues that security is jeopardized more by a disaffected citizenry than by the threat of external attack.

Toward the end of the Park regime, the opposition expressed radically different views. Kim Young Sam, for example, said that without freedom there is no reason to fight the Communists; the free will of the people is the nation's strength. Liberal politicians, church leaders, journalists, and academics objected to what they considered an authoritarian government's use of the threat from the North as an excuse for repressing the masses and perpetuating its own power. They were practically unanimous in protesting the withdrawal of U.S. troops. As long as the Americans were present, they said, the United States could pressure the government to move toward democracy. Nothing seemed to protect the dissidents against the excesses of their own government more than the American presence.

For their part, the Americans were not too precise in their attitude on human rights. Although unanimously devoted to traditional ideals, usually as defined in the Bill of Rights, Americans differed widely on the proper role of human rights in foreign policy. Some argued that it was inconsistent with their heritage for Americans to be tongue-tied in the promotion of American ideals around the world. The vigorous championing of human rights should be a fundamental tenet of foreign policy. To them, the lesson of Vietnam was that defense depends not on arms, but on the will, loyalty, cohesion, and morale of a people. In their view, the lack of a politically viable system would doom the ROK. The methods associated with Rhee and Park (and by extension President Chun) were forged for subjects, not citizens; for privates and corporals, not for educated and sophisticated South Korean civilians. Only as the ROK moved away from authoritarianism toward democracy should American aid be forthcoming. Democratic progress should be a fundamental condition for continued military and economic assistance.

On the other hand, a large number of Americans, conceding nothing in their love of freedom, argued that U.S. relations with the ROK must be predicated primarily, if not exclusively, on the security commitment, without regard for the ROK government's conduct of internal affairs. Reliance on human rights as an instrument of foreign policy would bring the United States nothing but trouble. Human rights do not belong in foreign policy; harping on human rights was an indulgence in self-righteousness; it was unbecoming, futile, and immature. The lesson of Vietnam was that when a friendly government, no matter how imperfect, is overthrown by the Communists, it becomes the victim of a system that is infinitely worse.

In an independent study undertaken for the U.S. Senate, Senators Hubert Humphrey and John Glenn examined the human rights situation in South Korea. They explained that the American people have a humanitarian interest in encouraging freedom for all men; and the United States has a national interest in preventing political oppression in South Korea from causing a major domestic confrontation.[2] Internal conflict in the South and the ever-present threat from the North would place U.S. troops in a precarious position.

As early as 1963, President Kennedy told Park—without massive publicity—that failure to hold democratic elections would jeopardize U.S. aid to Korea. This threat was used to the full, and it worked. Elections were held, and for nearly a decade the ROK did enjoy an essentially democratic system.[3]

The democratic experiment ended in December 1971 when President Park declared a state of emergency; this was followed by the imposition of martial law in October 1972. This crackdown coincided with changes in U.S. policy (illustrated by the 1971 withdrawal of the 7th Division from Korea, the Shanghai communiqué, the return of Okinawa to Japan, and the slow withdrawal from Vietnam) and with the North Korean commando raid on the Blue House in Seoul and the revelation of the North Korean military buildup. President Park was convinced that he had to take stern measures to control the nation's economic development and to conosolidate his personal position against the challenge of Kim Dae Jung.

After 1971, few political freedoms—but most social and economic rights—survived. Groups adversely affected were opposition political parties, universities, churches, and the press. Many individuals suffered from the repressive measures, but there was little outward evidence of popular unrest that might lead to massive civil disturbances. The pattern after 1971 was for the government to react harshly to any attempt to subvert its power. When tension subsided, the government would relax its controls, but never enough to satisfy the dissidents. They, in turn, would reject the government's leniency and demand a return to democracy. Then the government would again tighten controls.

During one cycle of this chain reaction, the KCIA kidnapped Kim Dae Jung from a Tokyo hotel in August 1973. At the same time, the ROK government passed harsh emergency decrees. Prominent politicians, religious leaders, and students were imprisoned or disappeared. The best known were the two Kims: Kim Chi Ha, the poet, and Kim Dae Jung, the politician. Several persons linked to the illegal South Korean communist party were sentenced to death on charges that could have been trumped up.

Many Americans indicated their displeasure with these actions. Responding to the frustrations of Vietnam, the protest movement at home, and perhaps to letters from some of the 900 American missionaries in South Korea, Congress wrote into the Foreign Assistance Act of 1974 a provision directing the president to reduce or terminate military or economic assistance to any government engaged in a consistent pattern of gross violation of internationally recognized human rights. As amended in 1975, the act required the State Department to prepare reports on the status of human rights in countries receiving U.S. aid. Representative Donald Frazer of Minnesota voiced a widespread fear that the continued violations of human rights in the ROK could lead to a degree of instability endangering the lives of American troops stationed there.

The alternating periods of harshness and relaxation came to an abrupt halt in May 1975 following the ignominious American exit from Saigon. The wave of fear swept to the shores of South Korea. To counter a rise in student demonstrations, the government issued orders forbidding South Korean citizens, at home or abroad, to criticize the ROK government, even in private conversations with foreigners. For a time Korea University was shut down, and a new decree prohibited demonstrations against the government on any campus. At this juncture, the government issued Emergency Measure no. 9 prohibiting opposition to the *Yushin* Constitution, student assemblies for political purposes, removal from the country of Korean-owned property, and opposition to the decree itself. The decree permitted arrest, detention, search, and seizure without warrant.

The next scene in the evolving confrontation between Seoul and Washington took place in Washington. Philip C. Habib, assistant secretary of state for East Asia and Pacific affairs, testifying before the International Relations Committee of the House of Representatives, made it clear that the U.S. government was deeply concerned about human rights, but was neither involved nor associated with the South Korean government's internal actions. "Since our policies toward individual countries represent a mix of interests, objectives, and relationships," he said, "we know that neglect of human rights may well adversely affect the achievement of other important objectives."[4] He called attention to Henry Kissinger's statement to the Japan Society that it was unquestionable that popular will and social justice were, in the last analysis, the essential underpinning of resistance to subversion and external challenge.

Habib assured the congressmen that the Ford administration had a continuing concern in the development of functioning representative institutions within a framework of respect for human rights. Nevertheless, recognized the overriding importance to the stability of the peninsula of the security commitment, which served the interests of Korea, the region as a whole, and the United States. The preservation of peace on the peninsula remained the essential prerequisite for political development and the exercise of human rights in South Korea.

The next episode in the drama occurred at the Catholic cathedral in the Myongdong section of Seoul. On March 1, 1976, a dozen prominent South Korean opposition figures signed a "Declaration on Democracy and National Salvation" (otherwise known as the Myongdong Declaration), calling for repeal of Emergency Measure no. 9. Again, President Park reacted forcefully by arresting eleven of the twelve signers, including Kim Dae Jung and former President Yun Po Sun, as well as fifteen coconspirators. After a trial, all were found guilty and sentenced to jail.

During the 1976 presidential campaign in the United States, Ford stood for no change in the American position on human rights as summarized by Ambassador Habib. His Republican rival for the nomination, Ronald Reagan, chided Ford and Kissinger for inattention to moral issues in their conduct of foreign policy. Reagan would oppose the Communists not only on grounds of national interest, but also on grounds of their evil ideology. His idealism was targeted against the Communists, whereas the Democratic nominee, Jimmy Carter, took the stand that allies as well as enemies should honor the cause of human rights.

Carter found support from a number of congressmen, primarily Democrats, who, decrying the trend toward authoritarianism in the ROK, argued that the time had come to consider whether the relationship existing between the United States and the ROK was in the best interests of the United States. They called for raising the priority given human rights in U.S. foreign policy and insisted that the United States should not support a government that oppressed its own people. In their view, freedom was virtually dead in South Korea.

The issues of human rights and troop withdrawal were linked during the campaign. The Democrats pointed out that from the outset U.S. aid to the ROK was predicted on the existence and growth of democratic institutions, which, in the course of twenty years, had failed to materialize. At the same time, they argued that the current level of troops need no longer be maintained because of the growing strength of the ROK. In 1976, President Park himself had indicated that U.S. troops could be withdrawn by 1980. He said that if the USSR or the PRC did not become engaged in any Korean conflict, the ROK would not need U.S. ground, air, naval, or even logistical support. Therefore, it would be safe for the United States to withdraw its troops gradually and to reduce or eliminate its aid to the ROK unless the human rights situation improved.

After the inauguration, President Carter set up a Human Rights and Humanitarian Affairs Bureau in the State Department, which immediately began aggressively advocating human rights. President Park's reaction was negative, but he temporarily loosened the reins on the dissidents. He felt that he could be more lenient to his opponents since even they opposed the U.S. troop withdrawal. A position paper of the Korean National Council of Churches affirmed its belief that the plan to withdraw American troops would deal a death blow to its struggle for freedom, justice, and human rights.

The Carter emphasis on human rights as a cardinal tenet of diplomacy quickly sailed into troubled waters. The diplomatic and military bureaucracies opposed overemphasis on idealism in the ordinary conduct of international affairs. Japan disliked the Carter twists in U.S.-ROK relations and brought great pressure to bear to keep them in familiar grooves. President Carter, himself, backed away from his own pretensions. When carrying the responsibilities of security, he was unwilling to reduce or eliminate aid to the ROK as a device to make them adopt a more democratic line. The more he was weighed down by the Strategic Arms Limitation Treaty, the Egyptian-Israeli negotiations, the Iranian revolution and the American hostages, and the Soviet invasion of Afghanistan, the less he was able to campaign for human rights. He became neither idealist nor realist. He was criticized by some for talking too liberal and by others for acting like Henry Kissinger.

The Carter administration's annual reports to Congress on human rights in the ROK were of little value. Few in the State Department wished to criticize South Korea at the risk of glossing over the sorry state of human rights in North Korea, and no one wanted the odium that would inevitably result from public criticism of a valued ally. American officials in Seoul and Washington talked constantly, quietly, and forcefully to their South Korean counterparts disapproving the excesses of the ROK government, but they shied away from putting the substance of unofficial pressures on the official record. Their common concern was to make South Korea look as good as possible.

As a matter of record, the reports put the best possible face on the status of human rights in the ROK. Negative aspects were underplayed in the sense that unsubstantiated allegations were not used and unnecessarily high-handed language used by partisan critics was avoided. Favorable comments were underscored. The reviews stressed, repeatedly, that South Korea was exceptional among developing nations in its lack of class distinctions, rapid social mobility, use of the merit system to determine access to higher education, and efforts to reduce the disparity between rural and urban income. The ROK was praised for its rising standard of living and its improving quality of life.

Restrictions on personal liberty were admittedly excessive, but the reports excused them on security grounds. They explained that although many political prisoners remained in jail, many had been released. Brutal treatment of prisoners had been lessened. Only a tiny proportion of the population fell under the heavy hand of the law—few of them unjustly. Deviations from constitutional guarantees were temporary and justified by existing circumstances. President Choi had relaxed repression immediately after Park's death, but the situation had deteriorated under President Chun. The report released in February 1981 noted that at the end of 1980, many basic political freedoms and individual rights were in a state of suspension, but that improvement might be expected as the internal situation stabilized.

Liberals complained that the reports were misleading and laundered. It was impossible for Americans to ferret out the worst violations of human rights in the ROK. The worst abuses were hard to prove and, if not thoroughly documented from open sources, were omitted. Compilers of the reports often dismissed or ignored testimony of reputable witnesses. Some cases were simply too hot to handle. In liberal opinion, the reports were ineffective in pressuring South Korea toward reform and amounted to little more than thinly disguised whitewash. Thus, critics on the left and the right were inclined to agree that the reports, as they were presented during the Carter administration, were counterproductive and should be discontinued.

As long as President Carter remained in office, he proclaimed his faith in human rights policies and insisted that our deepest affinities were with nations committed to the democratic path of development. He directed his establishment to pursue his aims by every means available, including frank and private discussions with foreign leaders, repeated public affirmation of American ideals, and symbolic acts such as official visits. Carter himself visited the ROK, perhaps hoping to make a good Baptist out of an indifferent Buddhist. Some American missionaries in Korea, warning against raising Park's prestige, cautioned Carter that a visit would not sway Park in the slightest from his repressive ways.

In making human rights a basic aim in foreign policy, President Carter felt that he was reflecting America's best values and was contributing to a growing world awareness of them. He was unwilling to go as far as those members of Congress who, angered by President Chun's forceful assumption of power, asked Carter to suspend $450 million in pending Export-Import Bank loans to the ROK. Carter's answer was to back Secretary of State Cyrus Vance's statement that security overrides human rights. After the Reagan inauguration, Carter may have seen reports that Chun was glad Carter could no longer lecture him, but he was undoubtedly buoyed by the hope that his administration had helped create an atmosphere in which improvements in human rights were more likely to occur.

6 | THE SECURITY COMMITMENT

At no time since 1969 has either the United States or South Korea disavowed the interpretation of the Mutual Defense Treaty given by the U.S. Senate during the debate on ratification or advocated abandoning the treaty. Conflicts have concerned its implications rather than the meaning of its words. Many argue, both in the ROK and the United States, that the treaty implies a U.S. obligation to protect the ROK and to guarantee its survival. Strict constructionists insist that the treaty guarantees nothing. Some Americans feel that the treaty brings the American nation closer than it wants to go toward another land war on the Asian continent. In committing the United States to act in accordance with constitutional processes, it is difficult to escape the conclusion that the treaty commits the United States to no action beyond that which would be taken even if the treaty did not exist.

It is frequently assumed, however, that there is an extra-treaty commitment stemming from the U.S. dispatch of thousands of soldiers to fight, if necessary to die, for American national objectives in Korea. The entire American nation and its military establishment are committed to those objectives—the preservation of the country and its way of life—shared by Americans and South Koreans. It is only to achieve these common objectives that U.S. forces are stationed in Korea. Their proper number is the subject of constant review and debate.

After the departure of the 7th Division from Korea in 1971, U.S. forces consisted of the 2d Infantry Division, the 38th Air Defense Artillery Brigade, the 4th Missile Command, a full air wing split between the 8th Tactical Fighter Wing and the 51st Composite Tactical Wing, the 19th Support Brigade, and small engineer, transportation and signal units. In 1978, U.S. military forces in Korea numbered 40,800, including 32,600 army, 7,600 air force, and 600 navy and marine personnel. The army contingent consisted of 15,000 combat troops backed by 4,800 logistics personnel, 3,500 in communications, surveillance, and intelligence, and 9,300 identified simply as "other."[1]

One battalion of the 2d Division is stationed north of the Imjin River, close the the DMZ. The remainder of the division is deployed south, with division headquarters at Camp Casey, twenty miles to the rear of the ROK army's forward defense position, but still astride the main invasion route from the DMZ to Seoul. In the event of a North Korean attack, the advance battalion, and presumably the rest of the division, would be involved immediately. In effect, this strategic deployment, often referred to as the "trip wire" deterrent, guarantees the ROK the immediate automatic response to which the United States refused to commit itself by treaty.

As a backup to conventional forces, the United States maintains a stock of tactical nuclear weapons in South Korea. While details of deployment are closely guarded, it is public knowledge that 650 is a reasonable estimate of the number of nuclear warheads; that the weapons are included in both army and air force armaments; and that they are held well south of the DMZ to protect the storage sites and to ensure that in the event of hostilities, there would be time for a presidential decision regarding their employment. The 7th Fleet offshore has aircraft capable of delivering nuclear bombs to Korean battlefields.[2]

The U.S. troops are in Korea to help train and develop Korean counterpart forces; to augment Korean forces if actual warfare began; and to serve as a deterrent to military aggression by North Korea.[3] Under the system of command established by the 1950 U.N. Security Council resolution and the 1953 armistice agreement, the president of the United States, through the military chain of command, has directed operational control over the entire ROK military forces—with the exception of the Capital Guard. Until October 1979, the president's command was exercised through a four-star U.S. Army general who was at once commander in chief, UNC; commander U.S. Forces/Korea; and commanding general, U.S. 8th Army. At that date, a new command structure—the ROK/United States Combined Forces Command—was established, in anticipation of changes that might follow agreed modifications in the UNC force structure.

In addition to U.S. forces on actual duty in Korea, U.S. forces in the western Pacific, Asia, and the continental United States are available for reinforcement. Since contingency plans call for massive ground, sea, and air reinforcement in time of emergency, crisis, or war on the Korean Peninsula, periodic military exercises are conducted to test and perfect this capability.

In assisting with the defense of the ROK, U.S. forces provide many of the ingredients needed to make the forward defense concept viable. These include:

> Intelligence gathering and analysis to maximize the probability of early warning;
>
> Commanders experienced in high intensity, modern combat;
>
> A highly mobile reserve armor and anti-armor capacity to partially offset ROK ground firepower disadvantages and reinforce ROK defense lines;
>
> Air power capable of gaining air superiority and providing vital tactical air support;
>
> Experienced forward air controllers that can direct air strikes without communications problems;
>
> Effective communications and logistic operations; and,
>
> The ability to quickly call in reserve ground, naval, and air forces from outside South Korea should they be needed on any emergency basis.[4]

In the minds of many Korean and American officials, the military role of the U.S. forces is less important than the psychological, political, and diplomatic effects of their presence. As Secretary Schlesinger stated in 1974, U.S. forces in Korea symbolize America's continued interest in the overall stability of that part of the world during a period of some tension. Their primary purpose is political. In the Korean view, one soldier is worth twenty speeches, and the physical presence of American troops comforts and strengthens South Korea.

The U.S. military presence in South Korea is an anathema to North Korea. Kim Il Sung once characterized the occupation of South Korea by the U.S. imperialists and their policy of aggression as the root causes of his nation's misery, the main obstacles to reunification of our country, and constant sources of war in Korea. It was clearly his conviction that an attack on the South was far too dangerous as long as the Americans were alert and stationed just below the DMZ.

American representatives in East Asia have frequently underscored the psychological value of the physical presence of U.S. forces. In Seoul, Ambassador William Gleysteen (1977–1981) affirmed to the South Koreans his belief that a strong U.S. military presence was the most basic of the United States' East Asian policies. Basing his observations more on the effects of U.S. forces on other countries in the area than on Korea itself, he said that without such a presence the United States would undermine the confidence of its allies and long-standing friends; reverse the fundamental benefits associated with new policies, such as the developing relationship with the PRC; dangerously reduce the deterrence against aggression in certain critical areas, such as Korea; and risk the danger that key countries in the area would recalculate their options and alter their basic policies in ways highly adverse to regional and global stability.[5]

No specific level of forces was ever stipulated as a necessary ingredient of effective deterrence. It is apparent that a military presence, regardless of size, is perceived to be as important as the Mutual Defense Treaty itself in preserving the credibility of the U.S. security commitment.

Scarcely less vital and meaningful to the ROK has been the United States' Security Assistance Program. When the Nixon Doctrine shifted the main burden of defense to the Asians, the United States strengthened and implemented a Foreign Military Sales Program (FMS) to make the doctrine effective. On the departure of the 7th Division, the United States turned over to the ROK a certain number of Phantom fighters, tanks (including 50 M-60 main battle tanks), armored personnel carriers, heavy artillery pieces, and missiles—all financed under MAP. When President Park announced a five-year program (1971–1976) for modernization of his forces, the United States promised $1.25 billion in security assistance over that period and $250 million in excess defense articles, subject to congressional approval. The items to be made available to the ROK included aircraft, ships, vehicles, weapons, ammunition, missiles, communications equipment, rehabilitation and repair facilities, supplies, training installations, and other equipment.[6]

Although the importance of the Security Assistance Program was recognized on both sides, it was much buffeted by political fallout from Watergate during its early life. In addition, the United States was not always able to live up to its commitments due to critical turns in the fighting in Indochina. An increasing number of Americans also objected to security assistance to a nation as corrupt and repressive as the ROK. Moreover, the imposition of martial law in the ROK distressed congressional liberals.

The Ford-Kissinger team obviously believed that a reduction in U.S. military assistance to the ROK was senseless in terms of realpolitik. Nevertheless, the Foreign Assistance Act of 1974 obligated the president to reduce or terminate military or economic assistance to any government that consistently violated internationally recognized human rights. The president could make exceptions warranted by national interest, but he was obliged to send an annual report to Congress on certain specified countries, including Korea. A later act placed arms export control in the hands of the president acting through an interagency committee, but subjected such exports to a great extent to the scrutiny and approval of Congress.

Through 1975, President Park received some $3.7 billion in military assistance for his modernization program. But for Korea to achieve its goal of self-reliance by 1981, he would need much more from the United States to supplement domestic efforts. American assistance was essential for expansion of Korean industries. Park's goal was to produce everything needed by the ROK military except sophisticated electronic equipment, high-technology fighter aircraft, and, of course, nuclear weapons.

With the money raised primarily through an 18 percent domestic sales tax, the Korean president was free to purchase arms wherever he could find them—Japan, Germany, Brazil, France, Canada, the United Kingdom. The United States, however, was his best source of supply for aircraft, missiles, helicopters, and electronic and communications equipment. The Security Assistance Program was still the major source of funds for the $1.5 billion needed to make his newly adopted five-year (1976–1981) Forces Improvement Program a success.

The Record: from Nixon to Carter

Of the three aspects of the security commitment—the Mutual Defense Treaty, the stationing of ground forces in Korea, and the provision of security assistance—the issue of troop withdrawal generated the most controversy. In 1970, a lower military profile in East Asia seemed a good idea. Judging from the assumptions of the Nixon Doctrine, one can conclude that Americans did not expect a disastrous end to the Vietnam war. The Sino-Soviet split, especially after the Manchurian border clash in 1969, gave hope that Beijing, in its own interest, would pursue conciliatory policies with Japan and the United States and possibly consent to a peaceful solution of the Taiwan problem. In Northeast Asia, the outlook for peace brightened as a stable, prosperous South Korea redressed the power balance with the faltering North. Under the circumstances, a reduction in U.S. forces stationed in East Asia, including South Korea, appeared logical and acceptable.

Since the ROK was so dependent on the United States, the Nixon Doctrine had a traumatic effect in Seoul. President Park admitted that the doctrine of "Asia for Asians" was good theoretically, but charged that it was dangerous for South Korea because of the ever-present threat of invasion. Park believed that the United States should not withdraw its forces or its influence from Asia before completion of the ROK's arms modernization program. He was desperately afraid the United States would order its forces home as soon as the Korean units returned from Vietnam. After taking measures to make his constitutional position more impregnable, he took off for San Francisco to discuss the situation with President Nixon.

While praising Park for his courageous leadership of a brave people,

Nixon showed restraint in his statements on security. He avoided the Johnson formula of "rendering prompt and effective assistance to *repel* an armed attack against South Korea" and merely promised to observe the Mutual Security Treaty. Because of continuing acts of aggression on the part of the North, he said, both ROK forces and U.S. forces stationed in Korea must remain strong and alert. Nixon noted with approval the increasing contribution of Asian nations to their own security and their growing efforts to strengthen existing institutions for East Asian and Pacific regional cooperation. The Nixon meeting was short rations for a Korean president hungry for substantial sustenance.

Meanwhile a debate arose in the media and the Congress whether the United States should be an *Asian* or a *Pacific* power. Korea became a test of whether the postwar U.S. policy that had led to Vietnam was to be changed—Should the U.S. continue to be an Asian power, or should it withdraw from its military position on the Asian mainland to concentrate on becoming the strongest Pacific power? Despite Korea's problems of security, economic progress, and political stability, the United States proceeded with its plans to withdraw the 7th Division. Secretary of Defense Melvin Laird planned to orchestrate the U.S. withdrawal with the progress of the ROK's program for military modernization.

The prospect of American withdrawal heightened the concerns of South Korean officials who feared partial withdrawal might be a prelude to total withdrawal. For the first time, Americans noted rifts in the euphoric U.S.-ROK relationship. The highest circles in Korea charged that in pulling out its troops, the U.S. was reneging on solemn security commitments iterated and reiterated by U.S. authorities over the years.

Facing up to the inevitability of at least a partial withdrawal, President Park remained apart from the chorus of protests. Expressing confidence in the self-reliance of the South Koreans, he exhorted them to put forth greater efforts for their own defense. He told an American correspondent that 1975 would be the earliest date that the United States could safely withdraw. "We do not want the U.S. to stay here forever," he said, "but we need them."[7] By 1975 the ROK would be superior to the North in every respect. He warned, however, that if the United States pulled out before that time, many poor Koreans would switch their allegiance to the Communists.

Writing from Seoul on November 23, 1970, *New York Times* correspondent John B. Oakes observed that some ROK officials argued that a withdrawal would give Japan an excuse to assume greater responsibilities for the ROK's defense. This they vehemently opposed. In their view, the planned reduction was premature since the ROK as yet lacked the manpower, training, arms, and equipment to match the North. They were confident that the goal of resisting any conventional assault with their own resources would be attained within a very few years. Until then, they needed the psychological support of the American presence.[8]

Spiritually bolstered by his re-election in 1971, President Park notified President Nixon on the eve of the latter's visit to China that South Korea would not be bound by any decision of the big powers made without the participation of the ROK government. Nixon assured Park that he would not discuss Korean affairs with Mao Zedong and Zhou Enlai or make any commitment adverse to the ROK. At that time, South Korean officialdom appeared to accept the view expressed by Prime Minister Kim Jong Pil: "Now is no time to survive by depending on others—U.S. troops in our country will go home sooner or later, which means that we must defend our country through our own strength."[9]

The first phase of withdrawal of American troops from Korea, the departure of the 7th Division in 1971, was a far more traumatic experience for the South Koreans than for the Americans. Preoccupied as Americans were with the drama of Indochina, they paid little attention to the potential security crisis developing in South Korea. To fill the security gap caused by the departing Americans, President Park immediately implemented his controversial emergency decrees. He felt that these would minimize the dangers of subversion. At the same time he recalled the South Korean troops from Vietnam to assume defense responsibilities in South Korea that had previously been borne by Americans.

As an echo to the American rapprochement with China and the Soviet Union, President Park staged his own détente with Kim Il Sung. When Park's peaceful overtures produced nothing but verbal shadowboxing, he became unusually apprehensive about the future. In the summer of 1975 he received intelligence reports that North Korean troops were preparing for a surprise attack. He was convinced that Kim Il Sung's visits to China and Eastern Europe, though unsuccessful, were ominous indications of the North Korean's adventurism.

In a mood of near desperation, Park witnessed the departure of approximately one-third of the 60,000 American troops stationed in Korea. He shared the pain of the American experience in Indochina, but he must have wondered whether his country would be the next to suffer the fate of South Vietnam. His desire was not for "Yankee Go Home," but for "Yankee Please Stay." His heartfelt sentiment—shared by practically every official, every politician, every individual who remembered the suffering caused by the Communists during the war—was that the U.S. forces were friendly, welcome, and needed until such time as tension was eliminated from the Korean Peninsula or a satisfactory peace was devised by the powers. Before the summer of 1975, the only consolation offered to President

Park had been that the U.S. government had no plans to reduce the level of American forces in Korea further.

Resigned to the U.S. withdrawal, President Park strove to calm his own people and to use his influence to persuade the Americans not to act too hastily. On August 20, 1975, in an interview with Richard Halloran reported in the *New York Times*, Park said that in five years the ROK would no longer need American ground, air, or naval forces, or even logistical support, if North Korea, unsupported by either China or the Soviet Union, were to attack the South. "We want the capability to defend ourselves, and that will take four or five years. Until the modernization of our forces is completed, it is absolutely necessary to keep U.S. Forces here at the present level."[10] (Note that "five years" was also the anticipated time limit in 1970.) Park also suggested that if U.S. détente with the PRC and the USSR developed to the extent that the USSR-PRC alliance were abrogated, the ROK might reconsider the whole situation.

Nineteen seventy-five marked a great watershed in U.S. policy in East Asia. In the aftermath of the savage ending of the Vietnam affair, U.S. allies, including the ROK, raised new and probing questions about the will and the capability of the United States to guarantee their security. For their part, Americans worried lest the allies, losing confidence in American credibility, tilt toward neutralism or appeasement of the USSR. These concerns were reflected in Washington.

The president and Congress were convinced that it was time for a new look. The low military posture inherent in the Nixon Doctrine had led some allies and foes alike to believe that a reduction in U.S. military presence was tantamount to abandonment of the national interest. Perceptions of weakness, vacillation, and disinterest had to be corrected if the traditional defense structure of the United States in East Asia and the western Pacific were not to fall apart.

The Ford administration realized that reduction of American forces looked less attractive than it had five years earlier because of the deteriorating situation in Indochina. Nonetheless it proposed to reduce troops in Korea by another 15,500 men. The entire picture changed drastically with the final American evacuation of Saigon on April 30, 1975. On May 20 the House of Representatives rejected the administration's proposal. The new and critical task for the United States was to counter the growing sense of uneasiness about American power and intentions not only in the ROK but in the ROC and Japan as well.

The most spectacular move to bolster U.S. credibility was Secretary of Defense James Schlesinger's well-publicized visit to South Korea to deliver President Ford's firm pledge to aid in immediately repelling the North Koreans should they again invade the South. Schlesinger's ebullience replaced Nixon's restraint. On arrival he said, "I have come here to exemplify both the high regard of the American people for their Korean ally and the continuing commitment to a common cause. Our purpose is to avoid conflict by any possibility of miscalculation on the part of others."[11] His purpose was to build up the confidence of the South Korean political and business leaders, who sorely needed it; Schlesinger immediately struck the right note by repeating the U.S. assurance that it had no plans to reduce the level of its troops in Korea.

At a news conference in Seoul, the secretary of defense announced that the United States would provide more F-4 and F-5 fighters to beef up the ROK's defense capabilities; if Congress approved, the United States would quickly make up its 30 percent arrearage in contributions to the ROK arms modernization program and deliver weapons, supplies, and equipment worth $1.5 billion to enable the ROK to fulfill its 1975 target by the end of 1977.

When asked about the nuclear situation, the secretary remarked that it was well known that the U.S. had tactical nuclear weapons in Korea, but he did not anticipate that it would be necessary to use them in the event of a conventional attack from the North. He did not rule out the possibility that they would be used if required. Given the force posture in the ROK, the DPRK would be unwise to contemplate attack. He stopped short, however, of committing the United States to the longtime Korean desideratum of immediate, automatic action to repel an armed attack.

In reviewing the troops of the 2d Division, Secretary Schlesinger remarked that the United States alone served as the counterweight to the power represented in particular by the Soviet Union. "Without that military balance the U.S. would shrink back into the North American continent as a beleaguered country . . . Everywhere, the deployment of U.S. Forces influences the total balance, and this is inevitable because with the increase in transportation and the progress in communication, the entire world has become a single strategic theater." He told the troops: "You are part of that larger strategic theater, and I believe the country owes you a debt of gratitude."

On August 29, 1975, the *Korea Times* reported that Lieutenant General James F. Hollingsworth (I Corps, ROK/US Group) had briefed Schlesinger on the nine-day war plan. The general was quoted as saying that "if the North attacked, it would be a violent, short war because I have the number-one field army in the world, and my mission is simply to defend the ROK and its capital city, Seoul." He added: "I am going to destroy the enemy with artillery firepower, and 700–800 aircraft sorties a day—around the clock." In explaining this aggressive strategy, Hollingsworth said: "If the North attacks, we will go across the [Imjin] river and go after the heart of the enemy's military power." Schlesinger reportedly responded that Hollingsworth's forward plan was "a very nice idea."

Schlesinger's visit and its extensive coverage elicited approval and praise. Although a significant faction among the Republicans (including ex-Secretary of Defense Laird) clung to the philosophy of withdrawal as a means of easing tension, Schlesinger accomplished his objective of restoring Korean confidence in the integrity of America's security commitment. When Schlesinger departed from Korea, ROK Minister of Defense Suh Jyong Chul remarked, "We Koreans can now sleep with our legs outstretched."

Following Schlesinger, President Ford himself visited Seoul and assured the Koreans that the United States remained committed to peace and security on the Korean Peninsula, as the presence of U.S. forces attested. In a subsequent address at the East-West Center in Honolulu on December 7, 1975, he reaffirmed U.S. support for the ROK. He let it be known that the United States would honor its commitments, although "we are not happy over the domestic policies of the Park Government." In his opinion, the specific level of forces was not immutable because it depended on the threat from the North, the ability of the South to meet that threat, and the prevailing international situation. He said that the United States had "no present plans for significant force reductions in the area."[12]

Secretary of State Kissinger spelled out the fundamentals of the United States' Korean policy in addresses delivered in Seattle and Portland in midsummer, 1976. In a carefully prepared introduction, he laid down four basic propositions for U.S. foreign policy: (1) American strength is essential to world peace and the success of our diplomacy; (2) alliances with the great democracies of North America, Western Europe, and Asia are the bedrock and the top priority of our foreign policy; (3) in a nuclear age, it is a moral as well as a political obligation to strive for peace; (4) security and peace are foundations for addressing the positive aspirations of people— prosperity, human rights, protection of environment, economic development, scientific and technical advance, and cultural exchange.

He implied that while bringing our commitments into balance with our policy, we have achieved much, but there were no grounds for complacency. He called attention to the growing Soviet activity in Asia and the continuing bitter confrontation between North and South Korea. In linking global and Asian security, he argued that the repercussions of a change in the Asian balance of power would be worldwide. Neither in Asia nor in Europe, he said, can we permit others to dictate our destiny or the destiny of others whose independence is of concern to us. As imperatives, he insisted that security policy in Asia must address global concerns, the linchpin of the U.S. security effort in Asia must be a strong and balanced military posture in the Pacific, and the United States must be perceived as able and willing to help its friends.

Turning specifically to Korea, he recalled that Americans fought and died to preserve South Korea's independence.

> Our experience and our sacrifice defined our stake in the preservation of this hard-won stability; treaty obligations of mutual defense define our legal obligations, [and] our support and assistance will be available where it has been promised . . . In fulfilling our commitments we will look to South Korea to assume the primary responsibility for its own defense, especially in manpower. And, we will continue to remind the South Korean Government that responsiveness to the popular will and social justice are essential if subversion and external challenge are to be resisted. But, we shall not forget that our alliance with South Korea is designed to meet an external threat which affects our own security, and that of Japan as well.[13]

Kissinger also outlined the objectives of the North. The DPRK wished to alter the institutional arrangements of the armistice agreement by disbanding the UNC. If the command were dissolved, the armistice agreement (signed only by the United States, the DPRK, and the PRC) would cease to exist. After the unilateral withdrawal of U.S. forces, the United States and North Korea would discuss peace and security—alone.

In response, the secretary declared that the United States would not accept these proposals, but was willing to negotiate a new armistice or replace the armistice with a more permanent arrangement in any form acceptable to all parties. But it would not negotiate behind the backs of its South Korean allies or agree to terminate the UNC without establishing a new arrangement to preserve the integrity of the armistice agreement. It would not undermine stability and hopes for negotiation by unilateral withdrawal. It would urge resumption of serious negotiations between the North and South. If North Korea's allies were prepared to improve relations with South Korea, the United States was prepared to take similar steps toward North Korea. It would like to see full membership in the United Nations for both Koreas without prejudice to eventual reunification.

On other occasions before the end of the Ford administration, Secretary Kissinger called for a preliminary conference of the main participants in the war—South Korea, North Korea, China, and the United States—to discuss ways of preserving the armistice and reducing tensions and to explore the possibilities of a larger conference on Korea to which others, including the USSR and Japan, would be invited. He also warned that the United States would react firmly should the forces of North Korea attack the five islands in the Yellow Sea off the Han estuary (considered the territory of the ROK) and that the United States would support the ROK if the North made any aggressive moves during the upcoming U.S. presidential election. These warnings were reinforced by impressive military displays occasioned by the ax-murders of the American officers in the DMZ.

Despite Koreagate and the repressive aspects of the Park Chung Hee regime, the security relationship between the United States and the ROK was mutually acceptable. The ROK was comfortably enroute to self-reliance and assured of financial support to bolster its own defense efforts. Although some American pressure to limit the amount of military assistance to the ROK existed, American military presence was regarded in principle as essential for maintaining political stability and a military balance in Northeast Asia.

Security Commitment and President Carter

The dilemma that plagued the Nixon-Ford administration—to pursue the low profile of the Nixon Doctrine or to take more forceful measures to bolster American credibility as seemed advisable after the fall of Saigon—disappeared with the election of Jimmy Carter. The new president brought to Washington his own ideas on gearing the U.S. security commitment to the ROK into the general goal of world peace. He had no doubts about the need to remain a strong Asian and Pacific power or about honoring American treaty obligations. He was positive regarding U.S. defense policy and the ground forces in South Korea.

As early as January 1975, while an aspiring candidate for the presidency, Jimmy Carter had revealed his conviction that the United States should withdraw all its forces, both ground and air, from Korea and negotiate assurances from China and the Soviet Union that North Korea would not invade the South. He was quickly persuaded that "restraints on North Korea" were nonnegotiable subjects with either the PRC or the USSR. Basically inclined to question the stationing of American troops overseas, Carter declared that he had yet to see a convincing argument for keeping American troops in Korea in perpetuity. In his opinion, Korea was much less important to the United States than were Europe and the Middle East. He had more faith in air and sea power operating from offshore than in land forces tied down in static and vulnerable positions. As for Korea, he believed that the trip-wire location of the 2d Division was an unacceptable risk that could involve the United States in another land war in Asia and tear the country apart.[14]

Once in the White House, he announced his attention of withdrawing all U.S. ground combat troops from the ROK within four to five years. He ordered his advisers not to question this decision but to make recommendations for its implementation. From the outset, many of the bureaucrats and military personnel long involved with Korea opposed the president's action as hasty, ill considered, and positively dangerous. Whatever their views, they were in a position where they were obliged to support Carter loyally or resign.

The Carter plan called for a three-stage troop withdrawal. The first stage would end in 1978 with the transfer of 6,000 men (one brigade). During this phase, a dozen F-4 aircraft would be added to the U.S. tactical fighter wing, and a new combined U.S.-ROK command would be established. The second stage would involve removal of support troops. Timing of the third stage would depend on political developments, but the headquarters and the last two combat brigades of the 2d Division would remain in Korea until at least July 1982. After that date, U.S. forces in Korea would total 12,000 men and consist of an air division; a small naval group; and army intelligence, logistics, and communications personnel. Most would be stationed south of Seoul, but could be involved in fighting in the first days of a war. [15]

President Carter took the position that the burden of proof rested on those who wished the troops to remain in Korea indefinitely. Discounting the risk of upsetting the military balance on the Korean Peninsula in favor of the North, he made his plan public on March 9, 1977. American troops were no longer needed, he argued, because of the ROK's economic strength and self-confidence. The improvement in U.S. relations with the USSR and the PRC made withdrawal possible. Carter re-emphasized the U.S. commitment to South Korea and pledged extensive military aid to compensate for the weakening of the ROK's defense structure.

As expected, the initial South Korean reaction was anger and dismay. The Japanese and other friendly Asian governments feared a reduction and possible abandonment of the basic American commitment to Asia. In Korea, the withdrawal was tacitly viewed as the American way of expressing displeasure over Koreagate and the alleged abuse of human rights.

Convinced that they had to make the best of an unwelcome situation, the Koreans set to work with Americans to formulate conditions for the withdrawal that would preserve the military balance and not endanger South Korean security. These conditions were worked out between Secretary of Defense Harold Brown and his Korean counterpart, Suh Jyong Chul, in July 1977 at the Tenth Annual Security Consultative Meeting. They agreed that the threat from the North was serious, that U.S. military support was important, and that it was essential to maintain the defense capability of the ROK at a state of readiness to deter a renewal of hostilities. Brown repeated President Carter's affirmation that the planned withdrawal signified no change in the U.S. commitment to the security of the

ROK, that the U.S.-ROK Mutual Defense Treaty of 1954 remained in full force, and that the U.S. determination to provide prompt and effective support to assist the ROK to defend itself against armed attack *in accordance with the treaty* remained firm and undiminished.

Secretary Brown explained that the United States had concluded that a carefully phased withdrawal of ground combat forces over a four to five year period would not affect the military balance on the peninsula provided it was accompanied by measures to strengthen and modernize ROK forces. He took the position that compensatory measures would be implemented in advance of—or parallel with—the withdrawals. The U.S. air, naval, intelligence, logistic, and support units remaining in the ROK, in combination with other U.S. land, sea, and air units in the area, would be a clear demonstration of U.S. determination to preserve peace and stability in the region.

Subject to congressional approval, Secretary Brown promised to transfer certain equipment to the ROK at no cost; supply substantial FMS credits; continue support for the ROK's Forces Improvement Program; transfer certain military items to the ROK on a priority basis; support the ROK's self-sufficiency efforts in arms manufacture by making advanced technology available; conduct joint military exercises; and set up a combined U.S.-ROK forces command to improve operational efficiency and symbolize a joint commitment to the maintenance of peace and security on the Korean Peninsula. He declared, however, that the UNC would continue to function as the peacekeeping machinery in the absence of a viable alternative for enforcing the armistice agreement.

The two defense officials agreed that these measures should make it clear to North Korea that no armed attack could succeed and that cooperation to reduce tension was the only possible approach to the Korean question. Finally, they noted the significant policy initiatives undertaken by the ROK and the United States to reduce tension and to consolidate peace on the Korean Peninsula, including the ROK's proposal for a nonaggression agreement between the North and South. They therefore urged the North Koreans to·demonstrate their readiness to resolve the Korean question peacefully by resuming the North-South dialogue suspended in 1973. The U.S. delegation reiterated the standing U.S. proposal for a four-power conference on Korea and reaffirmed that the United States would not negotiate immediately with North Korea on the future of Korea.

Spelling out these understandings may have seemed superfluous, but the procedure served a double purpose. It was another assurance, in the long list of American assurances, given to the public, President Park, and the South Korean government. More important, in specifying the obligations undertaken by the United States to strengthen the defense of the

ROK, it showed that the troop withdrawal was to be evaluated not as a hasty, isolated event, but as one segment of a carefully calculated change in the United States' global defense policy.

High-ranking officials of the Departments of State and Defense participated in the effort to sell the new policy—phased withdrawal of ground troops for deployment elsewhere, plus compensation in weapons and equipment to the ROK—to opposition elements in the military, the U.S. Congress, and the American public. Starting with the premise that a U.S. military presence was essential because of its substantial firepower, its importance as a deterrent, and its restraining influence in the Korean Peninsula, the Carter administration contemplated no *precipitous* change in the existing balance of forces. Ambassador Richard Sneider (1974–1977) argued that the redeployment of U.S. forces represented a better use of manpower and resources against the mounting Soviet threat elsewhere (in the Middle East, Western Europe, and the Persian Gulf area) as the danger of combat on the mainland receded. He added that deterrence on the Korean Peninsula arose not from the presence of the ground troops, but from the threat of the forward strategy and the ability to level Pyongyang by air.

Congress received the Carter program skeptically. Some congressmen saw no reason to change a policy that had kept the peace in Northeast Asia at a reasonable cost for the last twenty years; others argued that it was counterproductive to continue a policy that a changing strategic environment had outmoded. The Senate refused to give blanket endorsement to the withdrawal plan and immediately passed a resolution that the president and Congress should continue to formulate U.S. policy toward Korea jointly.

The bill to implement the Carter program to transfer $800 million in weapons and equipment to the ROK (in addition to the $275 million in military assistance) aroused further debate. The argument was all the more bitter due to the prevailing American sentiment over Koreagate and the state of human rights in the ROK. Among the government witnesses were Secretary of Defense Harold Brown, Deputy Assistant Secretary of Defense Morton Abramowitz, and General John Vessey, commanding general of the U.S. forces in Korea. Distinguished members of the intelligence community and the military establishment, in addition to some well-known academicians, led the opposition.[16]

From the outset it was understood that any phaseout of U.S. ground forces in South Korea should be accomplished by agreement of the president *and* Congress; it should take place in stages and with proper regard for the interests of the ROK, Japan, and other nations in the area.

Administration spokesmen pointed out that permanent stationing of American troops had never been intended and that phased withdrawal had been an objective since 1970. In 1977, partial withdrawal seemed practical due to manifest strategic changes in Asia, primarily the seriousness of the Sino-Soviet split and the ongoing normalization of relations between the United States and the PRC. It was an article of faith that strengthened air and naval units in the western Pacific, continued adherence to the treaty commitments, maintenance of the strategic military balance in the area, and a continued U.S. nuclear umbrella provided the deterrence needed to prevent North Korean aggression.

In that light it was determined that by 1980 ROK ground forces would be capable of assuming the burden of defending Korea if backed by the United States and its forces in Japan and elsewhere in the western Pacific. The United States intended to proceed cautiously so as not to alarm friends or embolden adversaries. The entire policy would be re-examined continuously and its military aspects tested by annual Team Spirit exercises. Withdrawal and redeployment were not to be considered solutions, but components of an overall effort to reduce tension on the Korean Peninsula and to meet the mounting global threat of the Soviet Union to U.S. interests more effectively.

From the standpoint of American national defense, the strongest argument for the Carter program was its anticipated advantages. A phased withdrawal of the ground forces would decrease the likelihood of automatic American involvement if hostilities again broke out in Korea. The United States would have time to consider its options. It was no longer necessary for U.S. ground troops to serve a trip-wire function or to act as a bond for the American commitment when no bond was needed. Fifty thousand deaths and billions of dollars in assistance were ample guarantees of American integrity and seriousness of purpose.

The prime military consideration for the United States was whether stationing some 40,000 ground troops in Korea was the best possible use of its limited manpower and scarce resources in a possible confrontation with the Soviet Union. Troops tied down in the exposed land base of Korea lacked the necessary mobility to face the 51 Russian divisions on the Manchurian border, a Russian amphibious effort in Northern Japan, or Russian aggression in Western Europe or the Persian Gulf. President Carter's strategists reasoned that the excess troops committed to Korea should be redeployed to be more readily available for action where needed.

The Carter administration recognized that withdrawal would profoundly shock all South Koreans, whatever their political loyalties. They had come to take the American military presence for granted. Nonetheless, its attitude was that withdrawal would benefit the Koreans. Although pretending to be young, weak, and inexperienced, South Koreans were a strong people. With 600,000 well-trained and well-equipped troops—many with combat experience—and with the fastest growing economy in Asia, they could take complete charge of their military and economic develop-ment, without crippling dependence on the Americans. The realization that the Americans were at last leaving might prompt them to work harder to solve their internal problems and to try harder to reach an accommoda-tion with the North.

The changing strategic environment, however, seemed the strongest support of the Carter program. Admittedly, Japan was vitally concerned with peace in Northeast Asia and stability in the Korean Peninsula and was comfortably secure with Americans in command in Seoul. It was reluc-tant to see any change, but expressed its understanding of American con-cerns. Above all, Japan did not want war. The maintenance of American ground troops in Korea was less important to the Japanese than the main-tenance of overall American strength throughout the entire region. Al-though many Japanese publicists voiced doubts of American credibility and the American desire to shoulder defense burdens in distant Asia, the Japanese government agreed to the Carter initiative. The Japanese insisted on being consulted on every contemplated move, saying they would be satisfied as long as the combined overall defense capabilities of the United States, Japan, and the ROK did not diminish.

Recognizing that many thought American withdrawal might provide Kim Il Sung a propitious moment for attack, President Carter argued that the PRC and the USSR would restrain him. Administration spokesmen aired their view that neither communist power wanted war in Korea, locked up as they were in their own rivalry. They believed that a partial American withdrawal would not give Kim Il Sung the go-ahead.

Perhaps the strongest argument of all was the impetus withdrawal gave the long-range objective of a unified Korean nation. Presumably, phased withdrawal would promote a more serious effort by both Koreas toward reunification, the best possible hope for reduction of tension on the Korean Peninsula.

Opposition to the Carter program was professionally well grounded and emotionally highly charged. Many of the arguments about redeployment, about the best place to station the 2d Division, were beyond the compre-hension of the ordinary observer. Even staff officers disagreed over the best strategic policy for the United States to pursue. In Korea, the Ameri-can military were practically unanimous in wanting to keep the troops exactly where they were. Carter was blamed for acting precipitously and irresponsibly. If the American presence had been the cheapest and most certain deterrent for 25 years, why should the U.S. change its policy now?

It was poignantly argued that the Americans had thrown 25 years of blood, sweat, and tears away by merely announcing the Carter policy. The shock of being left alone was traumatic. Naval and airborne tactical nuclear weapons could never replace ground soldiers. Airplanes can fly away quickly, and one never sees ships offshore. "One soldier in Korea is worth a thousand speeches." Major General Jack Singlaub, chief of staff of United States Forces/Korea, testified that in his opinion, withdrawal would invite a North Korean invasion and thus lead to war.

Koreans felt that if a Soviet confrontation, or a Soviet-inspired confrontation brought about by a surrogate, took place, Korea would quickly become a scene of battle. As long as U.S. troops were on the ground and in the neighborhood of the DMZ, the defense of the strategic Northeast Asian sector, including both the ROK and Japan, was well taken care of. It was foolish to weaken an existing strongpoint for the sake of a hypothetical need.[17]

Some American critics of the Carter program expressed the apprehension that even a phased withdrawal might force Japan into nuclear as well as conventional rearmament or cause the Japanese to readjust their policies toward the USSR in a manner unfavorable to the United States. Others argued that the Chinese might take withdrawal as a signal of declining American interest and might possibly again lean toward the Russians. Still others insisted that, at the very least, an American exodus would reduce American leverage over the military situation on the Korean Peninsula; adversely affect the economic development of Korea; and sharply curtail U.S. political influence in Seoul. Whatever the merits of the various opinions on withdrawal, the Carter program was effectively halted by events in Korea and the sharpening U.S.-USSR global confrontation.

The Carter Policy in Operation

The turn of events after the inauguration of the Carter program tended to cast further doubt on its wisdom. South Korean resentment forced Americans to become defensive, almost apologetic, about withdrawal. Repeated assurances were deemed necessary to persuade the Koreans that the Americans really had no intention of abandoning the ROK or hightailing it out of Asia in a fit of neo-isolationism.

Secretary Brown took on the burden of correlating the United States' global policy with its Korean policy. He explained repeatedly that the global strategic balance—including Western Europe, the Middle East, and Asia—had to be the determining factor in the positioning of American forces. "Our concern," he argued, "is, and should be, to meet any attack from the enemy, whether that attack should occur in Asia, Africa, the Middle East, or anywhere else." Within those parameters, President Carter began his withdrawal program.

Despite widespread misgivings in Korea and the United States about the military balance on the Korean Peninsula, the first contingent departed within six months. The gap left by their departure was to be filled by transferring equipment for one Honest John surface-to-surface missile battalion, three tube-launched, optically tracked, wire-guided antitank companies; and one engineering battalion to the ROK.

At the same time, the United States decided to help develop the Korean defense industry and extend credit for more purchases of American aircraft and other hardware. The United States abandoned the idea of supplying the supersophisticated F-16's to the ROK on the grounds that these planes were unnecessary for its defense, and, if given, might prompt the Soviets to supply North Korea with the latest model MiGs. The United States did not want to give an excuse for an escalation in the arms race.

By April 1978 it was already deemed expedient to modify the original withdrawal program. The administration decided that 6,000 troops would be withdrawn by the end of 1979, not 1978. Two brigades of the 2d Division plus division headquarters would remain in place until after the final withdrawal, which now was scheduled for either 1981 or 1982—in any case, after the U.S. presidential election. The skepticism generally felt in many circles in the United States was expressed in a resolution of the House Armed Services Committee requiring the president to keep 26,000 troops in Korea until North and South signed a peace settlement ending the state of war.

Because of increasing worries about the local and global strategic picture, a squadron of F-4's from outside the Pacific theater joined the U.S. tactical air force stationed in Korea in the fall of 1978. North Korea had assumed a more menacing stance, Vietnam had become more aggressive in Southeast Asia, and the Soviets showed alarming military inclinations in the western Pacific and the Persian Gulf region. The United States was increasingly engrossed with normalizing diplomatic relations with the PRC and the unwelcome turn of events in Iran.

In a speech in Seoul on September 11, 1978, Ambassador William Gleysteen defined and defended the U.S. position. The United States had to measure its commitments to the ROK against demands elsewhere. It required a clear and impressive ability to move substantial forces rapidly to aid allies and friends everywhere. "Military stance is not the clue to national policy," he said. "Diplomatic and economic competence, backed by latent military power, are much more important."[18] He suggested that it might be better to remove some troops from Korea and station them elsewhere to meet a local crisis, whether in Korea, the Middle East, or Europe, or to make them a mobile military reserve. The United States was not withdrawing, it was redeploying. The remaining ground, air, and naval units in the ROK would become involved immediately in the event of a North Korean attack. Under war powers belonging to the administration, these units could operate for sixty days before congressional approval was needed. He might have added that Congress, at that time, appeared more action oriented than the president.

New factors surfacing in 1979 produced further profound modifications in the Carter program. New intelligence estimates claimed that North Korea was much more powerful than had been reported and the military imbalance between the ROK and the DPRK was much more serious than had been calculated. Furthermore, the Soviets had stepped up their activities in the western Pacific immeasurably and, on the eve of hostilities in Southeast Asia, had concluded an alliance with Vietnam. The revolution in Iran and the Soviet invasion of Afghanistan were climactic events.

These factors directly influenced the shifting direction of the Carter program. In June 1979, President Carter visited Seoul on a goodwill mission. The official North Korean newspaper called the visit a war-mongering trip aimed at permanent military occupation of South Korea and the continued division of the Korean Peninsula. Both Carter and Park Chung Hee wanted three-way talks—North Korea, South Korea, and the United States—to reduce tensions and explore paths to peace, but North Korea vetoed the proposal.

In July 1979, the U.S. government halted withdrawals from the ROK until there was a credible indication that a satisfactory North-South military balance had been restored and a reduction in tensions was under way. It was announced that only 3,670 troops had been withdrawn, further reductions of combat units would be held in abeyance, and the timing and pace of further reductions would be re-examined in 1981 (after the elections). There were those who stated that this was President Carter's way of acknowledging the defeat of his intended policy.

Events in Iran and Afghanistan temporarily diverted U.S. attention from East Asia, but the slaying of President Park in October 1979 and the military coup of General Chun the following December revived American interest in the ROK. On learning of Park's assassination, the United States issued a public warning that it would react strongly, in accordance with treaty obligations, to any external attempt to exploit uncertainties arising from the internal situation in the ROK. This put North Korea on notice that the United States would not stand aloof from any possible aggression by the North.

Toward the end of the Carter administration, the annual report of the secretary of defense to Congress and the supporting posture statement of the chairman of the Joint Chiefs of Staff summarized the security policy of the United States toward Korea. The United States was confident that the ROK could defend itself, given the U.S. defense commitement and the U.S. willingness to assist the Forces Improvement Program financially, to strengthen the ROK's indigenous defense industries, and to provide substantial but diminished funds to procure aircraft and other military hardware. The amount of cost-free transfers of equipment would depend on the rate of withdrawal of U.S. troops, while appropriations for security assist would be sufficient to allow the ROK to assume a greater share of its defense responsibilities.[19]

Pending reassessment of the military balance and the advisability of further withdrawals, the United States had added AWACS (Airborne Warning and Control Systems) aircraft and a squadron of F-4's to its Korean deployments and intended to add longer-range artillery, better helicopter gunships, and a squadron of close-support aircraft. In the meantime, the military spending of the ROK increased from 5.5 percent of GNP in 1979 to 6.0 percent in 1980. The ROK buildup of its defense industries was progressing, and the United States had provided $1.5 billion in credits for military purchases from 1976 to 1981.

These arrangements gave the Joint Chiefs of Staff confidence that the deterrent on the Korean Peninsula continued to look reasonably firm and the North Koreans would not have an easy time of it should they decide to attack the South. No change of military plans that raised doubts about the joint U.S.-ROK capability for deterrence and defense was acceptable.[20]

As the global threat of the USSR mounted in the 1980s, Secretary Brown continued to emphasize that U.S. policy toward the ROK, indeed toward any nation whether friend or ally, had to be formulated in terms of the total national interest. In reports to Congress, he consistently delineated the parameters of Asian and global defense, within which the security of Korea must be evaluated. Repeating his arguments for rapid deployment of forces that could meet the Soviet threat in places chosen by the United States, not the USSR, he stated that deterrence requires locally ready forces, U.S. forces present in a troubled area, and U.S. forces that could be moved quickly into any trouble spot. According to him, the United States did not have the capability to defeat all initial enemy moves, but it did need the personnel, mobility, and firepower to preclude adversaries from reaching vital points. He stated that there was no need to wait the firing of the first shot or the prior arrival of hostile forces; many of our forces could be moved on receipt of strategic warning.

In Brown's view, effective response to enemy action primarily involved (1) naval forces giving the U.S. tactical air superiority; (2) prepositioning of equipment to give the United States the equivalent of permanent bases; (3)

air and sea-lift capabilities; (4) access and transit rights; and (5) frequent exercises to perfect techniques. These were not steps toward war, he argued, but prudent means to prevent or moderate Soviet action.

In the Defense Department's annual status report for 1981, Secretary Brown stressed the importance of the western Pacific to U.S. defense planning:

> Furthermore, our continuing alliances with Japan, the Philippines, our ANZUS partners—Australia and New Zealand—and South Korea are essential if the increasing burdens of defense in the western Pacific and Indian Ocean are to be met.
>
> In addition to maintaining a strong military presence on the Korean Peninsula and close defense relations with the Republic of Korea, we continue to seek close ties with the ASEAN countries (Association of Southeast Asian Nations), all of whom have been growing economically. Their cohesion and unity help not only to counterbalance Vietnamese pressures, but also to discourage Soviet ambitions in the area. Finally, we have begun a new relationship with the People's Republic of China (PRC). [21]

Further elaborating on defense measures, the secretary added that the United States was upgrading the 7th Fleet with new Spruance-class destroyers, Perry-class guided missile frigates, Los Angeles-class nuclear attack submarines, and Tarawa-class amphibious assault ships. By the early 1980s, four of our six attack carriers in the Pacific would carry F-14 aircraft instead of the older F-4's; meanwhile, 72 of the air force's 192 F-4's were being replaced by F-15's.

As a final element in the security of Northeast Asia, the secretary called attention to the 46,000 U.S. military personnel stationed in Japan. In short, Brown concluded, the United States maintained a major presence in and around Asia and, should circumstances warrant, would not hesitate to expand it. The intent of these parting shots of the Carter administration was to convince the American public that however criticized policy of withdrawing forces from Korea had been, the administration had not neglected the nation's defense capability against the USSR.

7 | LOOKING TO THE FUTURE

As a fitting conclusion to this background study, it is appropriate to examine variable and potentially damaging factors in the Korean-American relationship and to direct attention to the constants, or the continuing conditions, on which agreement must be preserved. The policies of the United States and the ROK are dynamic, executed in an ever-changing strategic environment. They are like whirring gears in a fast-moving machine. Although they may appear to mesh perfectly at any given moment, it requires consistent effort and a high degree of statesmanship to keep them synchronized or to repair them quickly if they jam.

President Chun's View from Seoul

As President Chun surveys the situation in Seoul, his chief concerns are domestic politics, the welfare of his people, the North, diplomatic relations with the great powers, particularly the United States, and the prestige of the ROK in the international community.

Chun was inaugurated on March 3, 1981, for a regular seven-year term as president. His record indicates that he is not a moderate alternative to harsher authoritarian rule by other militarists. He is the one who arrested senior military officers, muzzled the press, extended martial law, imprisoned dissidents, excluded dangerous political rivals from the democratic process, conducted the purification movements, and gave the orders for the forceful suppression of the Kwangju riots.

While taking significant steps toward healing old wounds and seeking reconciliation with those he had punished, he made it clear, on assuming office, that he would not tolerate lawless or disorderly acts. He granted amnesty to 5,221 people and released 3,385 prisoners. Some 630 political dissidents, including clergymen, students, professors, writers, and opposition leaders, were set free. Of those involved in the Kwangju rioting, 176 were released. Former Chief of Staff Chung Seung Hwa, sentenced to seven years imprisonment for failing to prevent the murder of President Park, was pardoned. Chun's removal of the names of over a thousand Koreans living overseas from the government's blacklist allowed them to return home if they wished.

President Chun has asserted that he wants democracy to take root in South Korea in accordance with its own culture. He wants his people to enjoy freedom of political expression and freedom of enterprise. He will shape his policies, however, in accordance with Confucian ethics of harmony and social responsibility rather than in conformity with legalistic Anglo-Saxon concepts of individual rights. In the interest of instilling the spirit of service in public employees, he granted clemency to thousands reprimanded for wrongdoing. For the sake of institution building and preparing the way for orderly succession to power, he has paid unprecedented deference to former Presidents Yun Po Sun and Choi Kyuh Hah and to the leaders of rival political parties.

Chun Doo Hwan has shown as deep a sensitivity as any other Korean leader to the welfare of his people and the economic development of his nation. There is a danger that in looking after the prosperity of business he will overlook the interests of the consumer. But there is also evidence that he is continuing the beneficial social policies of his predecessor and relying on tested economic advisers to meet the recurring crises inevitable in a market economy. He has indicated no desire to replace civilian technocrats with ambitious but incapable military colleagues. The upward course of economic development seems no less promising under Chun than it might have been under Park. Like previous presidents, Chun looks primarily to the United States for sympathy and substantive help.

In the matter of relations with the North, President Chun has a keen appreciation of the ideal and the practical. He shares the deep emotional yearning for a unified Korea—one people, one nation, one state—but he is also aware that when peace failed, the fratricidal war cost four million casualties. Such a catastrophe must not happen again. He would like to relieve his people of the burdens of an arms race. He would like to muster out some of his soldiers for civilian jobs and commit his factories to the production of civilian goods. He would be more at ease if he and the North could agree to neither manufacture nuclear weapons nor permit them on

Korean soil. But he dares not take the risk. As life throbs in Seoul and the beautiful Korean countryside, the sentries tighten their watch on the DMZ. The threat of invasion is as ominous as ever.

On January 12, 1981, President Chun solemnly proposed an exchange of visits between the highest authorities of the North and South. He invited Kim Il Sung to visit Seoul without preconditions and free of any burden. President Chun implied that he was prepared at any time to visit North Korea if invited by President Kim under the same terms. Kim's only response was an official North Korean news release calling Chun's proposal nothing but a foolish burlesque designed to whitewash his dirty, nation-splitting nature and gain public favor prior to the election. It is obvious that in the near future the ROK cannot entertain any hope of easing its burden of national security through progress toward peaceful unification.

President Chun has every reason to believe that his nation benefits from the diplomatic status quo and the existing balance of power in Northeast Asia. Of course, he wants his allies, the United States and Japan, to be stronger and more committed to the survival and prosperity of the ROK. But he is satisfied with the American determination not to succumb to Soviet blandishments and takes a certain amount of comfort from the inhibiting effects of the Sino-Soviet split. Having no cause to fear the existence of Japanese ambition for greater influence in Asia, he supports American desires for a greater Japanese defense buildup.

Most of all, Chun accepts the American commitment to the defense of the ROK in accordance with the Mutual Defense Treaty as credible. He sees the Korean Peninsula as the locus of great power rivalries and, being under the gun of Kim Il Sung, is convinced that the *only* thing that guarantees deterrence is the combination of strong U.S. and ROK military forces. He is not disposed to put a time limit on the need for American combat troops in the ROK.

Although President Chun has demonstrated his own independence and his resentment of occasional American arrogance, he does not harbor a latent racist sentiment against Western imperialism. In Korea, anti-imperialism is not antiwhite, it is anti-Japanese. It is sometimes alleged that President Chun has given signs of anti-Americanism, but his opposition has been directed only against specific American policies or attitudes. He is painfully aware of the fate of Chiang Kai-shek in China, Nguyen Van Thieu in South Vietnam, and the Shah of Iran, and he cannot be blamed for taking whatever measures he deems necessary for self-protection. As the American power position declines and that of the ROK rises, the Koreans are less inclined to seek or heed American advice. American influence in Seoul is declining—some South Korean leaders even feel that they have America in Korea's pocket.

The more Americans badgered Koreans on human rights, the less they liked it. On a visit to the United States early in 1981, President Chun expressed his relief that President Reagan had dissipated the old attitudes of tension and distrust. Chun credited Reagan with restoring confidence as quickly as it had been destroyed in 1977. He testified eloquently to his faith in the U.S. commitment, saying that the bonds of friendship were as strong today as they had been thirty years ago. He reaffirmed that the U.S.-ROK relationship is sealed in blood and not something that could be built overnight; it is a long-standing friendship that grows healthier as the years pass.

President Chun has no intention of limiting his diplomacy to the United States and the major powers. He is aware of the value of enhancing his nation's prestige and seeking broader economic relations wherever he can promote them. He is particularly sensitive to the opinions of the leaders of the nonaligned states and the entire Third World.

His strategically oriented swing through Southeast Asia in July 1981 illustrated his concerns. His major purpose was perhaps to expand economic contacts and promote export of Korean goods. His political objectives were no less obvious. He sought, with undeniable success, to heighten awareness of the ROK in the ASEAN countries and to inspire a feeling of greater confidence in the South Korean nation and its new leader. He projected an image of himself as a man of peace in contrast to the bellicose Kim Il Sung. He tightened the linkage between the ROK and the ASEAN in supporting a common strategy of stopping Soviet expansionism and opposing the communist threat, which—in the words of joint communiques—extends from Vladivostok north of the Korean Peninsula to the Malacca Strait.

At a press conference in Singapore, Chun put on the record his well-known desire for close economic relations with Beijing. He expressed his view that China was a large enough market to absorb Korean products and that the ROK could supply China with capital goods useful in its modernization. In bringing up the matter of relations with China in the Southeast Asian environment, President Chun demonstrated convincingly that his diplomatic perspective is global, not limited to Tokyo or Washington. He seeks for the ROK a more important, completely independent role in every aspect of world affairs.

President Reagan's View from Washington

President Reagan is as optimistic as President Chun on the future of U.S.-ROK relations. Reagan's view from Washington is in direct contrast to President Carter's. Without any conditions or reservations, Reagan promises Chun full diplomatic, military, and economic cooperation.

In the course of the first visit of a head of state to Washington after the inauguration, President Reagan assured Chun, without hyperbole, that the United States would remain a reliable partner, would fulfill its treaty obligations, and would be a staunch ally, standing by its friendship. In the joint communiqué issued after the meeting, Reagan declared that the United States would maintain the strength of its forces in the Pacific area and had no plans to withdraw its ground combat forces from the Korean Peninsula. Thus ended the Carter policy of phased withdrawal.

Reagan also announced that he was beefing up the American air contingent in the ROK. Without specific reference to time or numbers, he agreed in principle to sell sophisticated F-16's to the South Korean air force. He vowed that the United States would sell the ROK appropriate weapons systems, defense materials, and the technology necessary for enhancing that nation's capability to deter aggression. He would keep annual military assistance around the $160 million level. He could not promise more because of the necessity for congressional approval, but he would lend a sympathetic ear to new requests. President Chun could scarcely have asked for better consideration.

The goal of Reagan's policy on Korean reunification is to make the ROK capable of defending itself against the North and to support its efforts to achieve step-by-step reunification by peaceful methods. It is in the American interest to decrease tension in the peninsula and to work to prevent the outbreak of hostilities. The United States is pledged to strengthen the joint U.S.-ROK capability to defend against the North but not to make the South sufficiently strong to invade the North. In the belief that the North's military might still dangerously exceed that of the South, consequently posing a constant threat of attack, the United States wants its friends in the South and its adversaries in the North to understand clearly that there will be no relaxation in the firmness of its military commitment. Reagan continues to honor the promise of the Ford and Carter administrations that the United States will not negotiate with North Korea without the presence of the South.

American intentions were reaffirmed in the joint communiqué issued at the end of the thirteenth annual ROK–United States Security Consultative Meeting in San Francisco, April 29–30, 1981. Defense Secretary Caspar Weinberger confirmed that the United States intends to remain a Pacific power and reiterated the firm commitment of the United States to render prompt and effective assistance to repel armed invasion against the Republic of Korea—which represents a common danger—in accordance with the

Mutual Defense Treaty of 1954. He also confirmed that the United States nuclear umbrella would continue to provide additional security to the ROK.

In the matter of economic cooperation, President Reagan is as yet content to limit his policy statements to a general reiteration of his faith in the free enterprise system. As long as he is president, it is certain that neither military nor economic assistance will be tied in any way to the democratic performance rating of the South Korean government. He wants to see continuing economic growth in Korea because of his conviction that security must rest on a strong economic foundation. For the time being, it seems safe to rely primarily on the vagaries of the free market to determine the course of the U.S.-ROK economic relationship.

It is in the controversial field of human rights that President Reagan has departed most radically from his predecessor. He let it be known from the outset that there would be no more jawboning, no more of what columnist Pat Buchanan called Carter's children's crusade for human rights. Believing that the United States is in greater danger from Stalinists than from authoritarian allies, Reagan abandoned the policy of criticism of allies and substituted tactics of private persuasion and public reward. The first fruits of the new policy were harvested in South Korea. The private persuasion was seen in President Chun's commutation of Kim Dae Jung's death sentence to life imprisonment, and the public reward was exhibited in Chun's state visit to Washington almost immediately after Reagan's inauguration. To paraphrase Secretary of State Alexander Haig's definition of the policy of the Reagan administration, the United States will give high priority to protecting human rights, but there will be no more report cards on human rights practices. If problems arise, the Reagan administration will speak to governments through diplomatic channels.

Future Variables

It would be highly gratifying if the euphoric status of U.S.-ROK relations at the beginning of the Reagan-Chun administrations could extend into the indefinite future. However, new situations, some foreseeable and some not, will develop within the ROK, the United States, and the global environment that will call for new decisions. These variable factors may bring new strains to U.S.-ROK relations or strengthen existing ties.

Within the ROK, the authoritarianism of President Chun faces a challenge. The assassination of President Park revealed hidden sources of opposition that may still exist. The Kwangju riots and the perennial uneasiness in university communities show how close to the surface are the currents of unrest. Some older professors lament that they had to fight for academic freedom under Rhee, then under Park, and now under Chun. Admitting Chun's good points, they are painfully aware of his excesses. Those who suffer under the surveillance of the authorities or who are deprived of their political rights by presidential fiat genuinely yearn for more democracy. There may well be a limit to their tolerance.

A substantial minority in the ROK does not want to see the United States support President Chun unreservedly. It welcomes the Americans as protectors against the North, but worries lest the United States lose its leverage to pressure the South Korean government to liberalize. Many South Koreans do not want to see the Carter policy totally abandoned. They would like the United States to keep its options open to support a more liberal government should one succeed to power.

The domestic economy could profoundly affect the future course of U.S.-ROK relations. If aid, trade, and investments continue to bring mutual profits, all will be well. The American private sector will use its resources and its influence to strengthen the basic economic relationship. The costs of borrowing will continue to be justifiable for the ROK as long as its GNP continues to grow and productivity increases. But if inflation, unemployment, low wages, and maldistribution of income become unbearable, the situation within the ROK may become something akin to a depression in the United States. Economic dissatisfaction is a dangerous additive to political unrest. Korean capitalists and technocrats without outlets for their talents or laborers unable to feed their families could tax the capabilities of the government and, consequently, strain the relationship with their close American ally. The ROK might ask the United States for more help than it could supply; the ROK might then in its own interest adopt policies not exactly welcome in Washington.

Domestic pressures might also force the ROK government to modify its policies on reunification with the North. Many South Koreans come from the North and desire more progress toward one nation, one state. No South Korean criticizes his government for prudence and caution, but many suggest that the ROK could safely explore possible areas of compromise. No South Korean will accept the confederation idea, but no North Korean could be expected to consent to one man, one vote, with elections held under U.N. auspices.

Each side is likely to please its backers according to its willingness to concentrate on reducing tension on the peninsula. If the danger of war were either to recede or to mount significantly, the United States would have to assess alternative policies carefully.

The variables affecting U.S.-ROK relations likely to appear within the United States cover a wider spectrum than those noted within the ROK. The American democratic system responds to diverse interest groups, all of whom want to influence national policy. Elections are won or lost on domestic issues, not foreign affairs. Korea is overlooked as candidates argue about the economy, defense spending, social security modification, crime, states' rights, big government, and the Moral Majority.

Although lacking well-reasoned views about Korea, many Americans have strong convictions about American policies. Many think in terms of Europe first or fortress America or Korea as the last in Asia. Others, remembering Vietnam, believe that the United States should never again become mired in Asia; still others hold that it should never start a war that it cannot finish. Some Americans are pacifists, condemning war as the most stupid and costly of human institutions; others are anti-nuclear war because of their fear of human annihilation. In thinking about Korea, the first consideration of any of these groups is that the United States must do nothing that risks making Korea the spark that ignites a global war.

Few Americans express doubts about the value of the treaty commitment. Indeed, very few have precise ideas about the obligations implied in the agreement, but many Americans are quite ready to aid the ROK if it is attacked from the outside. Short of an actual invasion, Americans might not be willing to commit combat troops, although they would surely dispatch air and naval contingents to help their ally. Koreans fear that the United States might chicken out of Korea, as it did in Vietnam.

Few arguments about the stationing of existing levels of U.S. troops in South Korea are likely to arise in the near future. The general belief is that the military advantages outweigh the costs. Some Americans still support the Carter concept of phased withdrawal, fearing that an outbreak of war while U.S. troops are in a trip-wire location would leave the United States without options. If troops are no longer on station when hostilities erupt, the United States will be in position to decide if it wants ground forces to stay out or to return—as its interests at the moment dictate.

The economic variable is unlikely to cause spectacular shifts of policy in the United States. The importance of Korea as a trading partner pales in comparison with that of Japan. Americans will not worry about dislocations in the national economy caused by Korean competition in textiles, footwear, ladies handbags, and leather goods as long as they are affected so seriously by Japanese competition in automobiles, cameras, televisions, stereos, and electronic equipment. The profits accruing to Americans from the South Korean connection are not worth the political action to protect them. Americans scarcely notice the comparatively small amounts currently budgeted for military or economic assistance to the ROK.

It would be a mistake to think that the human rights issue is settled, once and for all, in American minds. Many Americans, with profound faith in principles and ideals, think that the United States should advocate human rights as actively as did President Carter. Some Americans, still a minority, feel that Chun is a ruthless military leader whose standards are unacceptable to civilized society and that South Koreans must begin anew to build democracy. This group bluntly says that the United States should tell President Chun that it will not continue to provide economic and military aid to a government that shows itself less and less concerned about civil liberties for its citizens. It is for that government to decide how it wants to treat its own people, but it is the privilege of the United States to decide whether to give economic and military aid.

The last variable is rooted in the evolving character of the strategic environment. The threat of war is always present. In each new crisis, the value of the ROK as an American ally becomes increasingly apparent. Whether a hawk or dove in American debates over foreign policy, the sentiment is unanimous that the cooperation of the ROK is absolutely essential for protection against any potential Soviet thrust in Northeast Asia.

Although Russian actions in other parts of the world at any given moment may be more critical the United States must note carefully the unfolding of Russian policies in Northeast Asia. As long as the USSR supplies sophisticated weapons to North Korea and backs it diplomatically, the United States must agree with the ROK on security issues.

Some Americans, eager to undertake any initiative that promises to reduce the chance of nuclear war, believe that tensions would be eased if the Russians agreed to treat the reunification of Korea as an international issue. Although rebuffed on such proposals as two Koreas in the United Nations, a four- or six-power conference on Korean questions, or cross-recognition, some Americans (and their South Korean allies) would like to explore further with the North Koreans (and the Soviets who back them) the possibility of a series of arms control agreements providing, for example, mutual reduction of forces by both Koreas, limitation of weapons supplied from outside, nuclear nonproliferation, and possibly a nuclear-free zone in Northeast Asia. This broader treatment of the problems of the Koreas may greatly enhance the prospects for stability and peace in Northeast Asia. No amount of diplomatic finesse, however, can attract a balky power to the negotiating table.

Toward a Long-Term Strategy

In the face of so many variables, the United States must keep its eyes on its own goals. It is essential to have clear concepts of American interests in Northeast Asia and to protect them by every available means. Progress toward an acceptable world order and assistance to allies to protect their interests are inseparable parts of basic American objectives.

Although devising a simple strategic formula for achieving American goals is impossible, decision makers must attempt to solve each problem as it arises, while moving forward toward ultimate goals. They must consider the power and intentions of their adversaries and be sensitive to the needs and demands of their allies. Recognizing the limits of military power and keeping commitments in line with capabilities are extremely important.

To overcome the United States' diminished credibility and to influence Asian leaders along favorable lines, policymakers should refrain from rhetoric and concentrate on making the United States strong militarily, politically, economically, and spiritually. Inherent strength is its own propaganda and projects its own image. It is the best way to arrest the dangerous tendencies far enough ahead to keep them well away from ourselves and our most vital allies.

In dealing with the ROK, some things are more important than the number of troops stationed or withdrawn or the amount of aid given or withheld. It is essential to reach a common concept of shared interests. Both the United States and the ROK want a stable, secure environment that allows them to advance the well-being of their citizens. Both accept the ideals of freedom and democracy. Both favor a freer international trading system, and both want a world order in which conflicts are solved peacefully. What is most needed is steady cooperation, so unchallengeable that it will remove all doubts about the United States' intention to defend its position in Northeast Asia. It is crucial that the perceptions of Koreans, Russians, Japanese, and Chinese correspond to the reality of the American commitment.

As the ROK advances in strength and prestige, with the largest and best-equipped military force in noncommunist Asia, the United States must continue to deal with its ally as its sovereign equal. The two nations will continue to have disagreements and problems, but they must solve their disputes on the basis of mutual confidence and mutual trust. A better-balanced, more mature relationship, realistically attuned to the dynamics of both nations, is the best assurance that together they will devise the most effective strategies to protect their mutual interests.

NOTES

Chapter 1

1. Korean Overseas Information Service, *Handbook of Korea,* 1979 ed. (Ministry of Culture and Information), p. 609; and ROK, "Fourth Five-Year Economic Development Plan, Agricultural Sector."

2. For assistance in economics, I am indebted to my colleagues at the Naval Postgraduate School, Professors Edward Olsen and Robert Looney. I also appreciate the assistance given by Dr. Kim Ki Hwan of the Korean International Institute in Seoul and by economists on the staff of the American embassy in that city. Economic data are taken from "Economic Management Plan for 1981," published by the Economic Planning Board, Republic of Korea, released in Seoul, March 1981.

Chapter 2

1. See U.S., CIA, National Foreign Assessment Center, "Korea: The Economic Race Between the North and the South" (Washington, D.C.: Library of Congress, Document Expediting Project, 1978).

2. Official figures for the North are not available. For comparative purposes, I have used the figures in the *Far Eastern Economic Review, Asia Year Book,* 1981, pp. 173, 179.

3. The figures used in this section are taken from U.S., Department of State, *Report on Korea, 1979.* An alternate source is International Institute for Strategic Studies, *The Military Balance, 1980–81,* pp. 70–71. In some instances, minor dis-

crepancies may appear. In evaluating these figures and drawing conclusions from them, I have had assistance and advice from Richard Cassidy, Richard Curasi, R. D. Thompson, Tom Marenic, and John Williamson, all of whom are knowledgeable and experienced in analyzing relations between North and South Korea.

Chapter 3

1. U.S., Congress, House, Committee on Foreign Affairs, *World War II International Agreements and Understandings,* 83d Cong., 1st sess. (Washington, D.C.: Government Printing Office, 1953).

2. Both the National Security Council and General MacArthur approved the withdrawal. See Harry S. Truman, *Memoirs,* vol. 2 (Garden City, N.Y.: Doubleday, 1956), p. 329.

3. Ibid., p. 325.

4. U.S., Department of State, *Crisis in Asia—An Examination of U.S. Policy,* Bulletin, January 23, 1950. Also distributed as Department of State Publication 3747, Far Eastern Series 32, February 1950.

5. The complete list of perceived American objectives, contained in a telegram from President Truman to General MacArthur, is found in Truman, *Memoirs,* 2: 435–36.

6. This quote appears in the notes of the author's conversations with President Rhee. Similar statements appear repeatedly in President Rhee's public statements. See particularly the pamphlet published by the American-Asian Education Exchange, Inc., "Syngman Rhee, an Asian Leader Speaks for Freedom," with an introduction by Gen. James A. Van Fleet, n.d.

7. U.S., Congress, Senate, Committee on Foreign Relations, *Mutual Defense Treaty with Korea: Hearings,* 83d Cong., 2d sess., 1954.

8. Ibid., p. 47.

9. For the full text of the treaty, including the understanding of the Senate, see U.S., Congress, Senate, Committee on Foreign Relations, Subcommittee on United States Security Agreements and Commitments Abroad, *United States Security Agreements and Commitments Abroad, Part 6, Republic of Korea: Hearings* (hereafter cited as Symington Hearings), 91st Cong., 2d sess., February 1970, p. 1717. The treaty is also found in U.S., Department of State, *United States Treaties and Other International Agreements,* vol. 5, part 3, pp. 2368–374.

10. Dwight D. Eisenhower, *Mandate for Change,* vol. 1 (New York: Doubleday, 1963), p. 132.

11. Stockholm International Peace Research Institute, *The Arms Trade with the Third World* (Stockholm: Almqvist and Wiksell, 1971), pp. 146–47. Other sources indicate comparable magnitude, although precise figures may differ.

12. Nena Vreeland, *Area Handbook for South Korea,* 2d ed. (Washington, D.C.: Government Printing Office, 1975), p. 350.

13. Anne O. Krueger, *The Developmental Role of the Foreign Sector and AID:*

Studies in the Modernization of the Republic of Korea, 1945–1975 (Cambridge, Mass.: Harvard University Press, 1979), p. 12.

14. U.S., Agency for International Development, *Overseas Loans and Grants and Assistance to International Organizations, Obligations and Loan Authorizations, 1953–1974* (Washington, D.C.: Government Printing Office, 1974), figures for the ROK, p. 76. The total given there is U.S. $5.025 billion.

15. United States Information Service, *The Common Interest* (Seoul, 1960). A sympathetic account of the U.S. Economic Assistance Program.

16. Symington Hearings, p. 1530.

17. Ibid., p. 1719.

18. Ibid., p. 1725.

19. Ibid., p. 1555.

20. Ibid., p. 1721.

21. Ibid., p. 1723.

22. Ibid., p. 1525.

23. Ibid., p. 1556.

24. Ibid., p. 1547.

25. Ibid., p. 1549–550.

26. Ibid., p. 1550.

27. Ibid., p. 1545.

28. Ibid., p. 1547.

29. Ibid., p. 1585.

30. Ibid., p. 1578.

31. Ibid., p. 1656.

Chapter 4

1. Richard M. Nixon, *U.S. Foreign Policy for the 1970's; Shaping a Durable Peace* (Washington, D.C.: Government Printing Office, 1973), pp. 109–10. Also, U.S., Department of State, Report of the Secretary of State, *United States Foreign Policy, 1972* (Washington, D.C.: Government Printing Office, 1973), p. 332.

2. Address by President Carter at the Georgia Institute of Technology, Atlanta, Georgia, February 20, 1979. Text released by the White House.

3. Henry R. Kissinger, *White House Years* (Boston: Little Brown and Co., 1979), p. 115.

4. See Richard B. Foster; James E. Dornan, Jr.; and William M. Carpenter, eds., *Strategy and Security in Northeast Asia* (New York: Crane, Russak and Co., 1979), for an extensive analysis from this point of view.

5. Donald C. Daniel, "The Soviet Navy in the Pacific," *Asia-Pacific Community,* no. 4 (Spring-Summer, 1979).

6. *Newsweek,* April 21, 1979, p. 23; July 9, 1979, p. 43.

7. Symington Hearings, pp. 1433–438.

8. Hua Kuo-Feng [Hua Guofeng], "Political Report to the Eleventh National Congress of the Communist Party of China," *The Eleventh National Congress of the Communist Party of China: Documents* (Beijing: Foreign Language Press, 1977), pp. 1–111.

9. *Beijing Review* 1981, no. 20 (May 18): 10.

Chapter 5

1. Material in this section is based primarily on U.S., Congress, House, Committee on International Relations, Subcommittee on International Organizations, *Hearings: Parts 1–6,* and *Report: Investigation of Korean-American Relations,* 95th Cong., 1st and 2d sess., 1977–1978. The objective of this investigation was to uncover wrongdoing by American officials and other persons living in the United States and to clear the innocent. The hearings did not concern actions that took place in South Korea.

2. U.S., Congress, Senate, Committee on Foreign Relations (Senators Hubert H. Humphrey and John Glenn), *U.S. Troop Withdrawal from the Republic of Korea* (hereafter cited as Humphrey-Glenn Report), 95th Cong., 2d sess., 1978, p. 55.

3. William P. Bundy, "Dictatorships and Foreign Policy," *Foreign Affairs,* October 1975, p. 56.

4. U.S., Department of State, Bureau of Public Affairs, News Release, June 24, 1975.

Chapter 6

1. Stuart E. Johnson and Joseph A. Yager, *The Military Equation in Northeast Asia* (Washington, D.C.: Brookings Institution, 1979), p. 78.

2. Ibid., p. 47.

3. Ambassador Richard Sneider, speech in Seoul, December 12, 1977 (text available from U.S. Embassy, Seoul).

4. Humphrey-Glenn Report, p. 39.

5. Ambassador William Gleysteen, "The Republic of Korea and the United States in East Asia" (Seoul: U.S. Embassy, September 11, 1978).

6. For detailed research on this section, I am indebted to: Richard P. Cassidy, "Arms Transfer and Security Assistance to the Korean Peninsula, 1945–1980: Impact and Implications," M.A. thesis, U.S. Naval Postgraduate School, Monterey, Calif., 1980.

7. Philip Shabecoff, *New York Times,* June 17, 1970, p. 16.

8. John B. Oakes, *New York Times,* November 23, 1970, p. 37.

9. *New York Times,* November 15, 1972.

10. Richard Halloran, *New York Times,* August 20, 1975. Also printed in Park Chung Hee, *Toward Peaceful Unification* (Seoul: Kwangmyong Publishing Co., 1976), p. 179.

11. For details on the Schlesinger visit, see the *Korea Times* (Seoul), August 27–30, 1975.

12. Address by President Gerald Ford, East-West Center, Honolulu, December 7, 1975.

13. U.S., Department of State, *Bulletin* 75, no. 1938 (August 16, 1976): 221.

14. Don Oberdorfer, *Washington Post,* June 12, 1977.

15. Humphrey-Glenn Report, p. 19.

16. U.S., Congress, House, Committee on Armed Services, Investigations Sub-committee, *Hearings on Review of the Policy Decision to Withdraw United States Ground Forces from Korea,* 95th Cong., 1st and 2d sess., 1978–1979.

17. Han Sung Joo, "South Korea, 1977: Preparing for Self-Reliance," *Asian Survey,* January 1978.

18. Ambassador William Gleysteen, "The Republic of Korea and the United States in East Asia" (Seoul: U.S. Embassy, September 11, 1978).

19. U.S., Department of Defense, *United States Military Posture: Overview by General David C. Jones, USAF, Chairman of the Joint Chiefs of Staff for FY-1981* (Washington, D.C.: Government Printing Office, 1980), p. 227.

20. Ibid., p. 113.

21. U.S., Department of Defense, *Annual Report, Fiscal Year 1981, by Harold Brown, Secretary of Defense* (Washington, D.C.: Government Printing Office, 1980), pp. 49–51.

SUGGESTIONS FOR FURTHER READING

On the Growth and Development of the Republic of Korea

Allen, Richard C. *Syngman Rhee: An Unauthorized Portrait.* Tokyo: Tuttle, 1960.

Chung, Kyung Cho. *Korea, the Third Republic.* New York: Macmillan, 1971.

Cole, David C., and Lyman, Princeton N. *Korean Development.* Cambridge, Mass.: Harvard University Press, 1971.

Han, Sung Joo. *The Failure of Democracy in South Korea.* Berkeley: University of California Press, 1974.

Han, Woo-Keun, *History of Korea.* Honolulu: University of Hawaii Press, 1980.

Hasan, Parvez, and Rao, D. C. *World Bank Country Economic Report: Korea.* Baltimore: Johns Hopkins Press, 1979.

Henderson, Gregory. *Politics of the Vortex.* Cambridge, Mass.: Harvard University Press, 1968.

Henthorn, William E. *A History of Korea.* New York: Free Press, 1971.

Joe, Wanne J. *Traditional Korea: A Cultural History.* Seoul: Chung Ang Press, 1972.

Keon, Michael. *Korean Phoenix: A Nation from the Ashes.* Englewood Cliffs, N.J.: Prentice-Hall, 1977.

Kim, Se-Jin, *Politics of Military Revolution in Korea.* Chapel Hill: University of North Carolina Press, 1971.

———, and Cho, Chang H., eds. *Government and Politics of Korea.* Silver Spring, Md.: Research Institute on Korean Affairs, 1972.

Korea Development Institute, *Korea's Economy, Past and Present.* Seoul, 1975.

Korean Overseas Information Service, *Handbook of Korea.* Seoul: Ministry of Culture and Information, 1980. (Revised and distributed annually.)

Krueger, Anne O. *The Developmental Role of the Foreign Sector and AID: Studies in the Modernization of Korea, 1945–1975.* Cambridge, Mass.: Harvard University Press, 1979.

Lee, Chong Sik, *Politics of Korean Nationalism.* Berkeley: University of California Press, 1964.

Oh, John Kie-Chiang, *Korea: Democracy on Trial.* Ithaca, N.Y.: Cornell University Press, 1968.

Oliver, Robert T., *Syngman Rhee: The Man Behind the Myth.* New York: Dodd, 1954.

Osgood, Charles, *The Korean Culture.* Rutland, Vt.: Charles E. Tuttle, 1966.

Suh, Dae Sook, and Lee, Chae Jin, eds. *Political Leadership in Korea.* Seattle: University of Washington, 1976.

Wright, Edward Reynolds, ed. *Korean Politics in Transition.* Seattle: University of Washington, 1975. (Contains a useful bibliographic essay.)

ROK Foreign Policy, Including Relations with North Korea

Abramowitz, Morton. "Moving the Glacier: The Two Koreas and the Powers." Adelphi Paper no. 80. London: International Institute of Strategic Studies, 1971.

Barnds, William J., ed. *Two Koreas in East Asian Affairs.* New York: New York University Press, 1976.

Cho, Soon-Song. *Korea in World Politics, 1940–1950.* Berkeley: University of California Press, 1967.

Chung, Chin O. *Pyongyang Between Peking and Moscow.* University: University of Alabama Press, 1978.

Chung, Joseph Sang-Hoon. *The North Korean Economy: Structure and Development.* Stanford: Hoover Institution Press, 1974.

Institute for Asian/Pacific Studies. "Security and Stability in Northeast Asia." San Francisco: University of San Francisco, 1977.

Institute for East Asian Studies. *Foreign Policy for Peace and Unification.* Seoul, 1975.

Institute of East Asian Studies, University of California, Berkeley, and Asiatic Research Center, Korea University, *North Korea.* Proceedings of a Conference held in San Francisco, 1981. Manuscript to be published by University of California Press.

Kim, Se-Jin, ed. *Korean Unification: Source Materials with an Introduction.* Seoul: Research Center for Peace and Unification, 1976.

Kim, Young C. *Major Powers and Korea.* Silver Spring, Md.: Research Institute on Korean Affairs, 1972.

————, and Halpern, Abraham M., eds. *Future of the Korean Peninsula.* New York: Praeger Publishers, 1977.

Koh, Byung-Chul. *Foreign Policy of North Korea.* New York: Praeger Publishers, 1969.

Kyosaki, Wayne S. *North Korea's Foreign Relations: Politics of Accommodation, 1945–1975.* New York: Praeger Publishers, 1976.

McCormack, Gavin, and Selden, Mark, eds. *Korea, North and South.* New York: Monthly Review Press, 1978.

Park, Chung-Hee. *Toward Peaceful Unification: Selected Speeches and Interviews.* Seoul: Kwangmyong Publishing Co., 1976.

Park, Jae Kyu, and Han, Sungjoo. *East Asia and the Major Powers.* Seoul: Kyung Nam University Press, 1975.

Robert A. Scalapino, and Lee, Chang-Sik. *Communism in Korea.* Berkeley: University of California Press, 1972.

Simmons, Robert. *The Strained Alliance: Peking, Pyongyang, Moscow and the Politics of the Korean Civil War.* New York: Free Press, 1975.

On U.S. Interests and Policies Before 1969

Baldwin, Frank, ed. *Without Parallel: The American Korean Relationship Since 1945.* New York: Random House, 1974.

Eisenhower, Dwight D. *Mandate for Change.* Vol. 1. New York: Doubleday, 1963.

Kim, Se-Jin, ed. *Documents on Korean American Relations, 1943–1976.* Seoul: Research Center for Peace and Unification, 1976.

Manchester, William R. *American Caesar: Douglas MacArthur, 1880–1964.* Boston: Little Brown and Co., 1978.

McCune, George M., and Harrison, John A., eds. *Korean-American Relations: Documents Pertaining to the Far Eastern Diplomacy of the United States. Vol. 1, The Initial Period, 1883–1886.* Berkeley: University of California Press, 1951.

Nixon, Richard M. *U.S. Foreign Policy for the 1970's: Shaping a Durable Peace.* Washington, D.C.: Government Printing Office, 1973.

Noble, Harold Joyce. *Embassy at War.* Seattle: University of Washington Press, 1975.

Paige, Glenn D. *The Korean Decision.* New York: Free Press, 1968.

Palmer, Spencer J., *Korean-American Relations: Documents Pertaining to the Far Eastern Diplomacy of the United States. Vol. 2, The Period of Growing Influence, 1887–1895.* Berkeley: University of California Press, 1963.

Stone, I. F. *Hidden History of the Korean War.* New York: Monthly Review Press, 1952.

Truman, Harry S. *Memoirs.* 2 vols. Garden City, N.Y.: Doubleday, 1955–1956.

U.S., Department of State, *A Historical Summary of United States–Korean Relations.* Washington, D.C.: Government Printing Office, 1962.

————. *The Record of Korean Unification, 1943–1960*. Washington, D.C.: Government Printing Office, 1960.

Whiting, Allen S. *China Crosses the Yalu*. Stanford: Stanford University Press, 1960.

On the Changing Strategic Environment

Choi, Chang-Yoon. "Soviet Foreign Policy Toward the Korean Peninsula. An Evaluation of Policy Alternatives." In *Triangular Relations of Mainland China, the Soviet Union, and North Korea*. Seoul: Asiatic Research Center, 1977.

Foster, Richard B.; Dornan, James E., Jr.; and Carpenter, William M., eds. *Strategy and Security in Northeast Asia*. New York: Crane, Russak and Co., 1979.

Fukada, Tsuneari. *Future of Japan and the Korean Peninsula*. Elizabeth, N.J.: Hollyn International Corporation, 1978.

Hahn, Bae-ho, and Yamamoto, Tadashi. *Korea and Japan*. Seoul: Korea University Asiatic Research Center, 1978.

Kim, Jun-yop, ed. *Triangular Relations of Mainland China, the Soviet Union and North Korea*. Seoul: Korea University Asiatic Research Center, 1977.

Kosaka, Masataka. *Asian Security, 1980*. Tokyo: Research Institute for Peace and Security, 1980.

Scalapino, Robert A. *Asia and the Road Ahead*. Berkeley: University of California Press, 1975.

Shaplen, Robert. *A Turning Wheel*. New York: Random House, 1979.

Swearingen, Rodger. *The Soviet Union and Postwar Japan*. Stanford: Hoover Institution Press, 1978.

Watts, William; George, R. Packard; Clough, Ralph N.; and Osnam, Robert B. *Japan, Korea, and China*. Lexington, Mass.: D. C. Heath and Co., 1979.

Weinstein, Franklin B., ed. *U.S.-Japan Relations and the Security of East Asia*. Boulder, Colo.: Westview Press, 1978.

————, and Fuji Kamiya, eds. *Security of Korea*. Boulder, Colo.: Westview Press, 1980.

On U.S.-ROK Relations, 1969–1981

American Enterprise Institute. "Withdrawal of U.S. Troops from Korea?" Defense Review no. 2. Washington, D.C., 1977.

Callaway, Col. Jack G., USA. "Korea, Future Problems, Future Policies." National Security Affairs Monograph 77-3. Washington, D.C.: National Defense University, 1977.

Chay, John, ed. *Problems and Prospects of American–East Asian Relations*. Boulder, Colo.: Westview Press, 1977.

Clough, Ralph. *Deterrence and Defense in Korea.* Washington, D.C.: Brookings Institution, 1976.

―――. *East Asia and U.S. Security.* Washington, D.C.: Brookings Institution, 1975.

Harrison, Selig S. *The Widening Gulf: Asian Nationalism and American Policy.* New York: Free Press, 1978.

Institute for Asian Pacific Studies, *U.S. Policy in the Western Pacific.* San Francisco: University of San Francisco, 1978.

Institute of East and West Studies, *Korean-American-Japanese Conference on Northeast Asia.* Seoul: Yonsei University, 1977.

Jo, Yung-Hwan, ed. *U.S. Foreign Policy in Asia.* Santa Barbara, Calif.: CLIO press, American Bibliographical Center, 1978.

Johnson, Stuart E., and Yager, Joseph A. *The Military Equation in Northeast Asia.* Washington, D.C.: Brookings Institution, 1979.

Kissinger, Henry R. *White House Years.* Boston: Little, Brown and Co., 1979.

Lee, Woong-Hee, ed. *New Era of the Republic of Korea and the United States.* Seoul: Chong Wa Dae Secretariat, 1981.

Solomon, Richard H., ed. *Asian Security in the 1980's: Problems and Policies for a Time of Transition.* Santa Monica, Calif.: Rand Corporation, 1979.

Vasey, Lloyd R. *Pacific Asia and U.S. Policies: A Political-Economic Strategic Assessment.* Honolulu: Pacific Forum, 1978.

White, Nathan. *U.S. Policy Toward Korea: Analyses, Alternatives and Recommendations.* Boulder, Colo.: Westview Press, 1979.

On Contemporary Issues

Periodical Literature: A*–annual,* Q*–quarterly,* M*–monthly,* W*–weekly*

Asia-Pacific Community (Q). Tokyo: Jiji Press.

Asian Survey (M). Berkeley: University of California Press. Consult annual January survey of events; issues for November 1977 and November 1980 are of particular value.

East Asian Review (Q). Seoul: Institute for East Asian Studies.

Far Eastern Economic Review (W). Hong Kong: Far Eastern Economic Review Ltd.

Far Eastern Economic Review, Asia Year Book (A). Hong Kong.

Foreign Affairs (Q). New York: Council on Foreign Relations.

Foreign Broadcast Information Service (irregular). Springfield, Va.: National Technical Information Service.

Foreign Policy (Q). Washington, D.C.: Carnegie Endowment.

Joint Publications Research Service (irregular). Springfield, Va.: National Technical Information Service.

Korea and World Affairs (Q). Seoul: Research Center for Peace and Unification.

Korean Journal of International Studies (Q). Seoul: Korean Institute of International Studies.

Korea Observer (Q). Seoul: Academy of Korean Studies.

The Military Balance (A). London: International Institute for Strategic Studies.

Orbis (Q). Philadelphia: Foreign Policy Research Institute.

Problems of Communism (Q).Washington, D.C.: U.S. International Communication Agency.

Yearbook on International Communist Affairs (A). Stanford: Hoover Institution Press.

Useful information may be found in current publications of the U.S. State Department, the Department of Defense, and the various congressional committees dealing with the armed services, appropriations, and foreign relations. Kim Han-kyo and Hang Kyoo Park, *Studies on Korea: A Scholar's Guide* (Honolulu: Hawaii University Press, 1980), is an invaluable work.

INDEX

DATE DUE

DEC 17 1994 DEC 0 2 1995			